NAPOLEON'S PENINSULAR MARSHALS

Richard Humble

NAPOLEON'S PENINSULAR MARSHALS

A REASSESSMENT

TAPLINGER PUBLISHING COMPANY

NEW YORK

First published in the United States in 1974 by
TAPLINGER PUBLISHING CO., INC.
New York, New York

Library of Congress Catalog Card Number: 74-3874

ISBN 0-8008-5465-9

CONTENTS

ILLUSTRATIONS

NAPOLEON'S PENINSULAR MARSHALS

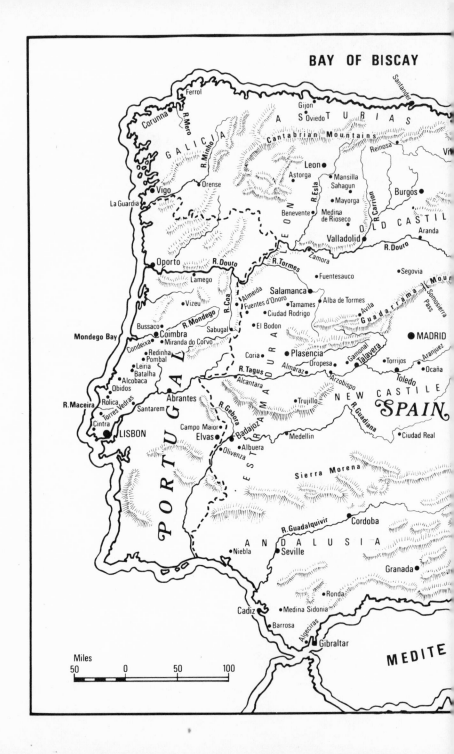

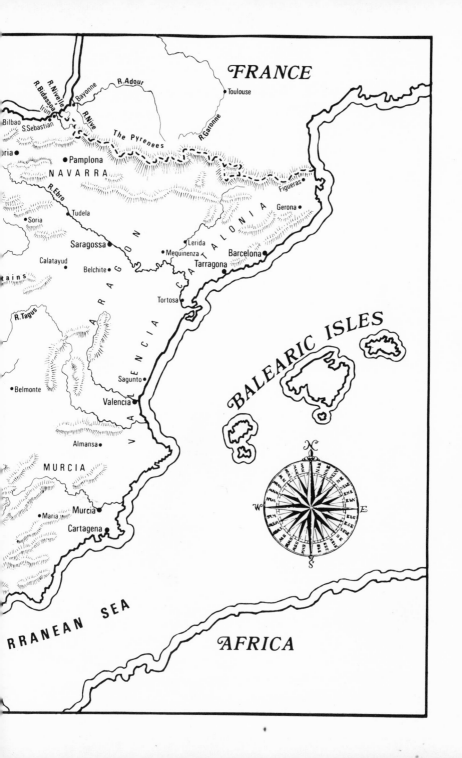

PROLOGUE

So many books have been written on the Peninsular War that to weigh in with another might almost be diagnosed as impertinence. Certainly a few words of introduction are called for. What one finds surprising is that so few studies of the Peninsular War have dwelled on the fundamental reason for the way that war was fought: the fact that Napoleon (apart from one personal appearance) turned the whole operation over to his Marshals and let them get on with it.

Admirers of the Emperor always find the treatment he prescribed for the 'Spanish ulcer' profoundly embarrassing. The puppet ruler of French-occupied Spain, Napoleon's brother Joseph, was considered an ineffectual nonentity by one and all, not least by Napoleon himself. This was particularly unfortunate because the hapless Joseph persisted in taking his role seriously and trying to tell the Marshals what to do. The Marshals would have none of this. They reacted by going over Joseph's head directly to Napoleon, who nearly always backed them up. The result was a total lack of any strong guiding hand on the French war effort in Spain and Portugal. Add the fact that the Marshals were bitterly jealous of each other and let each other down for personal or political reasons whenever possible, and you have the perfect setting for military anarchy.

Despite all this it took Wellington four years to get across the Pyrenees, and during those four years he came close to disaster more than once. The British general was never allowed to forget that he was up against some of the best military talent in the world. Divided as they were by bad orders from above and personal rivalries within, the Marshals in the Peninsula should have been easy to overcome. They were not. And this book is an attempt to explain why; to provide, in short, a look at the Peninsular War from the French side. I have tried to highlight the succession of French commanders who had to tackle Wellington in conditions varying from the totally favourable to the impossible.

Why did Napoleon make the colossal mistake of getting himself bogged down in the Peninsula when he needed all the troops he could secure to tighten his hold on central and eastern Europe? The answer is that he was amazingly ignorant in some matters and naive in others, and this applied to nearly everything to do with Spain — even after his brief campaign there in 1808-9. Napoleon believed that he would be able to cash in on sufficient anti-Bourbon resentment in Spain to put through a swift occupation of the country. Once safely under Imperial rule, Spain and her neighbour Portugal could be manipulated diplomatically and exploited econ-omically in the interests of France.

Napoleon never realized that the Spanish national mood was ruthlessly opposed to the idea of any foreign rule, while being especially resentful of the atrocious rule of King Charles IV and his despised favourite, Godoy. And when Napoleon took the step of jailing the entire Spanish royal family and sending occupation troops into Spain, the Spanish people began the Peninsular War. Resistance to the French began in the capital and spread across the entire country like a flashing, crackling powder-train. In previous campaigns the French had never known anything like this. Their comm-anders now found that their contingents were dotted across central and northern Spain under orders to complete the occupation of a hostile country. Several punishing lessons soon proved that the Peninsula defied every standard of soldiering which had been required in previous campaigns. Some of these lessons were never learned.

First came the difficulty of moving troops, in a hurry, along the shortest distance between two points in either Spain or Portugal. Worst obstacles were the *sierras* – the saw-edged mountain ranges – and the atrocious roads (where they existed at all). Another unpleasant discovery was that a hostile population meant that the natives along the line of march did not rally round with food stocks, transport, or draught animals. (To be fair, the British came up against precisely the same problem when they arrived in the Peninsula.)

Second came the astonishing lesson that Spaniards *could* be a match for French troops, despite the fact that the Spanish regular army had been a walking anachronism for decades. The Spaniards never forgot Bailen in the torrid summer of 1808, when a rag-tag Spanish army cut off and destroyed a French corps.

The third lesson for the French was not entirely a new one. It came in the same summer of 1808 when the British sent out an expeditionary force to expel the French from Portugal. Since the beginning of the Revolutionary Wars the French had had several reminders that British troops were nasty opponents on the battlefield, with an unpleasant tendency towards steadiness under fire and well-drilled fire-power. But at Vimiero in that summer of 1808 the French forces in the Peninsula suffered the first of a string of defeats which in time broke their hold on Portugal and then on Spain, and which finally laid southern France open to invasion. The British presence in the Peninsula became the crucial factor. And, like the non-existent roads, the forbidding terrain and the difficulty of keeping communications open in the face of a will o' the wisp enemy who constantly closed in behind the French armies, Napoleon never realized how effective the British intervention was until it was far too late.

Only once was there a moment when it seemed that Napoleon personally would get to grips with the British. This was in December 1808, when the small British force under

Sir John Moore struck at the communications of Napoleon's *Grande Armée* just after the Emperor had entered Madrid. Napoleon immediately shelved his master-plan for the all-in-one conquest of the Peninsula and charged north after the hastily-retreating British. The pursuit (December 1808-January 1809) changed the course of the war. The British were not trapped and annihilated; the Spanish resistance forces were not destroyed; Portugal remained open as the main base for operations against the French in Spain. Napoleon was forced to quit Spain with far more urgent business in central Europe; but when he left the war in the Peninsula had not been closed down and the military initiative had not been handed over to garrison troops. Instead Joseph Bonaparte was handed back his throne and left to carry on, helped by substantial forces commanded by all the top-ranking Marshals Napoleon could spare from his coming showdown with Austria.

The Peninsular Marshals, on paper, were responsible to Joseph — a synthetic ruler whom they despised. In practice they claimed full autonomy of command, appealing over Joseph's head to Napoleon whenever they saw fit. They were out on their own. Where they came from, how they rose to fame, how they ended up in the Peninsular theatre, and how they fared there is the subject of this story.

CHAPTER ONE

THE MAKING
OF THE MARSHALS

The Napoleonic Empire was born when General Bonaparte, former commander of the Army of the Orient, became First Consul of the French Republic on 25 December, 1799. It was officially christened on 18 May, 1804, with the announcement of the bold paradox that 'the Government of the Republic is entrusted to a hereditary Emperor'.

Above all else it was a military Empire. France had been saved in the Republican wars by her soldiers. Now her foremost general was Emperor; and one of his first acts was to pay public homage to the institution which had raised him to supreme power: the French Army. On 19 May, 1804, eighteen leading French Army commanders were created Marshals of the Empire.

The justifications for these promotions were varied, but all had a common purpose: to unite the fortunes of the new Marshals with that of the new Emperor. Basically, 'Marshal' was an honorific title. Not all of the eighteen Marshals of 1804 were even on the active list. By no means all of them had been former comrades or subordinates of Napoleon in his army commander days. They included hard-bitten ex-Jacobin Revolutionaries and former Royalists. They included men who had risen from the ranks since the outbreak of war in 1792 and men who had been professional officers for years before the Revolution came in 1789. They included tradesmen's sons and offshoots both of the minor aristocracy and the gentry. And now, in May 1804, they were honoured as the Great Captains of the Army of France, in a unique and glittering brotherhood. Where had the Marshals come from, and how had they risen so quickly?

The standard answer is, sweepingly, 'the Revolution', with much reference to the subsequent discovery of marshals' batons in soldiers' knapsacks, but the fact that the Revolution was good for promotion only raises more questions. It also obscures the point that a vital part of the work which made the French Army so deadly by the middle 1790's – ripe, in fact, for manipulation by Napoleon and his Marshals – had been achieved *before* the Revolution. And this particular fact deserves a little examination.

By the year 1789, the military powers of Europe could hardly claim to have made many recent innovations in the art of war. It was now eighty-odd years since the murderous campaigns of Louis XIV and the dreaded 'Marlbrouck'. Armies were still small and highly expensive investments of state expenditure. They could never be risked in wild ventures. They were tied to elaborate supply-trains and could not move fast. And in general war itself, like pheasant-shooting, had its own season, beginning in the spring and ending with the deepening of the autumnal mud.

Even during the campaigning months of the year, a war would usually follow a pattern of elaborate sieges, conducted according to strict rules of geometric planning and military etiquette. Parallel trenches would be drawn around the besieged fortress. Zig-zag approach trenches would be pushed forward, then connected by inner parallels in which siege batteries could be emplaced to bombard the hard-core defences of the fortress. The main plan was to make a big enough breach in these defences to allow for a successful storming attempt. Once the attackers had made their breach, there was normally a gentlemanly pause for negotiations in which the defenders would be invited to surrender. If they did, their garrison would be allowed to march out with all the honours of war, saluted by their erstwhile attackers. But if the surrender demand were rejected, the unfortunate defenders would have nothing to expect but the horrors of a full-blooded assault and sack, in which the attacking troops, having won their objective, might run amuck for days before order could be restored. And throughout the siege the attackers' main field army would be on the watch for a relieving force, which might risk a set-piece battle to raise the siege.

When this happened, the result was formalized slaughter. The infantry lines of the two armies would be pirouetted into battle formation and manoeuvred within the extremely limited range of each other's crude muskets. The battle could then run a simple course, the idea being to pound the enemy line until it either broke or was sufficiently enfeebled to prevent it from standing up to a general advance.

In battles like this discipline was all-important. The infantryman had to be drilled and drilled until he could be relied upon to go through his reloading cycle under fire without losing his head and breaking the rhythm of the firing sequence. Methods varied. One of the most effective was the Prussian system where the foot soldier, ramming, aiming, and firing, knew that just behind his unit stood a row of NCOs with drawn swords, waiting for the first sign of a falter. Any soldier who dared look round or generally show signs of uneasiness with the way things were going, would be run through the body by one of these NCOs. This sort of background knowledge tended to make the 'poor bloody infantry' of Frederick the Great's army hard to panic and even harder to break.

Frederick the Great's legacy was a unique one, but for totally paradoxical reasons. He was the Napoleon of his day, a master of manoeuvre and a brilliant tactician on the battlefield, where his personal presence was assessed as being worth 35,000 men. But everything he did was dictated by the 18th-century system of war. He manoeuvred because he dare not hazard his troops, which were as 'period' as could be imagined: rigidly drilled, few in number, and *expensive*. No people's army there. And Frederick's army became a copy-book case of reactionary complacency after his death. His most fatal legacy, in fact, was the downfall of Prussia after the disastrous battle of Jena-Auerstädt in 1806, which was fought and lost by a Prussian Army which had progressed not a whit from the condition in which Frederick had left it. None of his contemporaries really understood what it was that made him win. Instead, most of the armies of Europe rushed to ape the Prussian Army's appearance and drill, apparently under the belief that pipeclay, pigtails, and the goose-stepping *parademarsch* were important ingredients of victory.

The only country which did not go in for these myopic attempts to create a neo-Prussian army was France. It was in the early years of Louis XVI's reign, which began in 1774, that army reforms of vital importance began to be made by the new King's ministers — reforms whose work would save the country from military defeat in 1792-93, and create the basis of Napoleon's armies.

Before touching on the main French army reformers of the period, mention must be made of the fascinating military theories of the Comte de Guibert. He was a young French nobleman who had seen some service in Germany and Corsica and who, at the age of twenty-nine, published in 1772 a book which for a while made him a favourite of the French *salons*. This book was entitled *Essai Général de la Tactique*, and it prophesied many of the methods which the Revolutionary and Imperial French armies would make commonplace within the next thirty years.

Guibert's *Essai* was a strange confection. He put his finger on the need for a citizen army which should fight out of a sense of duty and patriotism, but rejected the idea in his own argument as something unimaginable at the time of writing. (The 'citizen army' theme, taken out of context, is where Guibert has been most often misquoted as a sort of premature military *sans-culotte*.) He was extremely 'modern' both in the Napoleonic and the 20th-century sense, in his preaching of rapid, decisive wars, *Blitzkrieg* style — but he spoke like a man of his time when he argued that armies should be kept small. Large armies, he held, were neither practical nor desirable, and a really good general would not need a large army anyway. On the other hand, Guibert argued that it was ludicrous and ruinous for armies to depend on lengthy, civilian supply-trains for their provisions in the field. Troops should travel light and live off the country.

Guibert really broke new ground, however, when he discussed how armies should separate into divisions to move and concentrate again to give battle. The old idea that the order of march should as near as possible be the order of battle he rejected as unnecessary and inhibiting. Above all, it was slow: there has to be a limit to the number of troops you can march along the same road in a given time. Disperse to march, concentrate to fight — that was the ideal. By 1804, when Napoleon named his first Marshals, this was the usual system in the French Army. Under the Empire, with the component corps of the *Grande Armée* each entrusted to the command of a Marshal, this system remained the mainstay of Napoleon's strategy of movement from Austerlitz to Waterloo.

Guibert should have been the Liddell Hart of the 18th century — his ideas, qualified though many of them were, were certainly original enough. But he spoiled it all by writing another book (*Défense des Systèmes de Guerre Moderne*) in 1779, in which he repudiated the basic motivation of his earlier *Essai*. 'When I wrote that book I was ten years younger. The vapours of philosophy heated my head and clouded my judgement.' The *Essai* was certainly a hot-house plant, nourished by the *philosophe* atmosphere of France's intellectual upper crust in the 18th century; but the many sketches it contains of the shape of things to come in warfare still appear impressive today.

The French Army reforms were far more practical. In 1763 France had just suffered a shattering series of defeats in the Seven Years War. Canada, Louisiana, and the French bases in India had been lost. France had been repeatedly beaten on land and sea and her finances, as usual under the Bourbons of the *Ancien Régime*, were tottering. But under the leadership of Louis XV's energetic minister, the Duc de Choiseul, administrative and military reforms were initiated with the intention of helping France regain her former place as a world power.

As far as the French Army was concerned, the most important reform was that of the artillery arm. Artillery in 1770 was rather like aviation in 1914: at the crossroads. Were the guns to remain merely as a battlefield service for the infantry and cavalry – or should they become an arm in their own right? Opinions varied (Guibert saw artillery in the former role), but the radicals realized that artillery had not yet come into its own and planned accordingly. In France, the patient work of Jean-Baptiste de Gribeauval (whose reforms were not superseded until 1825) began under Choiseul. The end-product was an excellent range of cannon for the Army: light (8-pounder), medium (12-pounder) and heavy (24-pounder) field guns. Gribeauval's artillery reforms meant that when war broke out against the European monarchies in 1793, France had what was unquestionably the best artillery in Europe.

Almost as important was the start of a new look in the training of professional officers for both Army and Navy. This was begun by the creation of twelve provincial military schools for the education of the sons of impoverished gentry. This was the work of the War Minister Comte Claude-Louis Saint-Germain, and it was a deliberate challenge to the traditional monopoly of the high nobility and wealthy bourgeois over the French officer corps. The new provincial schools were founded in 1776, and it was in one of them – that of Brienne – that Cadet Napoleone de Buonaparte from Corsica began his military education in 1779, *par le bonté du Roi*.

Saint-Germain also tried to cut down the size of the decorative but expensive and patronage-ridden Household troops, to extend the recruiting of regular units, to improve the efficiency and reduce the corruption of the Ministry of

War. He also favoured stepping up the severity of discipline. In so doing he aroused the hostility of the Court, the high nobility – in short, running foul of all forms of vested interest in the system he was trying to improve, and even alienating the professional soldiers. This sort of opposition was only to be expected: it happened to all energetic statesmen in the last years of the *Ancien Régime* who tried to put France's institutions to rights. The result was the same, however, and Saint-Germain had to go.

But what had been achieved by Gribeauval and Saint-Germain had enduring results. By 1789 France had one of the most modern and best equipped armies in Europe, and when the traditional French officer caste disappeared – either as a result of emigration or of Revolutionary liquidation – the new commanders of the French Army found that they had a formidable weapon ready to hand.

The year 1769 stands as a red-letter year in the calendar of military history. The Duke of Wellington was born in that year. So was Napoleon. And so were three of his future Marshals: Michel Ney, Nicolas Jean-de-Dieu Soult, and Jean Lannes. All three of them were destined to serve in the most bitter and tragic theatre of the Napoleonic Wars: the Peninsula. In the case of Ney and Soult, however, both began their careers as soldiers of King Louis XVI, as did Napoleon himself.

Michel Ney was a provincial from the little town of Saarlouis in Lorraine. He was the second son of a Seven Years War veteran who had made a decent career for himself as a barrel-cooper. Pierre Ney intended a professional career for the red-headed Michel and eventually got him 'good' jobs in which he could learn the ropes; first as a clerk in the office of the *Procureur du Roi*, the King's Attorney, and later in the ironworks of Appenweiler and Saleck.

For the energetic young Ney, however, it was not good enough. In the late autumn of 1786 he turned up at his parents' home in Saarlouis. It was a farewell visit: he had thrown up his job, he told them, and was on his way to Metz to join the Army. And there, on 12 February, 1787, Michel Ney enlisted in the *Régiment Colonel-Général* of Hussars.

He was a natural hussar. His build was right: 5 feet 8 inches, long legs, stocky body. He was strong, and became a champion fencer. Above all, he was a good rider. But when he joined up in 1787 the man who was to become Marshal Ney, Prince of the Moskowa and Duke of Elchingen, could hardly have had ambitions ranging beyond joining the lower officer caste as a lieutenant on the eve of his retirement. It was still the heyday of the counts and marquises; the colonel of Ney's regiment was a princeling, the young Duc de Chartres; and the military heights of the *Ancien Régime* were not for the likes of a barrel-cooper's son from the provinces.

The Revolution of 1789, runs the popular legend, changed all that. But it did nothing of the kind. All that the summoning of the States-General of France (5 May, 1789) meant to the French Army was that His Majesty was making a decidedly unorthodox experiment in tackling the nation's acute financial embarrassment. The gory rough-and-tumble which ended in the capture of the Bastille on 14 July was a shock, to be sure, but it was really a local fracas: the actions of the Paris mob were not those of France. The legend that 1789 communized France overnight is totally false. And certainly the *Régiment Colonel-Général*, still stationed at Metz, was hardly affected at all.

Certainly not Trooper Ney. It was not until 1 January, 1791, that he was promoted to *brigadier* – the equivalent of corporal. Another thirteen months were to pass until he took the next step up the ladder: 1 February, 1792, saw him promoted to *maréchal de logis* – sergeant-of-horse. Two months more and he was *maréchal de logis chef* or sergeant-major. But it was those fifteen months which tipped the scale of the Revolution. They saw France's first experiment with constitutional monarchy fail – because of the King's duplicity, because of the disenchantment of the moderate politicians, and because the radical party leaders were better organized than anyone else in France. They pressed for war, which, they believed, would force the King into declaring himself either for or against the Revolution. It was believed that war would cement the gains of the Revolution to date, uniting France against her enemies within and without. And war was declared on 20 April, 1792, under the rubber-stamp authority of Louis XVI, against the neighbour which had shown itself most distrustful of the course of events within France since 1789: Austria.

This was hardly surprising. It was to Austrian territory that most of the *émigrés* made their way; it was with these *émigrés* and the Austrian court that Queen Marie Antoinette indulged in her feckless and incompetent plotting. Moreover, Marie Antoinette was an Austrian princess; the extremist leaders and mob cheer-leaders did not find it hard to translate *'l'Autrichienne'* as 'the Austrian bitch'. Nor did they find it hard, as the experiment with constitutional monarchy began to break down, to beat the drum against Austria as Public Enemy Number One.

It was also in this period – 1791-92 – that the Revolution began to impose significant changes on the French Army. The most obvious symptom was the emigration of aristocratic officers. This has been computed as a figure of 6,000 out of 9,000 officers of the pre-1789 Army, and these were losses which could not be made good overnight. Next came the fact that the Revolutionary government's ideal of creating a volunteer army of 100,000 men had not been achieved: only about a third of the desired total of volunteers had answered the call, and those who had were not yet trained. The result was that the declaration of war on 20 April, 1792, found the French Army in a critical 'half-and-half' situation – regulars and volunteers aligned for common service – and seriously weak in experienced officers who enjoyed the confidence of their men. This helps to explain the first disastrous encounters with Austrian troops in the Netherlands, with the French panicking at the first contact with the enemy and bolting from the field. Austrian sluggishness saved France, however. No prompt counter-offensive came from the Austrians in Belgium.

It was not until late July that the first real counter-move got under way, and it was launched by Austria's ally Prussia under the command of the Duke of Brunswick. Ney's regiment (by now re-christened the 5th Hussars) had not been involved in the initial fiascos on the Belgian frontier, but this time it was right in the line of fire, forming part of the French army under Dumouriez which was blocking the road to Paris.

As a result the first battle in which Ney took part was the so-called 'miracle of Valmy'. Miracle it certainly was. The hodge-podge French force won the day although Dumouriez had taken up an almost suicidal position (he had allowed the Prussians to flank him in their passage through the Argonne with the result that when the battle began they were actually between the French army and Paris). But the French victory had three important causes. First, the Prussian Army was in an extremely bad way; on the day of Valmy its antiquated, typically 18th-century supply system was so out of gear that its field bakeries were in Verdun and its flour supplies back at Trier. It was pouring with rain, the battlefield was swampy, the Prussian troops were fed up, jaded, and riddled with dysentery. When it became apparent that the French were going to stand, Brunswick decided to try an artillery bombardment to dislodge them. When this failed in its turn, he muttered his famous comment '*Hier schlagen wir nicht*' ('We will not fight here') decided to call it a day, and withdrew from the field.

Point two follows from this. Dumouriez won at Valmy because his troops stood their ground, and the main reason they stood their ground was because the green volunteers had disciplined regular troops like Ney's cavalry regiment at their side. Point three was that the action consisted almost entirely of an artillery pounding-match. It was in fact the biggest artillery duel yet known, and for this the French were extremely well equipped, as we have seen. It would have been a very different story if the French had had to take the fire of the Prussian guns without knowing that their own guns were hitting back just as hard, if not harder. But they stood, and the Prussians gave up first.

After the Prussian withdrawal and the immense morale-booster of Valmy, the French armies went over to the counter-offensive. Valmy was fought on 20 September. The French monarchy was abolished in Paris on the 21st. Year One of the Republic began on the 22nd. All this strengthened the democratic tendencies in the French Army which had begun the formation of the volunteer units. The advent of the Republic now made the title 'Citizen' precede all titles of military rank — but it was not Republican influence which earned Ney his promotion to *sous-lieutenant* on 29 October. He got it because the former colonel of the 5th Hussars, Lamarche, had always been impressed by Ney's capabilities and Lamarche was now Ney's army general. Ney's subsequent promotions would also be due to recommendations by his superior officers: he was a man who won favourable attention naturally.

This is not to say that Ney failed to earn the confidence of the men he led into action during 1793 and 1794, the glory days of the Republic, when the troops of the Tricolour conquered the Low Countries and the left bank of the Rhine and broke the armies of the Austro-Prussian Coalition in battle after battle. Ney was more often than not in the thick of the fighting, and an efficient fighting officer always wins the respect of the troops as well as catching the eye of his superiors.

At this stage the armies of the Republic still had geographical instead of numerical designations — 'Italy', 'Rhine', 'Eastern Pyrenees', and so on; others were named after the new administrative *départements*. The army with which Ney fought during this period was one of the latter: the 'Army of the *Sambre-et-Meuse*' earned for itself one of the most legendary reputations in the whole of the Revolutionary Wars. The men of the '*Sambre-et-Meuse*' were not only the saviours of France but the champions of the Revolutionary crusade – the conquerors of Belgium and Holland. To have done well in that army was as useful a reputation to have in 1800 as being a veteran of the 'Old Contemptibles', the *Afrika Korps*, or the 8th Army in the 20th century. And Ney did very well indeed.

His service in 1793-94 combined much fighting with much staff experience, the latter under the eye of General Kléber, one of the best generals in the Republic. By the end of 1794 Ney had risen first to lieutenant, then to captain and in turn to *Adjutant Général* or Staff Major. Badly wounded at Mayence (Mainz) on 22 December in an unsuccessful skirmish, he turned down a suggestion that he should be recommended for promotion to brigadier-general in recognition of his gallantry in the field. He spent the year of 1795 on Kléber's staff, still with the '*Sambre-et-Meuse*', and reached the rank of colonel. The following year Ney so distinguished himself in the intense fighting on the Rhine that Kléber promoted him to brigadier-general in August. Michel Ney had rocketed from cavalry trooper to general's rank in five and a half years; and it was still not four years since he had seen his first battle.

Ney's rise to brigadier-general may be taken as typical of the times. The war, which had begun so badly for the French Army, was now expanding at such a speed that there was a permanent lack of sufficient battle-wise officers; and men like Ney were bound to get rapid promotion. Another similar case was that of Nicolas Jean-de-Dieu Soult, born the same year as Ney and also destined for the Marshalate.

Soult was a southerner, born in Saint-Amans-Labastide near Albi. Like Ney, he opted for a military career in his teens, but unlike Ney he chose the infantry rather than the cavalry, joining the *Régiment Royal-Infanterie* on 16 April, 1785. Soult's early promotion came rather more rapidly than Ney's: corporal, 13 June, 1787; sergeant, 1 July, 1791; sergeant-instructor, 17 January, 1792; *sous-lieutenant adjut-*

ant-major, 16 July, 1792. Soult continued to climb in the service with the 'Army of the Moselle', reaching colonel's rank in May 1794 and gaining his brigade, after a transfer to the '*Sambre-et-Meuse*', on 11 October of that year. Even at this stage a quick comparison shows an essential difference between Soult and Ney that was to continue down through the stormy history of the First Republic, the Consulate, the early Empire, the Peninsular War, until Waterloo itself. Soult was more the staff man, the planner; Ney, whenever possible, preferred to lead from the front line, with a sword in his hand rather than a telescope or message-pad.

A third general from the central front of the Republic from Belgium along the Rhine — was Edouard Mortier. His career started very differently to those of Ney and Soult. He was born in 1768 to a prosperous merchant of Le Cateau who planned a career in commerce for his son and had him educated at the *Collège des Anglais* in Douai. When Louis XVI summoned the States-General of France May 1789, Mortier's father was elected as a Third Estate deputy, and during the reforming years of the monarchical experiment (1789-91) Edouard Mortier served in the volunteer National Guard, first of Dunkirk and then of Le Cateau. Thus his advancement initially depended on democratic election rather than regular army seniority. Mortier was elected captain in the 1st Volunteer Battalion of the Department of Nord on 1 September, 1791, fought under Dumouriez in the following year, distinguished himself under fire, and was transferred to the '*Sambre-et-Meuse*' in 1794. Mortier did not get his brigade until 1799, after some five more years of hard campaigning, but his early career neatly reflected the other training-ground of Napoleon's future Marshals: the volunteer troops of the Revolution.

The central and northern fronts, where Ney, Soult, and Mortier all made their names, were the focus of attention until Prussia dropped out of the coalition in 1795, but in the spring of 1796 the Republic decided to launch a fresh offensive against Austria by invading her territories in northern Italy. This offensive sowed a fresh crop of future Marshals, for it was Napoleon's first independent army command. He took over a frustrated, tired, and appallingly-equipped army in March 1796; by April 1797 he had led it to within sixty miles of Vienna, conquered North Italy, knocked Austria out of the war, and confirmed the Republic's earlier conquests in the Netherlands and the Rhineland. Naturally the commanders of the Army of Italy, after such an achievement, were men of mark. The '*Sambre-et-Meuse*' and the Rhine Army had produced men like Ney, Soult and Mortier; the Army of Italy produced Augereau, Berthier, Bessières, Lannes, Massena, Murat, and Sérurier. All became Marshals in 1804.

Charles-Pierre-François Augereau was a colourful, swashbuckling, Parisian tough — one of the proudest sons of the Rue Mouffetard, where he was born in 1757. His early career was so chequered that it is hard to describe it in detail. We know that he joined up in the *Régiment de Clare Irlandais* in 1774, but after that his story becomes more than somewhat confused. Suffice it to say that he was unique. None of the other Napoleonic Marshals had so many anecdotes attached to them, containing such a frightening total of seductions, duels, life-or-death escapes, and army units of various countries from which he was either flung out for insubordination or from which he deserted. (He served with the Prussian Army for a time and the penalty for desertion from that army was death.) Augereau was back in France by 1790, having acquired the approximate rank of sergeant-major-instructor in various foreign armies, and served in the Parisian National Guard. His magnificent presence (and deadly efficiency with the sword) got him rapid election to officer's rank in volunteer units. Augereau returned to regular service as a captain with the 11th Hussars in June 1793 and reached junior staff rank with General Rossignol, putting down Royalist insurgents in the Vendée. It was in the fighting in the Pyrenees, against Bourbon Spain's participation in the First Coalition, that he reached general's rank, commanding the 1st Division of the Army of the Eastern Pyrenees. He soon proved that he was a master at handling a division, leading it from in front and adding to his reputation in several fierce engagements. When Spain and Prussia quit the First Coalition in 1795, Augereau was transferred to General Schérer's Army of Italy and took over one of its divisions. He stayed there during the infuriating autumn and winter months when Scherer butted ineffectually at the Austrian-Sardinian armies holding the Maritime Alps; and he remained a divisional commander when General Napoleon Bonaparte (as he now spelt his name) took over the Army of Italy from Schérer in March 1796.

In the whirlwind battles which followed – Montenotte, Millesimo, Ceva, Lodi – Augereau's division did more than its share, but his finest hour came at Castiglione in August. Even Napoleon considered retreat before the converging Austrian columns, but Augereau's battle plan and leadership won the day for the French. Bonaparte never forgot this achievement: Castiglione, 1796, won Augereau's baton for him in 1804.

Alexandre Berthier was totally different. For a start he was a minor 'aristo', the son of an ennobled military engineer in the service of Louis XV. Berthier first saw service in the War of American Independence, serving on Rochambeau's staff in the French expeditionary force sent to help Washington against the British. Returning to France as a colonel, Berthier was made Major-General of the Versailles National Guard by Louis XVI.

He survived the Revolutionary Terror thanks to a combination of political self-effacement and obvious military competence of the very highest order. He was, in fact, one of the most brilliant chiefs-of-staff in all military history. Getting the maximum amount of troops to the right place at the right time sounds simple, but it is in fact more like playing several chess games at once against time. How many roads lead in the right direction, and how many troops can use them without jamming them solid? Are those roads metalled or not – and if not, will they become movement-stopping quagmires if the weather breaks? How much forage can be found at the right stages on the march for the cavalry? All these myriad problems of logistics – and many more – had to be solved by the chief-of-staff if the full strength of horse, foot, and guns were to fight efficiently when required – and Berthier was a master at it. He planned every crucial march made by Napoleon's *Grande Armée* bar one: the march to Waterloo. And it was his work with the Army of Italy which proved his inestimable value to Napoleon.

The third of the future Marshals from the Army of Italy was Jean-Baptiste Bessières. Another southerner, born at Prayssac in 1768, he was elected captain in the local National Guard when the Revolution came and began his regular service in November 1792. Bessières was then a *chasseur* (light cavalryman) with the 'Pyrenean Legion', later incorporated into the Army of the Eastern Pyrenees, where Augereau was learning how to command a division. Bessières became a *sous-lieutenant* on 16 February, 1793, and captain in the 22nd *Chasseurs* on 8 May, 1794. He was transferred to the Army of Italy just before it began its epic campaign under Napoleon. And it was there that the hitherto unremarkable career of this junior cavalry officer began to undergo a transformation, for Napoleon chose Bessières to command the 'Company of Guides', the hand-picked bodyguard which rode with Napoleon in Italy and Egypt. This tough company became the hard core of the future Consular and Imperial Guard, which in turn was built up to corps strength, the élite force of the *Grande Armée* and a Marshal's command: Bessières's. It was a Caesarian appointment, and it caused much heart-burning among the other Marshals. Bessières had achieved nothing like as much distinction in the field as the others, and when in 1804 he was awarded a Marshal's baton in preference to over a score of really hard-bitten fighting generals it sparked off natural resentment.

Jean Lannes was one of the best fighting generals Napoleon ever had. A Gascon, born at Lectoure in 1769, he was apprenticed to a dyer in his teens but joined the local National Guard as a volunteer in the 2nd Battalion of the Department of Gers in 1792. There he was elected *sous-lieutenant* on 20 June. The 2nd Battalion subsequently joined the Army of the Eastern Pyrenees, where Lannes saw plenty of fighting and rose to colonel before being transferred to the Army of Italy in November 1795. He served as a brigadier during Napoleon's drive across northern Italy and proved he could lead shock troops like a fiend incarnate. Battles like Lodi and Arcola gave him plenty of scope, and he ended the campaign with one of the most impressive reputations in the Army. Napoleon immediately earmarked Lannes for the Egyptian adventure, in which he added to his laurels.

Next came the man who has been hailed by many as the greatest of Napoleon's Marshals: André Massena. His origins were very like Napoleon's: Massena was born on 6 May, 1758, the son of a small-time merchant of Nice. As Nice lay beyond the French frontier at that time, Massena was born a Piedmontese subject and grew up, like the Corsican Napoleon, to be bilingual in both Italian and French. Massena realized a classic dream of boyhood; he ran away to sea at the age of thirteen and became a cabin-boy. This adventure, however, ended in classic disillusionment and in 1775, now seventeen years old, he joined the local *Régiment Royal-Italien*, a unit which, as James Marshall-Cornwall puts it in his splendid biography of Massena, 'was a sort of Foreign Legion, mainly recruited from Italians and Piedmontese'.

Massena's service with the *Royal-Italien* is an excellent commentary on how the social prejudice of the *Ancien Régime* could frustrate the advancement of able men. His qualities brought him rapid promotion as an N.C.O.: corporal, 1776; sergeant, 1777. He was also given the duties of an instructor. In 1784 he was promoted further, to *adjutant sous-officier* – warrant officer – but that was considered to be his ceiling. Five years later, after fourteen years of impeccable service, he took his discharge, retired to Antibes, and married.

Massena accepted service in the Antibes National Guard as a 'captain instructor', but it was not until September 1791 that he was asked to join one of the new volunteer battalions as an adjutant. In his new unit, the 2nd Battalion of the Department of the Var, Massena shone at once; and on 1 February, 1792, he was elected colonel by his men. When the Republic declared war on the Kingdom of Sardinia as well as on Austria, Massena's battalion was soon in action and had done so well by the summer of 1793 that Massena was promoted to brigadier-general, on 22 August.

Five days after this the Royalists in Toulon handed the port over to Admiral Hood's British Mediterranean Fleet. During the long weeks when the fate of Toulon hung in the balance Massena had the responsibility of sending an artillery detachment under Captain Buonaparte to help the Republican besiegers. Napoleon's self-publicity has made his own role in the eventual captivity of Toulon famous. It is less well known that the final assault on the Toulon forts was led by Massena, and that while Buonaparte was promoted to brigadier-general (he had been advanced to major on 19 October) for his part in the siege, Massena was only promoted one grade to the command of a division, which was announced on 20 December.

Returning to the Austro-Sardinian front, Massena led his division with distinction under three commanders-in-chief (Dumerbion, Kellermann, and Schérer) throughout 1794-95. On 23-24 November, 1795, he won the battle of Loano and pushed on to take Savona on the 26th — a brilliant feat, accomplished in extremely tough conditions, which made him the foremost commander in the Army of Italy. When Napoleon began his offensive in March 1796, it was Massena who led the army's spearhead of two divisions (in one of which Lannes was serving).

Like Augereau, Massena made a permanent name for himself during the Italian campaign: it was due to his efforts that the last attempt to relieve the besieged Austrian garrison on Mantua was broken at Rivoli, and with it Austria's stranglehold on Venetia. And it was after the battle of La Favorita, which sealed Mantua's fate, that Napoleon embraced Massena before his troops and hailed him as '*L'Enfant Chéri de la Victoire*' — 'the darling child of victory'.

Joachim Murat was a Gascon, like Lannes. He was an innkeeper's son from La Bastide-Fortunière (later renamed La Bastide-Murat), and he was born on 25 March, 1767. Murat joined the French Army for a somewhat different reason than those of his colleagues: his parents wanted him to become a priest and he did not fancy the idea at all. He fled from his seminary in February 1787 at the age of twenty and joined the *Régiment Chasseurs des Ardennes*, later the 12th Chasseurs, in which he served for five years. In 1792 Murat served for a while as a horse guardsman in the King's Constitutional Guard, but returned to his regiment where he was promoted *brigadier* nine days after the outbreak of war in April. In 1792-93 he campaigned with the Army of the North, in which he got his commission and rose to the rank of captain.

The next three years — 1793-95 — were chequered ones for Murat. Always a great hand at playing to the gallery, he seems to have attracted the attention of the Revolutionary government with too much flamboyance and not enough political non-involvement. When the demagogue Marat was assassinated in July 1793, Murat seriously — and with fashionable ostentation — considered changing his own name to Marat. When Robespierre fell a year later, Murat was one of the many denounced as adherents of the Robespierre regime (Napoleon was under a similar cloud), but he escaped with demotion and suspension from active service. It was on the night of 5-6 October, 1795, that Murat first became personally associated with Napoleon, for Murat was the man who brought in from the artillery park at Les Sablons the guns that fired the famous 'whiff of grapeshot' on the orders of Napoleon and Barras and crushed the counter-revolutionary coup. Napoleon did not forget this, and when he began his campaign in Italy in 1796 Murat went with him with the substantive rank of colonel *aide-de-camp*.

In the battles which followed, Murat soon showed that he was an outstanding cavalry leader. His name is always mentioned high on the list of classic cavalry commanders like Prince Rupert, 'Jeb' Stuart, Rommel, and Patton. He was flamboyant, vain, jealous, with a fantastic and extravagant taste in fancy uniforms. (Napoleon, on one occasion, took one look at Murat's latest outfit and told him to go away and put on a proper uniform, as his present confection made him look like a circus-rider.) He cemented his ties with Napoleon by marrying Napoleon's sister — but that was not why Napoleon left the direction of the cavalry arm of the *Grande Armée* to Murat. For all his faults, Murat was a nonpareil when it came to a desperate charge or an all-out pursuit.

Of the seven future Marshals from the Army of Italy, Jean Matthieu Philibert Sérurier was the odd man out. He was fifty-four when the campaign of 1796 began and it had taken him thirty-four years to make the painful climb from militia lieutenant to major. He was simple, honest, uncomplicated, utterly brave, but he was completely out of touch with the new principles of war. Napoleon found him to be a thoroughly dependable divisional commander and rewarded him for his long years of loyal service before and after the Revolution by awarding him a Marshal's baton in 1804.

After the Italian campaign came the expedition which Napoleon led to conquer Egypt. Here two new names came to the fore: Louis Nicolas Davout and Jean-Andoche Junot. Napoleon was in Egypt and Syria from July 1798 until August 1799, when he handed over command of the Army of the Orient to General Kléber and ran the British blockade back to France. He took with him only Berthier, Lannes, Murat, Bessières, and another former *aide-de-camp* from the old Army of Italy: Auguste-Frédéric-Louis Viesse de Marmont, who as a young officer had served in the same artillery unit as Napoleon. The other generals were repatriated from Egypt with the army when peace was signed with Britain in March 1802. Kléber, however, was dead by this time: he had been assassinated in June 1800 by an Arab fanatic.

On the Continent, Britain had meanwhile brought Austria back into the war in what became known as the 'War of the Second Coalition'. Russia, too, joined the Allied camp, and the Republic had to fight for its life. The British and Russians landed in Holland at Den Helder but withdrew after prodding half-heartedly at the approaches to Amsterdam, and the French general who got the credit for 'expelling' the invaders from Dutch soil was another future Marshal, Guillaume Marie Anne Brune. Certainly the greatest feat of this stage of the war was Massena's defence of Switzerland (which the French had occupied and converted, like Holland and the states of northern Italy, into a puppet republic). An Austro-Russian force closed in on Zürich from the north, while another expeditionary force under the great Suvorov carved its way across northern Italy and headed across the St Gotthard Pass to join up from the south. By destroying the enemy army at Zürich, Massena forced Suvorov to withdraw or face destruction himself. Switzerland, which otherwise would have become a springboard for an Allied invasion of France, was saved for the Republic. Also serving under Massena during the battle for Zürich were Mortier, Ney, Soult, and two more future Marshals (though not of the first creation): Louis Gabriel Suchet and Nicolas Charles Oudinot.

The second phase of the War of the Second Coalition began after Napoleon returned to France in 1799 and engineered the coup d'état which made him master of France as First Consul of the Republic. This is not the place to describe the intrigues, manoeuvring, threats, and plain brute force which made the coup succeed; but it underlined the fact that the generals who backed Napoleon were not unanimous in their approval. There were the 'old Republicans', the ex-Jacobin generals, all ex-heroes of '93, and they needed quite as much delicate handling as Napoleon's political opposition.

Napoleon's seizure of power was made considerably easier by the fact that the only generals who mattered were those who were actually in Paris. It was also convenient, as far as French public opinion was concerned, that the ludicrous, neo-Classical constitution of the 'Directorate' (it was run by five Directors and had a 'Council of Ancients' and a 'Council of Five Hundred') was just about as corrupt and discredited as a government can get. But Napoleon knew very well that the support he got from the other French Army chiefs was in many cases conditional. Jourdan and Augereau were hardcore 'old Republicans'. So was Lefebvre, Governor of Paris; but Lefebvre, a very simple man, was easily beguiled by Napoleon into giving the coup his blessing. Far more intractable was War Minister Charles Jean Bernadotte, another ex-'*Sambre-et-Meuse*' general. He was an outspoken critic of Napoleon and a born intriguer who had earned Napoleon's justified mistrust ever since 1797. Bernadotte disassociated himself with the coup and had to make his peace with Napoleon when it succeeded. Above all there was Jean Victor Marie Moreau, the most prominent general in France apart from Napoleon himself. Moreau backed Napoleon's coup in 1799 but was a staunch Republican at heart, and remained a natural focus for intrigues against the Consulate.

Once First Consul, Napoleon had an immediate task which helped him keep the generals out of political mischief for a while: the war had still to be won. Italy was the most urgent trouble-spot. The north Italian plain was back in Austrian hands and the French Army of Italy was as tired, demoralized, and disorganized as it had been when Napoleon had first taken it over in March 1796. This time, however, there was a very real danger of a full-blooded Austrian invasion of France across the Maritime Alps. Napoleon gave the Army of Italy to Massena, the hero of Zürich and the defence of Switzerland in 1799. It was obvious that the only way to pin down the Austrians in northern Italy was to hold on to Genoa, which the Austrians dare not leave in French hands if they wanted to invade France. Massena and his second-in-command – Soult – therefore based themselves on Genoa with a garrison of three divisions (17,820 men) against which the Austrians under Melas could pit 95,000. To add to his problems Massena had a civilian population of about 70,000 to feed.

The siege of Genoa began on 20 April, 1800, when the French had been driven back to the city's outer defensive perimeter and had had their coastal communications severed to the west. Meanwhile Admiral Keith's British warships imposed a close blockade on Genoa, cutting off all possible French supplies or reinforcements by sea.

There were many appalling sieges during the Revolutionary and Napoleonic Wars, but Genoa, 1800, was one of the worst. Massena held on and held on until hair-powder was being issued to eke out the virtually non-existent flour ration and the starving population of Genoa (who got half the starvation-scale rations issued to the troops) were begging him to surrender. The French garrison, however, launched repeated sorties, in one of which Soult was badly wounded and taken prisoner. Massena had to keep going for as long as he could, for he knew that the First Consul's 'Reserve Army' was planning to cross the Alps and make a lightning descent on the Austrians' rear, and that it was vital for Genoa to hold out and prevent the Austrians from concentrating in full force to meet this new threat. At last, on 27 May, a despatch from Napoleon was brought through the Allied ring clamped round Genoa, telling Massena that the spearheads of the Reserve Army were across the St Bernard Pass. By this time Massena had about 3,000 troops in hospital and the daily death rate in Genoa was up to 400. Even so, Massena protracted the surrender talks with the Austrians and the British and did not capitulate until 4 June, marching out with a mere 8,110 emaciated troops.

Ten days later – 14 June – the battle of Marengo was fought near Alessandria. Thanks to totally inadequate reconnaissance, Napoleon's army was attacked by superior forces and driven off the field. The day was only saved by a brilliant counter-attack by General Desaix's division, and it was yet another stroke of luck for Napoleon that Desaix got himself killed in the process and left the lion's share of the credit for the victory of Marengo to the First Consul. Marengo was a tremendous shock for the Austrians in Italy, who at once sued for armistice terms. Napoleon's daring strategy had abolished the threat to France from Italy, but tactically he owed it all to Massena and the dead Desaix.

Defeat at Marengo would not necessarily have been fatal for Napoleon, for the Reserve Army was only the central force in an arc of French armies stretching from the Riviera to the upper Rhine. General Moreau's Army of the Rhine had opened its offensive on 25 April (five days after the siege of Genoa began), crossing the Rhine with Ney's division in the van. The weeks that followed amounted to a leisurely, cautious waltz across southern Germany, with Moreau waging a good old-fashioned 18th-century war of manoeuvre. He had started with considerably greater forces than those of his Austrian opponent, Kray; the idea had been for the Army of the Rhine to win a crushing victory and then divert troops south to reinforce the French in Italy. Throughout May and June, however, Moreau manoeuvred Kray eastward without forcing a general engagement. A truce with the Austrian army on the Danube was signed on 15 July, a month after Marengo; abortive negotiations broke down in late October and the campaign was resumed. The result was the battle of Hohenlinden (3 December, 1800) which smashed the Austrian army, opened the road to Vienna, and knocked Austria out of the Second Coalition for good. The weaker adherents of the coalition were then subjected to a diplomatic mopping-up which left a war-weary Britain alone in the fight, and which led in turn to the Peace of Amiens in March 1802.

Even before Marengo and Hohenlinden, Napoleon had cemented his hold over France by proving he could rule. By putting in an average of eighteen hours' work per day he set about smashing the administrative bottlenecks created by the various Revolutionary regimes and getting the wheels of government turning again. His strategy and diplomacy gave France peace abroad; his reforms gave France domestic order and the basis of a growing prosperity unheard-of since 1789. As far as this story is concerned, one of his most important reforms was seeing that the troops got paid – a detail which had been generally ignored by the Directorate. By 1802 Napoleon was in such a strong position that he was able to ship off many of the disaffected generals to the dead-end campaign against the slaves in San Domingo, while Bernadotte retreated to the provinces in disgrace. 1802 was also the year in which Napoleon founded the morale-boosting institution of the *Légion d'honneur* and made himself First Consul for life.

It was also in this period that Ney was drawn for the first time into the inner circle of the generals in Napoleon's favour. Before May 1801 Ney had never even visited Paris; he had never met Napoleon, nor concerned himself with politics. It was clear from his record, however, that he was a first-rate fighting general, and Napoleon wanted him on his side. This was accomplished via the boudoir. Josephine selected a suitable bride from her *entourage* – Aglaé Louise Auguié – and propelled Ney gently but firmly across her path. Nature only took its course after Ney had been persuaded to cut off his old-fashioned pigtail and shave his hussar's side-whiskers, and after Aglaé had been subjected to a deal of propaganda lauding Ney to the skies; but on 27 July, 1802, negotiations were concluded and the marriage contract was signed. The wedding was on 5 August, with Ney wearing a magnificent sword presented to him by Napoleon. Later that year Ney was given a new role, that of a diplomat. Counter-revolutionary patriots were getting too active in Switzerland, and a German-speaking general was needed to bring them to their senses with a combination of diplomacy and sabre-rattling. Ney was in Switzerland from October 1802 until March 1803; he paid a visit to France for the birth of his first son, to whom Napoleon and Joseph Bonaparte stood as godparents, and then returned to Switzerland. The basic negotiations were concluded in September 1803, and Ney returned to France in January 1804, having already received the congratulations of Napoleon for having completed a first-rate job.

By this time war was looming again. The tenuous Peace of Amiens ended in May 1803, although for weeks beforehand Britain had been press-ganging for the Fleet and Napoleon had ordered a start to be made on a new invasion flotilla. He was also planning the complete reorganization of the French Army into separate corps — each one a miniature army in its own right, with balanced proportions of horse, foot, and guns, and each under the command of a first-rate general. The objective was England, the 'modern Carthage', which the First Consul now pledged himself to invade and destroy. To this end he deployed the 'Army of the Ocean Coast', which at its peak in the early summer of 1805 contained seven army corps.

In 1803 the British landed Georges Cadoudal, a leading Royalist, on French soil. His task was simple: to eliminate Napoleon and open the way for the restoration of the Bourbons. Also party to the plot was General Pichegru, a former Republican commander who had been exiled for Royalist sympathies. Moreau, too, was approached; he was all for getting rid of Napoleon, but refused to be associated with the Royalists. In February-March 1804, Napoleon's security police pounced and arrested Cadoudal, Pichegru, and Moreau, together with about twenty other Royalist exiles who had secretly returned to France. Moreau was exiled; Pichegru died in prison (probably by suicide); and Cadoudal was sentenced to death. At the same time Napoleon had the young Duc d'Enghien snatched from neutral territory across the French frontier, dragged to Paris, and shot. Napoleon believed that Enghien was the Bourbon prince who was to be the figurehead in the Cadoudal plot — but there was no evidence for this whatsoever.

Damnable though the execution of Enghien was, the

Cadoudal plot and its implications led directly to the proclamation of the Empire. 'We have done more than we hoped to do', commented Cadoudal as he awaited his execution in jail: 'We meant to give France a King, and we have given her an Emperor.' Napoleon was proclaimed Emperor on 18 May, 1804, and the list of the new Marshals of the Empire was announced on the following day.

It included six elderly 'old Republicans' whose period of active service was well advanced, if not virtually over — Jourdan, Lefebvre, Moncey, Perignon, Kellermann, and Sérurier. It included the inner circle generals who had been with Napoleon in Italy and Egypt — Berthier, Massena, Davout, Augereau, Lannes, Murat, and Bessières. It included the three aces from the Army of the Rhine — Ney, Soult, and Mortier. Finally there was Brune, who had added a victory over the Vendée rebels in 1800 to his nominal victory over the British and Russians in Holland in 1799; and Bernadotte, the ace-intriguer who was nevertheless yoked to the inner circle by personal friendships with the other Marshals and by the fact that he was Joseph Bonaparte's brother-in-law.

Such were the Marshals of the first creation — Republican symbols, potential enemies, and completely devoted fighting men, all now given rich estates and incomes and the highest military status in the land. There would not be many weeks in which the new Marshals could enjoy their new fortunes in peace. Already, for the seven corps commanders of the 'Army of the Ocean Coast', the descent on England loomed large.

CHAPTER TWO

NAPOLEON'S EMPIRE

In later years Napoleon was to claim that the training-camps of the 'Army of the Ocean Coast' and the blatant preparations for the invasion of England were only a cover for the training of the *Grande Armée*, and that he had never intended to risk the invasion at all. This was certainly an attempt to explain away the embarrassment of having had medals 'Struck in London, 1805' to celebrate the *'Descente en Angleterre'*, but it contained a half-truth. The 'Army of the Ocean Coast' was certainly a double-edged weapon which could be just as easily swung against central Germany as committed to an invasion of southern England.

'Hanover, after all,' John Terraine has commented, 'is hardly a suitable departure-point for invading Kent' – and Hanover was where Bernadotte's I Corps was based in the summer of 1805. The II Corps was at Utrecht, commanded by Marmont, who had not been given a baton with the other eighteen (mainly because of his age: he was not yet thirty in May 1804). At Bruges there was Davout with the III Corps; Soult was at Boulogne with the IV Corps, and then, in close proximity, Lannes with the V Corps and Ney with the VI Corps. Last came Augereau at Brest with the VII Corps. A mere glance at the map shows that only Davout, Soult, Lannes, and Ney were really in position for a swift cross-channel assault.

Everything turned on whether or not the British battle fleet could be lured away on a wild-goose-chase for long enough to permit the French invasion flotilla to make the crossing. By the time that Napoleon had accepted that this was not to be – 24 August, 1805 – the 'Army of the Ocean Coast' knew its embarkation-drill backwards. But by then the British had brought Russia and Austria into a Third Coalition (Prussia, fatally for herself, maintained a selfish neutrality). Here were enemies within Napoleon's reach, and by the end of August the seven corps were heading east for the Rhine. The *Grande Armée* was beginning its march into military legend.

A brief description of the corps system is called for at this point. It was the logical development on a larger scale of the divisional breakdown which had become the norm during the Revolutionary Wars. A corps was a miniature army with its own complements of horse, foot, and guns. The basic unit around which *esprit de corps* was encouraged to jell was the regiment with its eagle. Sergeant Thirion of the 2nd Cuirassiers (heavy cavalry) has left us a detailed description of an eagle. He knew what he was talking about because he was given the job of carrying the thing when the *Grande Armée* retreated from Moscow in 1812:

'I must confess that I found the standard extremely heavy. At the end of a fairly long staff was a bronze eagle with open wings. Under the eagle, and nailed to the staff, was a square flag of white satin surrounded on three sides by a gold fringe made out of bullion the length and thickness of one's finger. On this flag had been embroidered in large letters of gold: *The Emperor to his 2nd Regiment of Cuirassiers*. The reverse side bore the names of all the battles in which the regiment had taken part, and on every square inch of satin left blank by these inscriptions was a swarm of bees half the size of one's thumb. To the eagle's feet was tied a white satin cravat which hung double for a yard and had at each end a tassel made from twisted fringes larger than a finger, all in gold. The whole thing was furled in a morocco sheath.'

Regimental battalions were grouped in brigades, and the

brigades into divisions. The number of divisions per corps varied considerably. Corps commanders in action frequently found themselves being ordered to give up one of their divisions to reinforce a more critical sector of the line. But to take Ney's VI Corps as an example, a typical corps of the *Grande Armée* in 1805 consisted of a cavalry division and three infantry divisions, with an artillery strength of 36 guns. Ney's cavalry division (General Tilly) consisted of three regiments. A total of 24 battalions formed six brigades, two per division: 1st Division (General Dupont), 2nd Division (General Loison) and 3rd Division (General Mahler). The movements of the corps – over 20,000 men apiece – were co-ordinated by Napoleon and Berthier at Imperial Head-quarters, where the intricate brainwork of getting the corps to the right place at the right time without collisions was carried out.

The Allies anticipated that the French would mount a strong offensive through northern Italy, as they had done in 1796 and 1800, but Napoleon was planning to follow Moreau's route in 1800 and drive directly upon Vienna across the Rhine, through the Black Forest and Bavaria to the upper Danube valley. Throughout September the long months of training on the Channel coast proved their worth as, with magnificent march discipline and staying-power, the seven French corps, with Bessières' Imperial Guard corps and Murat's Reserve Cavalry corps, closed up to their first concentration-line which curved north along the Rhine from Basle and eastwards to Würzburg.

At Ulm on the Danube was the Austrian General Mack with 60,000 men, his attention fixed by Murat's cavalry to the west. What he did not discover until too late was that Napoleon had wheeled his main force around the Austrian's northern front, closing them to the east of Ulm in superior strength to that of Mack's army. After a savage fight at Elchingen on 14 October, Mack's forces were driven back on Ulm. Elchingen was solely Ney's work; he led the French counter-attack in person, and when he stormed the Michelberg heights on the 15th the investment of Ulm was complete. Mack surrendered on 20 October, raising the score of captives which had fallen to the French since the beginning of the campaign to 60,000 prisoners, 18 generals, 200 guns, 5,000 horses, and 80 standards.

The next objective was Vienna, and the corps fanned out for the march — Ney to occupy the Tyrol, Bernadotte to enter Munich and Salzburg, Marmont to curve southwards towards Graz and make contact with the 50,000 men of Massena's Army of Italy which were supposed to be coming up from the south. A new corps was formed from reserve units, put in position on the extreme left, and given to Mortier — but Mortier got a battering in his first brush with the Austro-Russian forces under the command of Kutuzov as the latter fell back. The tremendous pace of the advance from the Channel was now beginning to tell; there was much straggling and fighting for rations on the march to Vienna, which Napoleon's troops entered on 14 November.

Even before Ulm the Marshals had shown that as individuals they were fiercely jealous of their own authorities. Napoleon had put Murat in command of the corps of both Lannes and Ney and this arrangement had proved to be disastrous. Ney's triumph at Elchingen, which retrieved the situation, laid the foundations of a lasting rivalry with Murat. Far more serious was the inevitable result of the pell-mell pace of the campaign; straggling, looting, inadequate rations and forage. If the Austro-Russian forces under Kutuzov had been in any position to counter-attack during the march on Vienna, the result might have been very different.

As it was, Napoleon headed northwards out of Vienna, making for Bohemia and the Austro-Russian army. A brilliant piece of bluffwork by Lannes and Murat enabled the French to seize the Danube bridge at Spitz before the Austrians guarding it could blow it up. Napoleon knew that he must tempt the Austro-Russian force to give battle before either Prussia joined the Allied coalition or before the Austrian Archduke Charles, who had disengaged from Massena after a fight at Caldiero on the Adige, could come up from Italy with his army. If Kutuzov had had his way Napoleon might have been fatally over-extended in his quest for a decisive battle, but luckily for the French the young Tsar Alexander I overruled his experienced old general and insisted on a stand-up fight. The result was Austerlitz, a battle which has become a classic of timing and the exploitation of terrain to split an enemy army. Lannes, Soult, Bernadotte, and Davout commanded the corps of the line, with the Guard and the Reserve Cavalry (Bessières and Murat) poised to take up the running.

After Austerlitz, as after Ulm, there was a rich crop of mutual complaints and recriminations among the Marshals. A bitter feud between Bernadotte and Davout was developing and there were respective rows between Lannes and Soult, Soult and Davout, and Murat and Lannes. To crown everything Lannes took offence at the Emperor's bulletir which, he felt, gave insufficient credit to the work done by Lannes' corps, and took himself off on a prolonged, self-awarded leave. It is significant that while Napoleon was swift to punish dereliction of duty by his Marshals in future years, he let this peccadillo pass.

Certainly he could afford to. Ulm and Austerlitz smashed the Third Coalition as Marengo and Hohenlinden had smashed the Second. Austria was out. The brutal fact was rammed down Austria's throat with the signing of the Peace of Pressburg (27 December, 1805). The Habsburg Empire was now shorn of all its former territories in Germany and North Italy, plus the Adriatic province of Dalmatia. Bavaria, Württemberg, and Baden passed to Napoleon as 'independent' client kingdoms. Napoleon hoped to bribe Prussia into becoming his most influential agent, policing the north German states in the interests of France. Prussia, ignobly, had already hastened to sign the Treaty of Schönbrunn, exchanging Anspach and Neuchâtel for the former Electorate of Hanover.

On 1 April, 1806, after Massena had chased the Neapolitan

Bourbons out of southern Italy, Napoleon made his brother Joseph King of Naples. In the summer a small British expeditionary force led by General Stuart landed in southern Italy and smashed a French division at Maida, using its well-drilled fire power to shatter the onrushing French. Massena meanwhile found himself tied down with 40,000 soldiers, trying to crush the guerrilla patriots of Calabria.

British fire power plus the intangible fury of guerrilla warfare – very soon, now these would be recognized as the two main ingredients of the Peninsular War. The experience gained in Italy in 1806 might have given the French Army invaluable experience in how not to tackle irregular warfare, but events moved rapidly in another, conventional direction. The guerrilla war in southern Italy was overlaid by another great campaign in Germany against the power whose presence at Austerlitz must surely have tipped the scales against Napoleon: Prussia.

Greed had induced Prussia to sign the Treaty of Schönbrunn with Napoleon, and greed drove Prussia into her decision to go to war with Napoleon rather than give up Hanover should Britain negotiate a separate peace. But this venture was not only selfish: it was stupid. The Prussians did not give themselves sufficient time for the Russian armies in Poland to come to their aid. In 1806 Prussia took the field alone, and was ruined in consequence.

The main body of the *Grande Armée* was lying in southern Germany when the Prussian war began on 7 October. The Guard had been withdrawn to France, while Marmont's II Corps had been sent off to occupy Dalmatia. When the Guard joined up after having been rushed into Germany by relays of four-horsed waggons, Napoleon had about 130,000 men – almost exactly the size of the Prussian field army which was lumbering south with the idea of cutting the French communications with the Rhine.

When the campaign began some of the Marshals had recently come up in the world and had been given new titles, and those who had not were determined to do their level best to do the same. Berthier was now Prince of Neufchâtel. Murat was Grand Duke of Berg. Bernadotte, whose adherence to Napoleon had always been the most ambiguous of all, was Prince of Ponte-Corvo. Titles were titles, after all: who would get the next? Would they be awarded for prowess on the battlefield, for governing provinces, or in memory of exploits in the former Army of the Republic?

Thoughts like these lay at the back of the Marshals' minds at the start of the Jena campaign, which has been hailed as a classic war of annihilation. Certainly, the destruction of the Prussian Army created by Frederick the Great in one month was an astonishing feat. True, Napoleon's first use of the '*battaillon carré*', the lozenge formation which he now adopted to move the army corps and bring them together on the battlefield, was also significant. But there could be no denying the faults committed by the individual Marshals — faults which were only retrieved by considerable luck, Prussian inflexibility, and desperate fighting.

The *Grande Armée* marched from the Nuremberg region in the following formation:

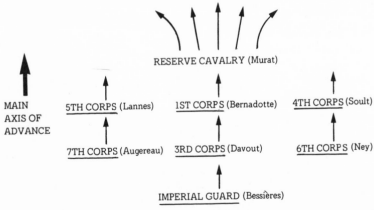

It was a rectangular formation, spread out across a front of about sixty miles to start with but drawing together as the march went on. The cavalry, riding ahead, probed for the enemy. The idea was that the formation could wheel left or right at a moment's notice depending on where the enemy turned out to be. But to envisage the advance to Jena as a steady crawl of seven black rectangles which wheeled neatly around the left flank of the Prussian Army and finally broke it at Jena and Auerstädt, though attractive, is misleading. The basic strategy was perfect but liaison between Napoleon and his Marshals was tenuous at best, and the staffs of the various corps were more often than not in the dark as to the day's objectives. But even if this had not been the case, the private rivalries between the Marshals meant that Napoleon never had the reins of a perfect team in his hands.

To sum up: by 13 October Napoleon knew that the Prussian army of Brunswick and Hohenlohe was somewhere near Jena, east of Weimar. He planned to wheel the *Grande Armée* to the left and lay it across the Prussian left flank. Lannes and Augereau wheeled to the left; the Guard moved up in the centre; Soult and Ney came across from the right; and Bernadotte and Davout were told to keep going and envelop the left rear of the Prussians. So far so good. But the deployment of the French during the night of the 13th could well have been disastrous; the exact position of the Prussian army at Jena had not been fixed with precision. If the French had not been screened by a fog on the morning of the 14th, they could have been broken up by artillery fire while their ranks were still jammed together. Then the battle was begun prematurely by Ney jumping the gun, leading his advance troops hell-for-leather against the Prussian line before the bulk of his own corps had moved up into the line, and before Soult and Lannes were in position on the French flanks. Only Ney's bravery, plus the luck of the devil and the unrolling of the main French attack, brought him through without defeat and disgrace.

Worst of all, however, was Napoleon's belief that he had the Prussian main body in front of him at Jena. He did not. While he was massing 90,000 Frenchmen against 40,000 Prussians, Davout was at Auerstädt, fighting for his life with his 26,000 men against the main Prussian army of at least

60,000. He was forced to hold out all day, alone, for Bernadotte's corps kept out of action and did not fire a shot in either engagement. Certainly it was Davout whose stand at Auerstädt pinned down enough Prussians to make the rout at Jena decisive.

After the victory came the pursuit. It went at breakneck speed and overturned the last Prussian hopes of carrying on the war; but at times it was as rapid as it was for the wrong reasons. Murat led it, with the cavalry, of course; but Ney's corps force-marched to Berlin via Weimar, Erfurt, and Magdeburg and the motive was as much due to Ney's rivalry with Murat as to his military genius. (The same applied to Lannes and Murat.) But whatever the motives the results were tremendous. The key cities and fortresses of Prussia fell like ninepins in great advances east to the Polish frontier and west to the Danish frontier. Twenty-three days after Jena and Auerstädt the last pocket of Prussian resistance — Lübeck — fell, and King Frederick William III of Prussia agreed to Napoleon's terms.

For the moment, these terms boiled down to letting the French use Prussia as a base of operations against the Russians in Poland. This new campaign followed the humiliation of Prussia without a break. It drove the *Grande Armée* to the limit of its endurance. It saw the French held for a time by an enemy as tough as themselves, and Napoleon fought to a bloody draw instead of winning a triumphant victory in pitched battle. But it ended successfully in the summer of 1807 with Napoleon absolute master of the European Continent, the French Empire at its zenith, and the Marshals heaped with new honours.

As the *Grande Armée* drove eastward across the plain of Poland during the November of 1806, the weather broke. Napoleon and Berthier found themselves confronted for the first time with the appalling problems caused by campaigning in the winter mud of the East European Plain. Even before Murat's squadrons entered Warsaw on 28 November, the *Grande Armée* had begun to flounder and curse just as the

German Wehrmacht was to do before Moscow in 1941. Napoleon represented the arrival of the French as a crusade on behalf of the Poles, and some 30,000 volunteer Polish legionnaires rallied to him. But the Russians were another matter. Not until February 1807 did Napoleon manage to force a full-scale battle: at Eylau on the 7th.

It was a near disaster for the French. Battle was joined before Davout and Ney had time to bring their corps into the line, which left Napoleon with 60,000 men against 80,000 Russians. Augereau, ordered to launch a spoiling attack with his corps, failed to attack at the right spot because of a blinding, driving snowstorm, with the result that the Russian gunners got unrestricted target practice at the flank of his corps. The losses in Augereau's corps were frightful and the balance swung heavily to the Russians' favour. A mass cavalry charge led by Murat saved the day for the French and both sides drew off — but the Russian army was still intact, the French had lost some 18,000 men, and Augereau's corps was too broken up to be re-formed. Its survivors were shared out among the other corps.

The next three months saw Napoleon urgently calling up more reinforcements from Germany and Italy to prepare for the summer campaign of 1807. They also saw Marshal Lefebvre, whom Napoleon had not yet entrusted with an independent command, capture the important port of Danzig on 24 May after a lengthy siege. Napoleon rewarded Lefebvre for this feat by making him Duke of Danzig. The summer campaign started badly with Murat's cavalry getting itself routed at Heilsberg on 10 June, but four days later the situation was restored by the battle of Friedland. At last Napoleon was able to fight the sort of battle he wanted, with every corps where it should be. At Friedland — 14 June, 1807 — the decisive advance was made by Ney, earning him the tribute 'That man is a lion!' from Napoleon. Friedland knocked the Russians out of the war in exactly the same way as Austerlitz eliminated Austria in 1805. The way was clear for the signing of the peace treaties and the drawing of the frontiers of the new Europe.

This was done at Tilsit on the Niemen eleven days after Friedland, when Napoleon and Tsar Alexander met and agreed on the terms under which France and Russia would now live in peace. First came Prussia, truncated, occupied forced to disgorge the territory swallowed in the partitions of Poland. This now became the 'Grand Duchy of Warsaw', a French-influenced Polish buffer state between Prussia and Russia. Prussia also lost her western provinces, which became the 'Kingdom of Westphalia' ruled by Napoleon's youngest brother, Jerome. Until she paid her war reparations in full, Prussia was to remain under French occupation. South of Prussia came Saxony, a French client. Further south still was Austria, a nominal ally of France, still shaken after Austerlitz. Across the Alps lay the northern 'Kingdom of Italy', an extension of the French Empire itself, and Joseph Bonaparte's 'Kingdom of Naples' in the south. Eastward across the Adriatic was Dalmatia, now given the title of the 'Illyrian Provinces' and doing very well under Marmont's governorship. Western Germany was now know as the 'Confederation of the Rhine', which had Napoleon himself as its 'Protector'.

Napoleon's policy being 'France before all', these new client states proved their usefulness by paying out royalties from their annual revenues to the Marshals and to other worthies of the Empire. The Grand Duchy of Warsaw was a good case in point. After the Eylau-Friedland campaign, for example, Marshal Ney's bank balance was enriched by an annual 28,000 francs from the exchequer of 'liberated' Warsaw by order of the Emperor.

On 13 July, 1807, a new Marshal (the nineteenth) was created: Claude-Victor Perrin, better known by his adopted surname of Victor. Born at Lamarche in the Vosges in 1764, Victor entered the pages of military history as a drummer-boy in the Grenoble Artillery Regiment in 1781. He left the Regular Army in 1791 and joined up as a grenadier in the

National Guard. Here he was obviously lucky with his elections, for by 15 September, 1792, he had become Lieutenant-Colonel of the 2nd Battalion of Volunteers (Bouches-du-Rhône).

Serving with the Republican armies of the south, Victor ended up in the army of Italy, having been promoted temporary brigadier-general for services rendered at the siege of Toulon. (Toulon, it will be remembered, was one of those episodes which was particularly good for promotion.) His rank was confirmed after serving with the Army of the Eastern Pyrenees, where he commanded the reserve; he then returned to the Army of Italy and commanded brigades under both Augereau and Massena during Napoleon's first Italian campaign. Napoleon made Victor a temporary divisional commander in January 1797 and he fought so well against the troops of the Papal States, capturing Ancona and Macerata in the process, that his new rank was confirmed yet again.

Victor did not go to Egypt with Napoleon's expeditionary force. Instead he ended up in a dead-end position in the so-called 'Army of England' and asked to be sent back to the Army of Italy. It might have been unfortunate for Victor that this particular request was granted because it plunged him into the disastrous series of French defeats in Italy at the hands of the Russians in 1799. But after Napoleon returned from Egypt, and after the coup d'état which made him First Consul, there were many generals whose loyalties were wooed to secure their allegiance to the new regime, and Victor was one of them. As a former comrade of the Army of Italy, Victor was given a corps command in the Reserve Army, an army which for eight heady days – 11-19 April – he actually commanded. In the Marengo campaign he did well in the fight at Montebello, the curtain-raiser to Marengo itself; but it was largely due to Victor's misleading reconnaissance of the Austrian positions at Marengo that Napoleon divided his army with such near-fatal results.

After the Marengo campaign Victor was given two significant posts which suggest that Napoleon regarded him as something of a second-rater; command of the occupation troops in Holland and Captain-General of Louisiana. The latter command would have been banishment indeed had Napoleon gone ahead with his plans to reinforce Louisiana; but the post evaporated with the sale of Louisiana to the United States of America in 1803, and Victor was returned to storage in Holland. He had nothing to do during the training of the 'Army of the Ocean Coast', and in February 1805 he was sent off to Copenhagen as Minister Pleni-potentiary to Denmark.

Over a year of inactivity followed for Victor. He was not involved in the epic Austerlitz campaign, but when the campaign against Prussia began in the autumn of 1806 he was assigned to Lannes as chief-of-staff and served at Jena. By the time of the miserable winter campaign of 1806-7 there were not many Prussian troops still under arms and fighting with their Russian allies, but Victor managed to get himself captured by a group of Prussian cavalry in January 1807; and he remained a prisoner until his exchange was negotiated after Eylau. A further stroke of luck for Victor came when Bernadotte was slightly wounded in early June and Victor took over the I Corps, leading it at Friedland. It was this last command which earned Victor his baton, plus over 50,000 francs' income, half from the revenues of Westphalia and half from those of Hanover.

Victor was the Marshal of schoolboy legend, the drummer-boy with the Marshal's baton in his knapsack. As far as military capacity was concerned, however, the kindest thing that can be said about Victor was that he was as brave at the next man, but dim. He was capable enough in his own way — but only when he was put firmly under a capable superior who could see to it that he was given work which he could actually do. Victor could be a disaster when let loose with an independent command. He was not unique in this: there were plenty of other Marshals (Lefebvre, for example) who were much the same. Unfortunately, however, the time was at hand when the new Marshal Victor would be given just such an independent command, with fatal results both for the troops he led and for the plans which he was supposed to carry out.

The essence of the Tilsit settlement was Napoleon's grandiose bid to close the ports of Europe to the commerce by which Britain lived — 'to defeat', as he put it, 'the sea by the land'. Unfortunately for his 'Continental System', which had been announced in the famous Berlin Decrees of November 1806, the mercantile powers of Europe — France included — got just as much profit out of trade with Britain as Britain got out of trade with them, and the Decrees gave the technique and practice of smuggling a mighty shot in the arm. But the Continental System did have teeth. There was a £4½ million fall-off in British exports to the Continent between early 1807 and early 1808, and the further burden of the Anglo-American naval war of 1812 had even more damaging repercussions.

It was natural that in his quest to seal off every mercantile loophole in the entire European coastline Napoleon should seek to dominate Spain and England's 'oldest ally', Portugal — but he did have other motives. The Neapolitan Bourbons had been chased out of Naples and across the Straits of Messina into Sicily, but Bourbon Spain was right on France's doorstep and was a natural direct route for any hostile army in British pay which wanted to strike at the very heart of the French Empire. With Russia neutralized and both central and southern Europe under his control, it could only be a question of time before Napoleon sought a showdown in the Peninsula.

He was not a clairvoyant. He had simply acquired the habit of getting his own way by military force, and in the French Army he had a superb weapon which had never let him down. In July 1807, at the pinnacle of his power, he sent out the first orders which resulted in the outbreak of the Peninsular War.

CHAPTER THREE

INTO THE PENINSULA

To start with, Napoleon only intended to use Spain as a bridge across which he could get at Portugal and bludgeon her into forswearing her alliance with Britain. Lisbon, not Madrid, was his initial objective. Britain had been basing her fleets and mercantile shipping on Lisbon since the original outbreak of the war. Spain, on the other hand, had been an ally of France since 1804 and was still an ally in 1807. With Spain's ports closed on Napoleon's orders, all that needed to be done was to shut the British out of Lisbon as well and the last commercial bolt-hole in western Europe would be denied them.

Portugal and Spain fell naturally into the opposite camps of Britain and France. The British could always put pressure on Portugal by sea; the French could always do the same to Spain by land. These were geographical facts; and to a large extent they explain the Peninsular War as a whole.

Napoleon, however, was greatly helped by the fact that in 1807 both Portugal and Spain were ruled by complete nonentities. Prince John, the Portuguese Regent, was a timid and vacillating man. King Charles IV and Queen Maria Luisa of Spain were even worse, and their son and heir, Prince Ferdinand, was a depressing carbon-copy of his parents. The power behind the Spanish throne was that familiar historical phenomenon, the ruling favourite — in this case Prince Manuel de Godoy, whose many grandiloquent titles were headed by the inappropriate label 'Prince of the Peace'.

Godoy had pushed Spain into the First Coalition against France and had got her out in 1795 just in time to avoid a crushing defeat. Later he had aligned his country with France (whose main concern was to use the Spanish fleet to help break Britain's stranglehold at sea), and even the crowning humiliation of Trafalgar, which virtually removed the Spanish battle fleet from the board, had not caused him to reverse his policy. Quite apart from his inability to play the part of a dynamic, successful war leader, Godoy was a thoroughly conventional favourite: he was cordially hated by one and all.

But when, after Austerlitz, it became clear that Napoleon's main concern had switched from invading England to subduing central Europe, Godoy began to think again. By the time of the campaign against Prussia in late 1806, Napoleon had begun to receive alarming reports of Spanish recruiting and levying of horses on Godoy's orders. As a result one of the conditions of the Berlin Decrees was a demand that Spain must not only join the Continental System but provide troops for garrison duties in north-west Europe.

Even an incompetent war-leader like Godoy could not fail to see which way the wind was blowing by the time of Friedland and Tilsit. He hastened to comply with Napoleon's demand for a Spanish expeditionary force to be sent to northern Germany, despatching the Marquis de la Romana with 15,000 Spanish troops to police the shores of the Baltic under French supervision.

Napoleon could not know it, but this would be the last success he would win by putting diplomatic pressure on the Peninsular powers.

Now only Portugal remained, and at first it seemed that straight bullying tactics would suffice. On 27 September, 1807, Napoleon barked at the Portuguese Ambassador: 'If Portugal does not do what I wish the House of Braganza will not be reigning in Europe in two months! I will no longer tolerate an English Ambassador in Europe. I will declare war on any power who receives one after two months from this time . . . !'

In fact, Napoleon had already made up his mind to intervene. In July 1807 he had given orders to prepare a French invasion force in the Bayonne area should intervention in the Peninsula become necessary. With the bulk of the *Grande Armée* still in Germany and Poland, this new strike force would have to be largely made up of raw conscripts, but with Spain on his side Napoleon saw few problems in getting them marched to Lisbon. And the man who got the job of leading the whole operation was a prime candidate for a Marshal's baton: Jean-Andoche Junot.

Junot, like Marmont, had so far been passed over for promotion to the Marshalate. He had been in all the right places at the right time, but had never yet been entrusted with an independent command. He had been Napoleon's secretary at the siege of Toulon in 1793 and had accompanied him through Italy and Egypt as an aide-de-camp. He was almost insanely brave in action and had run up a frightening tally of battle wounds. By 1801 he had achieved the rank of divisional general. Napoleon had sent Junot to Portugal as Ambassador in 1805 but he had thrown up the job, and he had served through the Austerlitz campaign as aide-de-camp to the Emperor. On 2 August, 1807, Napoleon appointed Junot commander-in-chief of the army euphemistically entitled 'The Corps of Observation of the Gironde'. And so it was Junot who led the first Imperial French army into the Peninsula, crossing the Rubicon-symbol of the River Bidassoa on 18 October. If you do well, ran his unwritten but obvious brief from Napoleon, you will be promoted to Marshal.

Junot is one of the most fascinating characters in the whole history of the Empire. Certainly he was one of the most tragic. He was utterly loyal; he was wildly unstable; he never became a Marshal; he died insane. Almost certainly his hectic campaigning in Italy and Egypt had made him a shell-shock case, and his tardy promotion suggests that Napoleon sensed this. Oddly enough, one of the best thumbnail-sketches of the man was made by an Englishma.

Bertie Greatheed was an English visitor to Paris during the Peace of Amiens; he had taken his family there to view the art treasures looted by the victorious Republic and crammed into the Louvre; and in the intervals between noting down his sour reflections on Parisian social life and manners under the Consulate he made the acquaintance of many eminent Frenchmen, both civilian and military. Junot was one of them. '3 February, 1803: Thursday . . . I dined with Green and met Junot and the two Divofs; we had a very interesting day indeed. The French had in Egypt to the full as many men as Abercromby, about 14,000, and their loss of that country resulted entirely from Menou's not collecting his men. Junot said, "I am 31 and by the time I am 41 I will be Governor of Egypt." This man is plain and frank: he has an enthusiastic love for Bonaparte, who shows his judgement in appointing him Commandant of Paris. He said, "If Bonaparte should order me to poignard 6,000 men I would do it without asking a question, and if I saw a dagger aimed at his breast, I would oppose my own. *Il m'a trouvé petit*", said he, putting his hands towards the ground, and raising them as high as he could, "*et il m'a fait grand comme cela.*" Mahomet had his Omar; why should not Bonaparte have his Junot?

'This man's parents must have been in some very humble station since he left them as a private soldier some 14 years ago. When he was serving with the army of the north he was raised to the rank of Sergeant in consequence of some brave action when his comrades brought him back on their heads. At the time when Bonaparte was General of Brigade before Toulon he wanted a person to gain intelligence and perform a service of great peril. Junot offered himself and did what he had undertaken. On making his report, Bonaparte, who writes a bad hand, dictated to Junot who wrote on his knee; he was pleased with the hand. At this moment a cannon-shot from an English ship took the ground close to them, and covered them all over with dirt. "This is good of the English", says Junot, "though they meant us harm; for I wanted some sand" [to blot his writing]. "*Cela n'est pas mal*", says Bonaparte to himself. So it was that these two men became acquainted.

'Junot has not the least conception of liberty, nor of any thing short of pure, unmixed, military despotism . . .

'Junot's nickname in the army was "*La Tempête*", and, said he, "*quand je n'avais pas l'ennemi je me battais avec mes camarades.*" *He has had two severe wounds on the head,* [author's italics] one from an Austrian sabre, the other a bullet, when they thought him dead and were going to bury him.

'4 February: Friday . . . One day Junot was asked what steps he would take if there should happen an insurrection of the people. He clenched his fists and with a terrible scowl replied "*Il n'en resterait pas un.*" Another time, when it was observed that Bonaparte would not let himself be brought from St. Cloud as Louis was by the mob from Versailles, "*Non*", says Junot, "*il vous ferait plaisir de voire comme il balayerait cette canaille.*" '

Later the same month February 1803, Greatheed met Junot again. 'Would that I had the whole conversation of the day on paper', he wrote. 'I would then present a picture the most perfect I can conceive of a thorough soldier with all his rough open virtues, and honourable murders on his head. A man kind-hearted, even tender I believe, till on the command of another man he thinks it is his duty to banish every feeling of humanity from his soul, and become more terrible than the tiger of Sumatra.' A typical piece of Junot-originated bombast came after the narration of a desperate escape. '*Non, non*', said he, '*ce n'était pas mon sort de périr là, je dois finir ma carrière dans St James Street.*' And again: 'He would have the soldiers wear more defensive armour, and particularly helmets instead of hats; as many offensive weapons as possible — "*on en a jamais de trop: je voudrais avoir cinquante pistolets.*" '

Such was the man who led the first French troops into the Peninsula on 18 October, 1807. They were not battle-hardened veterans from the *Grande Armée* but there were 24,000 of them, and their south-westerly march across Spain panicked both Prince John and Godoy. On 27 October, as if to rub in the true significance of Junot's presence in the Peninsula, Napoleon signed the Treaty of Fontainebleau with the Spaniards. It was a piece of typically squalid Bonapartism – an agreement in which Spain agreed to the partition of Portugal. Junot's forces would expel the Braganzan regime by taking Lisbon, after which southern Portugal would become a principality for Godoy while the north went to Charles IV.

Prince John of Portugal dithered frantically. The British were urging him to flee the country with his Government; he temporized, hoping for an eleventh-hour *rapprochement* with Napoleon, but he was hopelessly compromised by the Fontainebleau agreement. Meanwhile, goaded by Napoleon's repeated urgings, Junot's troops plodded miserably on towards Lisbon. Were it not for the fact that they were actually approaching their objective they would have been taken for a broken and retreating army. March discipline was appalling and straggling had reached epic proportions. Had the Portuguese been able to put up anything of a fight Junot might well have been stopped in his tracks, but luckily for him the march on Lisbon was unopposed.

On 13 November Napoleon's main propaganda newspaper, the *Moniteur*, proclaimed in Paris that the reign of the House of Braganza in Portugal had ended. And on the 30th Junot's leading troops staggered wearily into Lisbon. He had by this stage barely 2,000 men out of his original force of 24,000. The rest were spread out along his line of march in a state of dissarray which would have given Napoleon apoplexy if he could have seen it. But the trick had been won. Lisbon was in French hands – and Prince John had fled to the British, taking with him the court, the Government, and the ships of the Portuguese fleet.

Meanwhile a second Corps of Observation of the Gironde had been formed in southern France and was heading into the Peninsula to secure Junot's communications. It was commanded by yet another leading general ripe for the Marshalate: the Comte Pierre Dupont de l'Etang.

By 1807 Dupont was one of the most brilliant rising men in the *Grande Armée*. Born in 1765, he had joined the Regular Army in 1784. His first taste of action was in the disastrous Belgian campaign of April 1792, where he was wounded while defending his commanding general from mutineers. Dupont went on to serve with distinction with the Army of the North in Belgium, but he missed the Italian and Egyptian campaigns: the Directory had put him in charge of the Army Topographical and Historical Department. It was not until 1800 that he got back to active service; Berthier, nominal commander-in-chief of the Reserve Army (Napoleon only took command of the Reserve Army at the decisive moment), asked for Dupont's services as chief-of-staff. Dupont made his name during the storming of the Fort of Bard, which for a while threatened the Reserve Army's communications across the St Bernard; the fall of the fort enabled the Reserve Army to continue its southward rush into northern Italy, where Dupont duly served at Marengo.

After Marengo Dupont was put in command of the right wing of the Army of Italy and conquered Tuscany; he added to his reputation by winning the battle of Pozzolo on Christmas Day, 1800, soundly defeating 45,000 Austrians with a force of only 15,000. He then became a divisional commander in the *Grande Armée*, first under Ney, then Mortier, under whom he was beaten in the clash with Kutuzov's Russians at Dürrenstein on 11 November, 1805.

During the Jena campaign of 1806 Dupont commanded the 1st Division of Bernadotte's I Corps, but it was his service at Friedland which put him in the running for a corps command and a Marshal's baton. He came out of the Friedland campaign with an annuity of 19,261 francs (yet again at the expense of the Grand Duchy of Warsaw), the Grand Eagle of the *Légion d'honneur*, and the governorship of Berlin. And on 3 November, 1807, he was appointed commander-in-chief of the second Corps of Observation of the Gironde.

Dupont's initial task in the Peninsula was to establish

himself in northern Spain as a forerunner of the more experienced troops who were to follow shortly. This was not a formidable job. By 28 December Dupont had reached Vitoria, where his corps passed the winter of 1807-8.

Since Junot's entry into the Peninsula, Napoleon's communications with the Spanish Court had led him to believe that he would be able to kill two birds with one stone by exploiting the rift between Prince Ferdinand and his parents. Here again, Godoy was the key figure. 'This Prince of Peace, this mayor of the palace,' sneered Napoleon, 'is the rascal who will open to me the gates of Spain.' Ferdinand was in fact panic-stricken at the thought that Godoy would go so far as to usurp the throne if the King died, and he had made secret overtures to Napoleon for French support. Godoy had retaliated by urging the King and Queen to have Ferdinand arrested – but Napoleon had promptly ordered his release. The domestic rivaly in the Spanish Court was a godsend to Napoleon. Ferdinand, in fact, was a popular figure in Spain, regarded as the people's champion against the hated Godoy.

The New Year of 1808 saw Junot in Lisbon pulling his troops together and seeing to the garrisoning of Portugal, and Dupont's corps in winter quarters around Vitoria, More French troops soon followed. On 8 January Marshal Bon-Adrien-Jannot de Moncey crossed into Spain with the 'Corps of Observation of the Ocean Coasts', 30,000 strong. Like Dupont, Moncey halted in northern Spain.

Moncey was one of the more elderly Marshals. Born in 1754. he had twenty years' Army service behind him by 1789. His service in the Revolutionary Wars was far from the great battles in Belgium and on the Rhine: he served in the Pyrenean theatre. In fact he rose to the command of the Army of the Western Pyrenees and he was no stranger to Spain. In 1795 he had taken Vitoria, pushed the Spanish armies back to the Ebro, taken Bilbao, and had been generally instrumental in knocking Spain out of the First Coalition in that year. However, he was denounced as having Royalist sympathies in 1797 and received only secondary appointments until the Marengo campaign of 1800, when he commanded the back-up corps which descended on Lombardy across the St Gotthard Pass. He received his baton in 1804 not because he was a great Revolutionary hero or a trusted adherent of Napoleon, but because of his length of service and seniority in the Army. Moncey was stolid, unimaginative, but, if given an undemanding job, reliable enough. In the early months of 1808 the Peninsula was still an undemanding theatre in which to serve, and Moncey was as useful as any of the other Marshals to send to Spain and wait for the main action to begin.

By February 1808 Napoleon had insinuated a total of 54,000 French troops onto the territory of his apprehensive Spanish ally, with another 24,000 holding Lisbon. Napoleon had also begun an anti-Godoy propaganda campaign in the *Moniteur*, and even the desperate head-in-the-sand policy of the Spanish Government could no longer ignore the fact that it could not be long before he would show the iron fist.

It came on 16 February, a stunning blow: the French seized the Spanish frontier fortresses of Pamplona, San Sebastian, Figueras, and Barcelona. There was no declaration of war; there were no Spanish countermoves. By seizing these fortresses Napoleon had flung the entire Spanish frontier open to the passage of his armies.

Four days later he appointed Joachim Murat his 'Lieutenant-General in Spain', but several weeks went by before Murat had fully prepared the force which he planned to take with him to Madrid. This consisted of a hard core of 20,000 infantry and a hefty cavalry force, and their entry into Spain in March sparked off a popular rising at Aranjuez on the 17th. It was not an anti-French revolt at all: the enemy was Godoy. Charles IV panicked again and abdicated in an attempt to save his favourite, but when Murat arrived at Madrid on 23 March he put a stop to that. The last thing Napoleon wanted was for Ferdinand to become King with the enthusiastic support of the Spanish people, and so Charles IV was restored to his throne under protection of the

French.

Now Napoleon made his great mistake, the fatal error of judgment which killed every chance of his successful manipulation of the Peninsula. He decided to dispossess Charles and Ferdinand of the throne of Spain and put in a puppet king of his own choosing. Napoleon completely failed to grasp the fierce loyalty of the Spaniards to their traditional ruling house. He lumped together the King, the Queen, Godoy, and Ferdinand as a quadruple disaster from which Spain would be only too glad to be relieved, not seeing that Godoy alone was the real object of popular execration. He was absolutely right when he judged Spain as a poverty-stricken, primitive, and badly-ruled country. But he was absolutely wrong when he believed that the Spanish people would welcome the alien rule and military occupation of the invading French.

Once Napoleon's mind was made up events moved rapidly and dramatically. Napoleon invited the Spanish royal family to meet him at Bayonne in order to discuss their country's future relations with France. A series of meetings began on 30 April, and they were completely one-sided, the Spanish Bourbons receiving Napoleon's ultimatum to resign their rights to the Spanish throne. Napoleon must have felt some justification for his bullying tactics and the worthlessness of his opponents when he listened to Charles IV and his Queen denouncing their son and heir as a bastard in his presence in a vain attempt to save themselves. As the month of May opened, the sordid game was still being played out at Bayonne, with the Spanish King, Queen, Crown Prince, and favourite completely in the power of the French and wavering in the face of Napoleon's tempting offers of rich pensions and luxurious estates if they would only accept exile.

It was at this point that the people of Madrid began the Peninsular War.

Since 23 March the Spanish capital had been under the effective occupation of Murat's troops, a state of affairs that was tolerated as long as it was believed that the French had come to root out Godoy and, at the very worst, replace Charles IV with Ferdinand. But the disappearance of the royal family at the end of April caused growing disquiet in the capital; and when the news reached Madrid from the frontier that the King, the Queen, and the Prince were on French soil and in French hands the result was an explosion of blind, nationalist rage. On 2 May, the notorious *Dos de Mayo*, Madrid erupted in a frenzied citizen's crusade with one object: to drive out or massacre the hated French.

But that was what the French were there for, and Murat in particular knew all about crushing insurrectionary townees. It was a bloody affair while it lasted, but it was all over in four hours. The Madrid mob accounted for 150 French soldiers in their first disorganized rising, but the French got their revenge by killing some 400 Spaniards — by cannon fire, by the sabres of the cavalry and the bayonets of the infantry, and by the grim retaliatory firing-squads immortalized in Goya's terrifying painting of the *Dos de Mayo*. As night fell on the bloodstained streets and squares of Madrid, the Spanish capital was under martial law and securely in French hands again.

The *Dos de Mayo* was futile in itself but it was a deathless symbol with mighty results. When the news reached Napoleon at Bayonne it made the abdication of the Spanish Bourbons a foregone conclusion. This was signed and sealed by the Treaty of Bayonne on 5 May. All Napoleon had to do now was to get his brother Joseph recognized and crowned King of Spain, it seemed, and the problem of the Peninsula would be solved for good.

To make quite sure, Napoleon had sent Marshal Bessières into Spain to reinforce the contingents of Dupont and Moncey. This was the first independent command with which Bessières had been entrusted. It had the somewhat breathless title of 'The Imperial Guard and Divisons of Observation of the Western Pyrenees in Spain', and all Bessières had to do was to march these crack troops to Burgos, establish himself there, and stand by just in case there should be any trouble when King Joseph ascended his new throne. Meanwhile Murat had carefully selected a rubber-stamp 'Junta of Regency' made up of Spanish quislings from the nobility and former Court functionaries, and had got them to sign a petition to Napoleon asking for Joseph to be sent to Spain.

But the news from Madrid did not only travel to Bayonne. It radiated out across the provinces of the country, and the hitherto unforeseen factor of nationalist resentment took fire and spread with a terrifying speed. Less than a week after Napoleon wrote complacently to Talleyrand 'The Spanish business goes well and will soon be entirely settled' (16 May), the provinces began to revolt. In Badajoz on 20 May, the Spanish mob lynched the Governor, a puppet of the regime. Two days later and 250 miles away the same fate overtook the Governor of Cartagena. The province of Valencia broke out on the 23rd, and on the 24th came the revolt of Asturias, 500 miles away to the north-west and cut off from the heartland of Spain by mountain ranges. At Oviedo the Asturian insurrectionary Junta declared war on France in the name of 'King Ferdinand' and ordered the raising of 18,000 troops. Far more important, the Asturian patriots decided on 30 May to send a delegation to London to appeal for help from the British. The British Governor of Gibraltar, Sir Hew Dalrymple, had already been requested to send similar aid by the Junta of Andalusia at Seville, which had revolted on the 27th.

Nothing like this had been seen since the proclamation of the French Empire in 1804. None of the hereditary princes of Europe, with their powerful states and large armies, had been able to act in concert against Napoleon without meeting humiliating defeat. Yet the threadbare and ill-equipped provinces of Spain challenged Napoleon's attempt to take over their country in April-May 1808 with a grim, almost telepathic chain reaction. There was no conspiracy, no preparations, no wait for a given signal, and certainly no national leader — just this spontaneous rejection of alien rule.

As the summer of 1808 drew on, the French Marshals and generals in the Peninsula realized that they would have to fight to maintain their supremacy — and it was to be a fight with rules that none of them knew.

CHAPTER FOUR

SPAIN'S DEFIANCE

Joachim Murat was a lucky man — in one sense the luckiest of all the Peninsular Marshals. He was not the senior Marshal on the Army List, but he was Napoleon's brother-in-law; he had already received the Grand Duchy of Berg because of that fact; and as the first Marshal into Madrid he had seemed likely, for a while, to become the new King of Spain. Napoleon, however, held other ideas. As he saw it, Joseph Bonaparte, his elder brother, was the man for the job, even though this meant transferring Joseph from the Kingdom of Naples. This was all the more desirable because it would leave the vacant throne of Naples as a perfect sop to Murat. And so on 15 June, 1808, Murat quitted Spain. One month later he ascended his new throne, far away in southern Italy, and never returned. His role during the opening phase of the Peninsular War had been simple but dramatic, gaining him the kudos of taking and holding Madrid for the Emperor.

Even before Murat quitted the Peninsula, however, the Asturian deputation had arrived in England. The Asturians landed at Falmouth on 6 June, and immediately the awkward technicality that Britain and Spain were still officially at war was evaporated by a great blast of heated British enthusiasm for the Spanish insurgents. In Britain the news that Spaniards were challenging Napoleon came as an immense relief: the Union Jack was no longer alone.(In June 1941 the news that Hitler had invaded Russia had a very similar effect, even on those who had heartily loathed the Soviet Union and all it stood for.)

Oddly enough the British had a considerable expeditionary force ready to their hand. This force only existed because of Spain's alliance with the French, and because plans had been laid for the conquest of Spain's South American colonies. As soon as the news came in that the Spaniards had risen and were asking for help, all that had to be done was to send out new orders, and the troops could go to Spain's aid instead. Rarely has Britain been able to send military help to a new ally with such speed, and for such an ironic reason.

Whitehall hoped that the Spaniards would not try any risky moves until British troops could arrive in force, but this was not to be. Instead there now began a bewildering up-and-down zig-zag of changing fortunes. This is particularly hard to unravel because neither the French nor the Allies were under any single command or guiding will. Thus there was no tidy pattern of move and counter-move. The Spaniards compensated for their utter hostility towards the French by showing arrogant stupidity towards the British, creating problems as to where the British were to fight on their behalf, meanwhile fighting untimely and disastrous battles themselves. The French, on the other hand, to whom all this was completely favourable, headed straight into a series of unheard-of setbacks and humiliations which gradually taught them that this was a war in which the form-book was useless, and in which an apparent rabble could be as formidable as the Imperial Guard itself.

Certainly to start with, things looked good for the French. At the end of May 1808 Bessières and Moncey were in central Spain with a combined strength of about 52,000. Dupont was already under orders to march south with his 24,000 and occupy Andalusia, while Junot stayed put in Portugal. If the insurgents could launch powerful, unanimous attacks against these strong but scattered French units the latter would have to give up much territory and concentrate their forces; but this hardly seemed possible, let alone likely. On the other hand, the French reckoned that their trained troops must surely be able to shatter the patriot amateurs who dared to fight them, and then go on to complete their occupation of the country. So Dupont headed south towards Cordoba; Moncey prepared to strike east from Madrid at Valencia; and a smaller force under General Verdier was ordered by Bessieres to occupy Saragossa on the Ebro. In defining these widely separated objectives there seemed very little to worry about, as Napoleon saw it from the far side of the Pyrenees. It amounted to putting the finishing touches to the general occupation of Spain.

Dupont's march started well. He moved fast: by 2 June he had got as far as Andujar, down on the Guadalquivir. Here he began to come up against the motley army of seedy regular troops, down-at-heel militia, and peasant volunteers led by General Francis Xavier Castaños, the Spanish commander in the south. Militarily, the forces under Castaños were not up to much – but they were around 30,000 strong, the country was on their side, and they knew it. Much more important, they were prepared to put up a fight.

The regular Spanish army had never been a formidable force under the Bourbons, which was one very good reason for Godoy's timid temporizing with Napoleon. Under the Bourbon regime some foreign estimates had put its real strength at no more than 50,000 out of a theoretical strength of 130,000 men. Conscription existed but could be avoided: there were widespread regional exemptions. The best arm of the Spanish Army was the artillery but infantry and cavalry tactics were hopelessly obsolescent. Yet none of these weaknesses mattered in the war against the French. The national hatred of the alien armies created an entirely new mood which was reflected most clearly in the performance of the local *guerrillero* bands -- resistance groups held together by the personality and ruthlessness of their leaders. Their targets were French supply convoys, despatch riders, foraging parties – any force small enough to be surprised and annihilated. And the results were impressive enough. Between 1808 and 1813 the French in the Peninsula suffered a daily average loss of 300 men.

On 7 June Castaños' army got its fight, at the bridge of Alcolea. It was a resounding victory for Dupont, whose men ripped through the insurgent forces and went right on to storm Cordoba the same day. The taking of Cordoba was the apex of Dupont's career (on 2 June he had been named a Count of the Empire) and his Marshal's baton seemed very near. But after taking Cordoba Dupont decided not to risk a further advance. He gave his troops ten days' rest in Cordoba before evacuating the town on the 16th and falling back on Andujar. Dupont had been impressed by the extent of the insurrection in the south and certainly did not feel that he had sufficient troops with which to nail down Andalusia with garrisons, let alone to make an attempt upon Cadiz, which had been one of his final objectives. He decided to hold on at Andujar and wait for reinforcement from Madrid; but days became weeks, and no reinforcements came. And all the time Castaños' lop-sided agglomeration of irregular *guerrilleros* grew in size as volunteers swarmed in from the countryside.

One good reason why no help reached Dupont from Madrid was that the French commanders there had suddenly realized that the task before them was not as simple as they had thought. A convincing lesson had been learned when Marshal Moncey had marched east to take Valencia with 8,000 men but no siege train. Moncey attacked Valencia on 28 June and was soundly repulsed. He then realized that he would have to sit down for a formal siege in a hostile countryside without the right tools for the job, and he very sensibly decided to cut his losses and retreat to Madrid. All he had done was to give his troops an exhausting route-march with no results whatsoever apart from the after-taste of failure.

It was the same story up in the north-east, where the French tried to take the key cities of Gerona and Saragossa. General Duhesme, whose division had seized Barcelona during the surprise military take-over of the Spanish frontier forces in February, was hurled back from Gerona on 20 June and retired on Barcelona — a failure as depressing as that of Moncey before Valencia. Throughout June and July, General Verdier's division made repeated attacks upon Saragossa but Verdier was forced to content himself with putting the city under siege. This was the first of two desperate sieges which Saragossa heroically endured during the year, commanded by a remarkable resistance leader Count José de Palafox.

July opened with a brisk and one-sided campaign in Old Castile to the north of Madrid, when the Spanish insurgent armies took the field — hopelessly prematurely, hopelessly un-co-ordinated — under Don Gregorio Garcia de la Cuesta, Spain's generalissimo, and General Joachim Blake. On the 3rd Moncey recovered the self-esteem lost before Valencia by hammering Cuesta at Almanza and pushing on to reoccupy Valladolid; on the 14th Bessières routed Blake's army at Medina del Rio Seco. It was Bessières' first battle as an independent commander. He was lucky in the extremely low quality of his opponent, and equally lucky in that his own cavalry was commanded by the brilliant young General Lasalle; but all things considered it made for much better reading in the *Moniteur* than the setbacks at Valencia, Gerona, and Saragossa. It was a timely victory, too, for it enabled Bessières to ride triumphantly into Madrid with Joseph Bonaparte, who had come with 2,000 Italian troops to take up his new throne.

But within hours of Joseph's entry into Madrid on 20 July, appalling rumours — soon to be confirmed in every horrifying detail — were coming in from the south. Dupont's force was gone, finished, capitulated. He had accepted terms from Castaños and his surrendered army was at the disposal of the Spaniards. For the first time since the armistice in Egypt, a French army had laid down its arms.

What had happened was basically the result of a tenacious general trying to do the impossible with totally unsuitable troops. Dupont had hung on at Andujar for a month after his withdrawal from Cordoba. With no information as to the shifting fortunes of his superiors in the north, he never gave up hoping that he would be sent sufficient reinforcements to consolidate his tenuous hold on the line of the Guadalquivir and enable him to complete the job for which he had been sent to Andalusia. By the third week in July he knew that he would have to quit Andujar. In his army of unblooded conscripts — boys who had never had to put up with the hardships of Egypt, or the Swiss Alps, or the dreadful conditions of the winter campaign in Poland —morale was low and casualties from disease and sunstroke correspondingly high. Equally depressing was the hovering menace of Castaños' army which strangled the French lines of communication and supply and which had caused General Vedel's division to become separated from Dupont's main body. Supplies of food and ammunition were running low, and the troops knew it as well as Dupont himself.

As soon as Dupont put his demoralized troops on the march out of Andujar the Spaniards closed in and harried them. A running fight escalated into a full-scale engagement at Bailen on the 19th, with Vedel's division still far away. Dupont's soldiers had been all right during the march on Cordoba, but now they were on the receiving end against an enemy who did not bother to attack them when they formed square, but only when they were least ready.

It might just have turned out differently if Dupont had not been wounded in the first serious clash at Bailen on the 19th, but that decided it. His troops were simply not experienced enough to carry out the desperate fighting retreat which alone could bring them to safety, and to save them from piecemeal annihilation, Dupont agreed on surrender terms with Castaños on the 22nd. Castaños, a humane and honourable commander, accepted the French surrender on the understanding that the defeated French troops in Andalusia would be repatriated to France, but his action was repudiated by the civilian Junta of Seville. Dupont's surviving 20,000 went into Spanish captivity, received savage treatment — starvation added to brutal handling — and died like flies. It was an act of pointless, violent revenge, faithfully representative of the Peninsular War as a whole.

Dupont himself, wounded as he was, did return to France. He who had come so close to promotion to the Marshalate was now stripped of his command and imprisoned, emerging to serve under the Bourbons after Napoleon's abdication. He lived on until 1840, but for the rest of his service career a damning label clung to his name: '*le capitulard*'.

It can be argued that, as the commander on the spot, Dupont should have taken stock of his situation and realized that his orders from Madrid were impracticable. But this was not the way in the *Grande Armée* in which he had campaigned in Germany and Poland. He and his mediocre force did all that men could do according to their experience and the letter of their orders. The truth is that they were guinea-pigs: the proverb 'In Spain a small army is defeated and a large army starves' had not yet been coined as a result of bitter experience. Nor had the appalling difficulties in getting relevant and up-to-date orders and information through to the field commanders yet been realized. Napoleon himself never did understand the latter problem; and Dupont was by no means the first French commander in the Peninsular War to suffer the consequences.

Meanwhile, the first British troops were on their way to the Peninsula: 9,500 men embarked at Cork under the command of Major-General Sir Arthur Wellesley, and 5,000 more under Major-General Sir Brent Spencer at Gibraltar. Wellesley's force sailed from Cork on 12 July; he himself went on ahead in a fast frigate to make contact with the Junta of Galicia in northern Spain, while Spencer was ordered to approach the Junta of Seville in the south. On paper it all looked promising: two small but compact British expeditionary forces had the chance of striking twin blows in northern and southern Spain. But the Spaniards had other ideas.

Wellesley landed at Corunna on 20 July, the same day that Joseph Bonaparte entered Madrid. Wellesley's first impression was of the disordered and uninformed chaos which characterized the Spaniards' fight for their country's freedom. What was the current situation in Spain? How many men did the Spaniards have under arms? Much more to the point: where were the nearest French troops? Nobody at Corunna seemed to know. News had come in of the recent battle between Blake and Bessières at Medina del Rio Seco, but the Corunna authorities could give Wellesley no concrete information about it. One thing, however, was clear: the Junta of Galicia wanted no help from the British. Wellesley was advised to take his army away and land it in Portugal. Down at Cadiz, Spencer was being given the identical advice from the local Junta. Given this strategic brush-off, Wellesley decided that there was only one way in which he could carry out his mission: to tackle Junot in Portugal and try to take Lisbon.

Wellesley therefore went on to Portugal, landing at Oporto on the 24th. Here he did get news: the whole country north of the Tagus had risen and it appeared that the bulk of Junot's corps was holding Lisbon and the line of the Tagus with a frontier outpost still being held at Almeida. Wellesley got a cross-check on this information when he consulted Admiral Sir Charles Cotton, the British naval commander blockading the Tagus. Cotton made it clear that Wellesley had no chance of landing his force on any of the ideal beaches to the north of Lisbon, which Junot covered in force. This left Mondego Bay as the nearest uncontested landing-point; Wellesley sent word to Spencer, telling him to join him there, and headed north again to get on with the landing.

On rejoining his transports, however, Wellesley found dispatches from England waiting for him. In these dispatches H.M. Government informed Wellesley that he was being sent 16,000 more men and two senior commanding officers to both of whom he would be subordinate: two elderly dug-outs, Sir Hew Dalrymple and Sir Harry Burrard, with no distinction apart from their seniority on the British Army List. (This is one of those bureaucratic decisions which prompted Shaw to write 'The British soldier can stand up to anything except the British War Office', in *The Devil's Disciple*.) Until these reinforcements and his new superiors joined him in Portugal Wellesley would be on his own, and he determined to do the best he could. The first landings in Mondego Bay went in on 1 August, and after eight days of near chaos on the fringe of the Atlantic surf Wellesley and Spencer landed their combined forces. Wellesley immediately prepared to head south towards Lisbon (eighty miles away) and cross swords with Junot.

Wellesley's landing in Mondego Bay had caught Junot on the wrong foot. Loison's division was still falling back from the north, and this left Junot with about 15,000 men with which to keep his hold on Lisbon itself and to guard against the British making possible supplementary landings closer to the capital. Junot's initial reaction, however, was a sound one: to send General Laborde's division, 5,000 strong, to act as a blocking force until Loison could join up and enable the entire corps to attack the British in force.

Wellesley had set out from Mondego Bay on 9 August. He had his hard-core force of 13,000 British troops, together with the dubious reinforcement of 1,400 regular Portuguese infantry and cavalry put at his disposal by Don Fernadim Freire de Andrada, the Portuguese supreme commander. Wellesley decided to stay as near to the coast as possible to keep in touch with the Fleet, and he pushed his advance guard down the coast. The British main body followed the Leiria road which led through Batalha, Alcobaca, Obidos, Roliça, and Torres Vedras to Lisbon. The first Frenchmen they would meet would be the troops of Laborde's division; and Laborde did excellently.

Laborde had reached the Batalha area on the 12th, but on discovering the British line of advance he made the decision to post a rearguard at Obidos and place his main body in a formidable position at Roliça. The first shots were fired in a skirmish at Brilos, just to the north of Obidos, on the 15th. Thanks to the dash of the British infantry first blood went to the British, but Laborde refused to be hustled: he knew he had the bulk of the British coming down on his 5,000, but he coolly pulled in his outposts, called in his rearguard, and stood his ground at Roliça.

By now Wellesley knew that another French division was in the offing, and that he must eliminate Laborde before they could unite. (In fact, the situation was Waterloo back to front, with Laborde as Wellington, Wellesley as Napoleon, Loison's division as Blücher's Prussians, and the British having to make the pace before crucial enemy reinforcements could be brought to bear against them.) It is a tribute to the strength of Laborde's postion that Wellesley took the whole of the 16th to feel it out before ordering a general attack early on the 17th.

The full strength of Laborde's position was not felt. Wellesley had planned an all-out advance, which began by lapping round both French flanks. Laborde, however, merely backed up into the rocky Zambugeira heights and waited for Wellesley to come on. The answer to this delaying tactic was to press home the attack as soon as possible, pushing the outflanking forces still deeper into the French rear. But now the weaknesses in Wellington's army began to make themselves felt: his advance got out of gear. The British left-flank division attacked the French right instead of swinging in behind it; the Portuguese on the right lagged behind; and the 4,000 men in the British centre had to tackle Laborde's centre on equal terms with the high ground entirely in favour of the French. There was vicious fighting as the British drove uphill, and hot-headed tactics on the British side (much to Wellesley's fury) enabled Laborde to drive back the 9th and 29th Regiments, mauling them badly.

Wellesley, however, kept his grip on the battle, and gradually his heavy superiority in numbers began to tell. The French left — which Laborde was drawing in to reinforce his centre — was enveloped again, and Laborde had to withdraw. He beat a fighting retreat inland and fell back to the south-east, having lost three guns and 600 men killed and wounded in return for 500 British casualties. Wellesley could console himself that the fighting spirit of his troops was superb, but he had failed to destroy an inferior French force and could only congratulate himself on having postponed the link-up between Laborde and Loison. Battle-weariness apart, there could be no question of following up Laborde, let alone striking at Loison's untouched division. On the evening of the Roliça fight on the 17th news reached Wellesley that the two new brigades, shipped out from England, had arrived off the Portuguese coast fifteen miles to the north-west. Before pressing on to Lisbon, Wellesley would have to cover the landing of these fresh troops and their supplies.

There was only one place where this landing could be made: the nearby estuary of the Maceira river. Two miles up the river from the estuary lay an arc of hills around the village of Vimiero, and there Wellesley posted his army to cover the landings, which were made on the 19th and 20th. These reinforcements boosted Wellesley's strength to 17,000 British infantry and 18 guns, plus 1,500 or so Portuguese.

But on the night of the 20th Wellesley's plans were wrecked by the arrival of his new superior officer, Sir Harry Burrard. On Burrard's insistence the British troops around Vimiero were to prepare to hold their positions against any rapid counter-strokes by the French and to keep open the Maceira estuary until Sir John Moore's 12,000 men, expected from England, could join the expeditionary force. Wellesley argued in vain. He could not believe that Junot was in any state to try an immediate attack – but he was completely mistaken.

Within hours of Burrard's counter-order on the night of Saturday, 20 August, a breathless cavalry officer rode into Wellesley's camp with the news that contact had been made with heavy French forces approaching from the south. The British troops stood to arms until an hour after dawn – and then, shortly after 8 o'clock, heavy dust clouds were spotted to the south. Burrard's pessimism had been justified: the French were coming. Considerably helped by the ability of his divisional commanders, Loison and Laborde, Junot had achieved a remarkably speedy concentration of his field forces. Leaving 7,000 troops to hold Lisbon he had marched to Torres Vedras where, within 48 hours of the Roliça battle, he had concentrated 14,000 men and prepared a lightning counterstroke to avenge Roliça. On the evening of the 20th he issued orders for a night march and dawn attack which would smash the British at Vimiero and drive the survivors into the sea.

It was a bold plan, with much to be said for it in theory. It has long been an accepted maxim that freshly-landed troops should be counter-attacked as soon as possible before they can dig in (which was precisely what Burrard intended to do). But, as we have seen, Junot was an unstable and impetuous man. He did not back up his impulses with an assessment of the facts. His night march was a failure because of the unfamiliar and obstructive terrain between Torres Vedras and Vimiero, and his dawn attack had to be replaced with an assault in full daylight. Achieving complete surprise in a dawn attack is one thing; having to make a set-piece approach, deployment, and attack under the eyes of the enemy is another, and there can be no excusing Junot's blind charge at the British lines on the morning of 21 August.

Holding the ridges above Vimiero, Wellesley's troops looked south across the tangled terrain and choked watercourses which lay below them and into which the French columns were advancing head-on. By the time that Junot had appreciated that his floundering masses attacking the British centre were being held up, and sent off a flanking column, Wellesley had had ample breathing space in which to deploy troops to meet it and cut it off. The French frontal attacks, pressed home by Laborde and Loison, were hurled back by the British line; the French columns were riddled with bullets from the new explosive 'Shrapnel' shells and by massed volleys of musketry. The repulse of the French left and centre threw the Torres Vedras road wide open; the French right-wing division, under Solignac, was surrounded, and Wellesley prepared for an energetic advance which would keep the French running until they reached the Tagus.

Junot's army was saved, however, by the arrival on the battlefield of Sir Harry Burrard, who took one look at the flying French and ordered Wellesley to call off his men. Flat-out pursuits to destroy a defeated enemy were not the kind of warfare he understood, and not solely because he had never been in a position to achieve one himself. Burrard was a military child of the 18th century, strictly a limited-offensive man. All he could see was that Junot's attack had been successfully broken and to him that meant that the battle had been won. The fact that it would be wasted if the French were not destroyed as a fighting force never occurred to him. To a man like Burrard, winning a battle had to be followed by sufficient time to count losses and assess the situation.

Burrard's views were completely endorsed by the commander-in-chief, Sir Hew Dalrymple, who finally arrived from Gibraltar on the morning of the 22nd to take command. He overruled all Wellesley's objections and pleas for an immediate pursuit, and when the French General Kellermann (son of the Marshal) arrived in the afternoon to ask for terms that was the end of it. By this time Junot was back at Torres Vedras and the Lisbon road was blocked again. The French had lost some 2,000 men at Vimiero (the British losses were around 700), although Junot could call on the 7,000 reserves around Lisbon itself. Solignac's division, cut off at Vimiero, had taken its chance to break through and had joined up with the French main body. But Vimiero had been a tremendous blow at the morale of the French (much as the British rifle-fire at Mons in 1914 appalled every German who encountered it), and Junot was only too willing to try and talk his way out of a second battle. He was incredibly lucky in that the British War Office had arranged matters so that Dalrymple and Burrard would be handling the negotiations instead of Wellesley, who found himself required to acquiesce in the decisions of his superiors.

Kellermann did the talking on the French side, and Kellermann was an extremely hard and able man (he had led the decisive French charge at Marengo, had been wounded at Austerlitz, and soldiered on until Waterloo. In the notorious agreement known as the Convention of Cintra, signed on 30 August, the French agreed to evacuate Portugal – on condition that the troops, complete with their weapons and equipment, would be landed in France by the British Fleet. To men like Dalrymple and Burrard, who did not understand that the only point in fighting an enemy is to destroy him, this seemed an excellent arrangement which would liberate Portugal without another shot having to be fired. In modern terms it is unimaginable – as though the Wehrmacht High Command in May 1940 had agreed to ship the trapped British Expeditionary Force back to England, and to lay on the transports to take them home.

It was equally unimaginable at the time – so much so that when the news of Cintra broke in Britain on 15 September it nearly brought down the Duke of Portland's Government. Dalrymple, Burrard, and even Wellesley became objects of popular hatred, and a Court of Enquiry was hastily ordered by the apprehensive Government. Dalrymple was recalled to Britain on the 17th, and his tripartite command set-up was dismantled by his disappearance from the Peninsula. But the appointment of his successor was a momentous one: Sir John Moore, creator of the new Light Division of the British Army, whose ideal had been the training of the 'thinking fighting man'. Now he was to command the new British expeditionary force which would march into Spain to complete the liberation of that country, which seemed to have begun so well.

Bailen had been the catalyst. The news of the capitulation in the south had prompted Castlereagh, Secretary for War, to prepare a force of 30,000 men to co-operate with the Aragonese and Asturian partisans in the north. The advance guard, destined for Corunna – 18,800 troops under Lieutenant-General Sir David Baird – was ready to go by 3 September; and a week after Dalrymple's recall it was decided to earmark 20,000 of the troops already in Portugal and to put both forces under the overall command of Moore.

The Allied recovery after Napoleon's first attempt to nail down the Peninsula by force was nearing high tide. Portugal had been cleared. Castaños had followed up Bailen by marching on Madrid, and King Joseph Bonaparte packed up his Court and ran for the Ebro. There was no fight for central Spain; the French abandoned even Burgos and pulled back to Vitoria. Castaños entered Madrid in triumph on 23 August, and by the end of the month the advancing Spaniards – Blake on the left, Castaños in the centre, and Palafox with his Saragossa army on the right – were preparing to cross the Ebro and sweep the last pocket of French resistance out of north-eastern Spain.

Napoleon's reaction was simple. He would smash the Spaniards with the full weight of the *Grande Armée*. Ney's VI Corps was the first to get its marching orders for Spain, and Ney himself reached Irun on the Spanish frontier on 30 August. 'I have sent the Spaniards sheep whom they have devoured; I shall send them wolves who will devour them in their turn,' vowed Napoleon – but before he could withdraw his 'wolves' from central Germany and send them into the Peninsula he had to underpin the settlement made with Tsar Alexander at Tilsit. To suspend the military occupation of Germany would be a standing invitation for Austria to make trouble again, and this threat had to be provided for.

It stands in the history books as the Convention of Erfurt, 27 September–14 October, 1808: over a fortnight of pageantry and glitter, with servile princes and monarchs queuing up to pledge their adherence to Napoleon's system. It was a hollow if gorgeous sham and its effects were not to last – but Erfurt gave Napoleon all the time he believed he would need to restore Joseph to the throne of Spain and settle the Peninsula once and for all before returning to the policing of Europe. Throughout the second half of October the long blue columns trudged down through France, south-east across the Pyrenees, to concentrate on the Ebro for the return to Madrid.

On 5 November Napoleon himself set up his headquarters amid Joseph's émigré court at Vitoria. His plans were cast; the flower of the *Grande Armée*, 152,000 strong, was ready to strike at the divided Spanish armies. The last act, it seemed, was about to begin.

CHAPTER FIVE

THE EMPEROR STRIKES

The Marshals were of the Empire, and it was no coincidence that the apogee of the Empire — 1807-8, after the battles which cemented the French control of Europe and before the Spanish entanglement began in earnest — marked a turning-point in their own lives. From being leading generals they were now peers of the Empire, most of them titled, with rich estates and incomes which they wanted to enjoy. And it was becoming more and more clear that Napoleon's classic lure of 'the career open to talents' was beginning to backfire on him as far as the Marshals were concerned. For the Emperor continued to make it obvious that nobility and wealth were not the only goals to which the former cavalry troopers and sergeants might aspire. There were thrones.

The basic problem was one of nineteen leading generals with sharply differing talents, divided from the outset by professional rivalry. This was unavoidable. It even applied to comparatively simple souls like Ney, who was far less interested in title-hunting than in adding to his stock of *La Gloire*; and Lefebvre, who had had his title presented to him virtually on a plate but who still yearned to pull off an individual achievement in the field. Add to this the supplementary problem of ambitious characters like Bernadotte and Soult, eating their hearts out because that vainglorious buffoon Murat was now lording it as King of Naples, and the picture of the Marshalate in 1808 becomes even more complex. In the new Spanish campaign which was about to begin, these unavoidable rifts and rivalries between the serving Marshals would bedevil the chances of success even when Napoleon was present to keep his lieutenants in order and see that they worked together.

A review of the battle order of the *Grande Armée* at the beginning of November 1808, as it stood poised for the reconquest of Spain, offers a good opportunity to take stock of how the Marshals had fared since 1804.

Victor had the I Corps, and Victor had been created Duke of Belluno on 10 September, 1808. Soult had the II Corps, and he had been created Duke of Dalmatia on 29 June of that year. Moncey, one of the first Marshals of the first creation to enter Spain during the initial phase of the war, who had recently been involved in the inglorious retreat from Madrid, commanded the III Corps. Moncey had been created Duke of Conegliano on 25 July. Lefebvre had the IV Corps, and his Dukedom (of Danzig) had been awarded him on the same day that Victor got his: 10 September. Mortier, Duke of Treviso since 2 July, commanded the V Corps; Ney, still in command of the VI Corps, had been Duke of Elchingen since 6 June. A rising star commanded the VII Corps: Gouvion St Cyr, not a Marshal (he would earn his baton during the Russian campaign of 1812). Finally, commanding the VIII Corps, came Junot – of all people, one might be excused for thinking, after his ignominious expulsion from Portugal. When one recalls the savage sentence of official disgrace dealt out to Dupont after the capitulation of Bailen, one can see that Junot's retention in a corps command proves how much importance Napoleon could attach to personal friendships. Junot's title – Duke of Abrantès – dated from the fleeting six months which he had recently spent as Napoleon's governor in Portugal.

When Napoleon took command of the *Grande Armée* in Spain Lannes was given a two-corps command, co-ordinating the movements of Moncey and of part of Ney's corps. He had been created Duke of Montebello on 15 June. One unforgettable character – Murat – would not take part in this campaign, his Majesty King Joachim I of Naples being far away in southern Italy. Bessières commanded the Reserve Cavalry in Murat's place (an appointment which succeeded a brief spell in command of II Corps), and Bessieres still had his dukedom to win.

Thus the commanders of the *Grande Armée* in November 1808 represented a formidable concentration of *parvenu* nobility and military talent. The trouble was that they were rival individualists. Their skills — often misapplied but always impressive — would bring Napoleon's master-plan to within a hair's breadth of success, but not to its full achievement.

The basic plan was a strong central drive on Madrid with tentacles closing round the Spanish flanks. On paper it should have meant the destruction of the Spanish flanking armies under Blake and Palafox and the shattering of Castaños in the centre, but it was quite impossible to co-ordinate the movements of the French corps to secure this ideal result. The French juggernaut rolled forward, beat the Spanish field armies, and took Madrid — but it was a juggernaut with engine trouble, readily traceable to the timing.

For example, the French right-wing forces in Spain had been in action against General Blake for several weeks before Napoleon arrived at the front. Ney and Lefebvre had combined forces to take Bilbao on 26 September and a month of skirmishing had ensued. This was clinched by a resounding defeat for Blake, again administered by Lefebvre, at Durango on 31 October. Ten days later came the two-day battle of Espinosa (10-11 November) and another defeat for Blake. This was the battle which knocked Blake's army out of the Spanish line, and it was won by Victor. (C.S. Forester devotees will recall that the Spanish retreat from Espinosa is the back-drop for the opening chapter of his novel *The Gun*.) Blake had been subjected to piecemeal and very messy bludgeoning, but not to a crushing and final defeat, and his army, badly mauled though it was, was still in being.

The best performance, naturally enough, was put up by that part of the *Grande Armée* under Napoleon's eye: the centre corps. Soult smashed Belvedere's Estremaduran troops at Gamonal and took Burgos on 10 November before moving into a back-up position for Napoleon's descent on Madrid. Meanwhile, on the French left, Lannes, Moncey, and Junot were preparing to smash Castaños, then wheel south-east and finish the job by finishing off Palafox and taking Saragossa.

It was at this point that Napoleon's handling of the Marshals on campaign missed fire once more. He ordered Ney to swing his VI Corps away from the main line of the *Grande Armée's* advance. Heading east through Aranda and Calatayud, Ney was to act as the southern jaw of the pincers which Lannes and Moncey would close on Castaños from the north. If Ney had carried out the orders dictated by Napoleon Castaños must have been destroyed, and military historians would still be making enthusiastic noises over one of the most perfect and symmetrical strategic coups ever achieved.

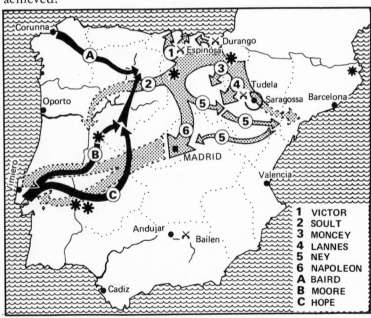

The campaign of 1808, showing how Napoleon's master-plan was thrown out of gear.

Ney set out on his march correctly enough, but for once in his career he felt his way like a blind man with a stick. Apologists have found plentiful excuses for his caution: the ever-present difficulty of movement, bad intelligence, uneasy thoughts of the dreadful precedent of Bailen (though it is hard to imagine Ney worrying about a fellow-general's defeats), and so on; but the fact remains that it was Ney who spoiled the plan to destroy Castaños. At Tudela on 23 November Lannes, having taken over command from Moncey, won perhaps the most decisive battle of his career, and Castaños fell back in outright retreat. According to the Napoleonic master-plan he should have been retreating right into Ney's arms, but Ney and the VI Corps were nowhere near the vital point, having wasted three days at Soria. Five days after Tudela, when it was much too late to intercept Castaños, Ney finally arrived on the lower Ebro to find that Moncey was preparing to besiege Saragossa and that the original plan was no more.

While Napoleon paused at Burgos, Soult was switched to the north to finish off Blake's force, which had straggled across the mountains after his last hammering at Espinosa to regroup at Reinosa, 12,000 strong. With Lefebvre, Victor, and now Soult on his heels — a total of over 70,000 Frenchmen — Blake threw in his hand. He marched what was left of his army to the coast in order to put them in touch with the British Navy, and resigned. Blake was replaced by the Marquis de la Romana, who had been shipped back to Spain with his troops by the British, and who was determined to keep the northern army in play. He marched it right back across the Cantabrians, based it on Leon, and recruited its strength back to over 15,000.

Although de la Romana had avoided check-mate for the moment, his position was hopeless. But now Napoleon, having accepted the fact that the northern Spanish army had not been destroyed, chose to believe that it had been too badly hurt to be worth further worry. Victor and Lefebvre were ordered down from the northern sector to add more muscle to the drive on Madrid. Soult, however, was to stay put between the Douro and de la Romana's army. His position there would be an ideal springboard for an invasion of Portugal aimed at the lower Douro and Oporto.

The march on Madrid was resumed the day before Tudela: 22 November. In front of the French was mere military debris. The surviving Spanish forces, a barrel-scraping of 21,000 men, had one chance of keeping the French out of Madrid: to hold the Somosierra Pass across the Sierra de Guadarrama, the mountain range which arches like a shield across the northern approaches to Madrid. They nearly succeeded, but only because Victor was given the job of storming the pass, and Victor decided on a typically unimaginative assault which made Napoleon lose patience. The Emperor hurled the Polish Lancers of the Guard into one of those classic cavalry charges which, like Scarlett's uphill charge of the Heavy Brigade at Balaclava, should never have succeeded. The Lancers boiled over the Spanish batteries and earthworks, losing heavily all the way as they forged up the pass — and the defenders broke and fled.

Four days after the storming of the Somosierra Pass, on 4 December, 1808, the *Grande Armée* marched into Madrid. The first important objective of the campaign had been secured: King Joseph's throne had been recovered for him in under four months from his first ignominious departure.

The occupation of Madrid was followed by a constructive period of troop redeployment. This studded the *Grande Armée* around Madrid in such a way as to set up links with Soult north of the Douro and Lannes and Moncey on the Ebro. At the same time, Victor was moved south of the capital to secure the Tagus crossings at Aranjuez and Toledo. Lefebvre was sent west to Talavera, while heavy cavalry forces pushed even further west to Oropesa and Almaraz. This whole period lasted some eighteen days, and it was intended to regroup the *Grande Armée* for its next task: to invade Portugal and avenge Vimiero by smashing the British. In this new drive Napoleon intended to bring Ney's VI Corps

— which had contributed little more than a non-productive route march during the first phase of the campaign — into more effective play. Ney was recalled from the Ebro, and his corps reached Madrid on 14 December.

The main question now was the whereabouts of the British. Napoleon believed that they would be found to the east of Lisbon, within easy retreating-range of their confounded ships. He never dreamed that they would venture into Spain in any strength or depth. When eight troopers of the King's German Legion, an ex-Hanoverian cavalry unit in service with the British, were captured near Talavera on 11 December, his hunch seemed confirmed. The direction was right, directly on his shortest line of march to Lisbon; even the prisoners were right: they must have come from an advanced cavalry screen. But on the 19th Napoleon received stunning news from the north: heavy British forces had struck at Soult's communications in Old Castile. Any setback to Soult could open the road to Burgos to the British, and this would put a knife to the main communications artery of the *Grande Armée* in Madrid. All hopes of a westward drive into Portugal must be abandoned until this new menace in the north had been dispelled.

'I hope my country will do me justice,' Moore gasped at Corunna as he lay on his death-bed, horribly mangled by a French cannon-ball. It was indeed the least he could expect. His foray into Spain not only saved Lisbon from the fate of Madrid: it was the most daring venture of the British Army since Marlborough marched to Blenheim some 104 years before.

Moore's brief from the British Government had been clear: to enter Spain and give all the help he could to the Spanish armies, which Whitehall fondly believed to be preparing to clear north-eastern Spain of the last French forces in the Peninsula. But Moore soon found that the Spaniards could not even give him accurate news of their latest defeats, let alone of the correct strength and position of the French. Moore took one of the most lonely and selfless decisions in military history when he decided to go it alone. By riding picador across Napoleon's lifeline he kept the Peninsular War — and Britain's most immediate hopes of victory against the French Empire — alive.

Moore had received his orders on 6 October. He was to leave 10,000 men to hold Portugal and take an expeditionary force of 20,000 to help the Spaniards. He was also told that another 17,000 would be sent out under Sir David Baird, landed at Corunna, and marched overland to join Moore's main body in northern Spain. Moore decided to set out as soon as possible, sending his cavalry and artillery undèr Lieutenant-General Sir John Hope along the Elvas-Badajoz-Madrid road and marching his infantry and a few 6-pounder guns via Ciudad Rodrigo and Salamanca to Valladolid. Baird and Hope would join him there.

But the British intervention in Spain nearly ended in instant disaster. Baird's transports arrived off Corunna on 13 October — three days before Moore set out from Portugal — but the Spanish Junta refused to let Baird's force begin to land until the 26th. It was not until 4 November that his last troops were disembarked, and then they had to tackle the 200-mile march across the mountains to Astorga. For this they were singularly handicapped by another administrative blunder: the British War Office had omitted to send any gold with which to hire local transport.

Moore's welcome to Spain was ominous. At the frontier fort of Ciudad Rodrigo on 13 November he was greeted with panic-stricken appeals for help sent by Count Belvedere, who had just been routed by Soult at Gamonal. And at Salamanca, which he reached on the 15th, Moore realized his true and terrifying situation for the first time.

He was alone. The French were only sixty miles away, in Valladolid, the intended concentration-point for his army; Baird and Hope were each 100 miles away, separated from him by mountains. The great Spanish offensive which he had come into Spain to assist had collapsed before it had even remotely approached reality.

But Spanish armies were still fighting, if only for their lives, and Moore felt that he had to hang on in the hope of stiffening their will to keep fighting. Yet there could be no question of moving forward until Baird and Hope joined him; indeed, given the circumstances, he had to order Baird and Hope to cut and run for Corunna and Lisbon respectively, if they should run into overwhelming French concentrations. At first it seemed that Baird would do just that. On hearing the news of Gamonal, Espinosa, and the French occupation of Valladolid, he had ordered a retreat — but when Moore heard of it on the 28th he called Baird to heel. 'If the enemy prevent us, there is no hope for it,' wrote Moore; 'but if he does not, I am determined to unite the army. When that is done we shall act according to our circumstances. There is still a chance that the presence of so large a British force may give spirits to the Spaniards.'

Then there followed a bewildering sequence of rumour-based news, any of which might have been true, which tripled the agony of Moore's position. The fact that he came to any concrete conclusion — let alone a brilliant piece of strategic deduction — is the highest possible tribute to the man.

Within hours of recalling Baird on the 28th, Moore was ordering him to retreat on Corunna, and sending off a message to Hope to head for Ciudad Rodrigo for a link-up before a joint retreat on Lisbon. The fatal news of Tudela and the rout of Castaños had arrived. The last major Spanish field army had been crushed; the fall of Madrid seemed imminent. On 2 December, Moore heard of the storming of the Somosierra Pass, and also that the French had been sighted before Madrid; on the 4th, after a level-headed march amid the most harrowing circumstances, Hope's force, bringing the precious guns, made contact with Moore by arriving at the nearby town of Alba de Tormes. The retreat to Lisbon could now begin: Moore's army, at last, was a balanced force of horse, foot, and guns. It had done its best, but now there was nothing to justify its remaining in Spain.

And then, on 5 December, the scene changed again. More

news, this time from Madrid: the city was preparing for a last-ditch stand, another siege, like Saragossa, which might pin down the French for months. Moore knew that he could not relieve Madrid by direct intervention. But by striking out to the east he could make it impossible for the French to winter in central Spain. Even the news that Madrid had fallen did not shake his determination. The French were definitely being drawn south; they had even evacuated Valladolid. Moore was not able to head for his original rendezvous with Baird, whom he recalled on the 5th; and his own rested army set out for Valladolid on the 11th.

On the 13th, a totally unexpected piece of luck informed Moore that he no longer had the chance of merely making a nuisance of himself in northern Spain: if he moved fast he could win a crushing victory. What had happened was, in miniature, the story of the whole Peninsular War. A French *aide-de-camp* carrying Imperial dispatches had thrown his weight about once too often at a post-house and the local Spaniards had murdered him. His papers were forwarded to the British — and they contained a dispatch from Napoleon to Soult. From this document Moore learned that Napoleon believed the British to be screening Lisbon, and that the Emperor was planning a westward advance to crush them. He learned what had happened to Castaños since Tudela: Bessières was pursuing him in Valencia. Mortier's corps was heading for Saragossa to tighten the siege, while Junot was moving up from Vitoria to Burgos. But the prime news was that Soult, for the moment, was isolated on the Carrion river. Thanks to the garrisons which he had left in the north, Soult's corps was not up to strength. If Moore and Baird could join hands before Junot could combine with Soult, the 35,000 British could attack Soult's 18,000 with every chance of annihilating an entire corps of the *Grande Armée*.

Moore's reaction was prompt. He headed north across the Douro on the 15th, when Baird's spearheads had got as close as Benavente. On the 20th the two British forces finally met at Mayorga. Everything was going Moore's way: his army was now united, it was keen for a fight, and it held all the cards over its nearby enemy. Within twenty-four hours the British were in action: a cavalry fight at Sahagun, where two of Soult's cavalry regiments were badly beaten by the spirited attack of Lord Paget's Hussar brigade. Already, however, Napoleon at Madrid had heard the news that large British forces had been located both at Salamanca and Astorga, and that they seemed to have the intention of moving, via Valladolid, against Soult.

What Napoleon did next is a classic of war. He scrapped his plans immediately and prepared for a lightning advance to the north. Lefebvre, Ney, and the Guard were to his hand; they were not enough. Desolles' division was brought in from its communications duties which had been linking Madrid with Lannes on the Ebro, and Lapisse's division was brought up from Victor's corps on the Tagus. Junot was ordered to move on Valladolid at once in order to close the gap between the advancing French main body and Soult's isolated corps.

Given Napoleon's uncertainty as to where the British actually were, his was a wonderful piece of deduction. The whole situation had been stood on its head. Instead of 35,000 British preparing to smash 18,000 French, over 70,000 French were now preparing to smash 35,000 British.

Meanwhile, on the Carrion river, Soult would have to hold on until these massive reinforcements could be brought into play. He had been badly shaken by the cavalry affair at Sahagun on the 21st, and had pulled back his outposts across the river. Moore was preparing to follow up his success at Sahagun with an all-out attack on Soult's lines around the town of Carrion, the assault being scheduled for dawn on the 24th.

'If the bubble bursts and Madrid falls,' he had written to Baird on 5 December, 'we shall have to run for it.' Now indeed the bubble had burst with a vengeance. The appalling news that the *Grande Armée* was hurtling north to trap him reached Moore on the 23rd. Now it was his turn to make a snap decision and unlike Napoleon he had only one choice:

to get out. Paget's five cavalry regiments and the reserve infantry division were left on the Carrion to make Soult feel that he was still going to be attacked, while the British main body fell back towards the Esla river. Behind the Esla lay the first essential stage along the line of retreat to Corunna: Astorga.

Paget's rearguard saved Moore's army by giving it a 48-hour start in the race. The crossing of the Esla had been completed by the end of the 27th, but the real pressure began to be applied on the 28th. The advance cavalry units of Ney's VI Corps and the Imperial Guard had arrived to help Soult. Paget's cavalry, outnumbered by well over two to one, fought like madmen to hold the French on the Esla for as long as possible.

In the fight for the Esla crossings the honours went to the British. What was more satisfying to Moore's troopers, it was done at the expense of the legendary Imperial Guards cavalry — the Chasseurs, under General Lefebvre-Desnouëttes. In a wild mêlée at Benavente on 29 December some 200 Chasseurs were taken or killed and the remainder driven back across the Esla. Lefebvre-Desnouëttes himself was captured. After this resounding success the British yielded the Esla crossings and withdrew to cover the retreat to Astorga.

The retreat to Corunna had begun. The British had not yet been trapped, but there was nothing to suggest that their pursuers might not manage to fight them to a standstill. It is often forgotten that on the British side Moore's problems were made far harder than they should have been by the simultaneous retreat of de la Romana's army, which had given up Leon. Napoleon and his Marshals would have had a far harder time if de la Romana had yielded to Moore's requests and headed north to Asturias, dividing the French pursuit. Instead he retreated on a collision course, as it were — right across the British line of march, heading west for Orense. Soult, expanding his front northward towards Leon, slaughtered the Spanish rearguard at Mansilla on 30 December, and hordes of starving, typhus-ridden refugees from the defeat caused near chaos by swarming through the British advanced depot at Astorga.

The first 48 hours of the New Year of 1809 made it clear to Napoleon that he had under-estimated the British reaction to his counter-attack, and that he had also misinterpreted their actual position. The rearguard cavalry actions fought by the British cavalry had led him to believe that Moore's army was still between the Carrion and the Esla when it was already well on the way to Astorga. Instead of a trapped prey, Napoleon had a fleeing enemy. It was to be a stern chase, with Soult in the van and Ney's corps in close support.

On 2 January, 1809, Napoleon accepted the facts. Soult was given the task of keeping the British on the run. He was also given a division from Junot's corps and could call on Ney if necessary. Napoleon himself left Astorga on 2 January. He had two major worries which made his return to France essential: fears of sedition in Paris, and ominous news that Austria was threatening to break out in open revolt against his Continental System.

Napoleon's departure from Spain, was, of course, a climacteric of the Peninsular War. As he saw it, British intervention in the Peninsula was finished and the Marshals could mop up. But in January 1809 there were two bad flaws in the expectations of the French for the final settlement of the Peninsular problem. First, Napoleon had designated no supreme commander – not even the freshly-restored King Joseph. He himself would continue to issue overriding orders for the prosecution of the war in Spain, with disastrous results. Second, he had failed to appreciate the practical difficulties of moving troops in the Peninsula, even though he had had occasion to reproach several of his Marshals for tardy manoeuvring, and even though he himself, during the snow-choked crossing of the Guadarramas during his north-ward pounce against Moore, had walked on foot amid the grenadiers of his Guard and had actually experienced adverse conditions from the point of view of the troops themselves.

There was only one real clash during the British retreat to

Corunna. It came just after Napoleon's departure: at Calcabellos on 3 January. Ney had sent up his cavalry to speed Soult's advance, but with tragic results. At Calcabellos a British marksman killed Ney's brilliant and irreplaceable cavalry commander, General Colbert. After this engagement the French pursuit was purely Soult's affair. As it went on his divisions became more and more strung out along the line of march; the appalling conditions in the mountains hit the French just as hard as the British, who were nearing not only the sea but their main supply depot. They were falling back on a source of comparative plenty which would be denied to the French. Sickness, plus the need to detach forces for garrison duties, were whittling down the strength of Soult's corps to a level which would make for a much more even confrontation with the British than had seemed possible back on the Esla.

By 13 January Moore's army had staggered into Corunna to find that the vital fleet of transports had not yet arrived to take off the troops. Soult's objective, the destruction of the British, seemed very near — but he had only two over-stretched divisions within striking distance of the Corunna perimeter and there could be no question of bringing on a general engagement until his other forces had joined up. This in itself is a striking testimony of the pace of the retreat, and how the very plight of the British acted in their favour.

Nevertheless, Soult's advance guards kept up the pressure. On the 13th they forced Paget's rearguard to fall back from the El Burgo bridge over the Mero river, which permitted the French to cross and to threaten Corunna direct. Soult spent the 14th and 15th establishing his forces along the arc of hills to the north of the approaches to the town — but on the 14th the British transports arrived off Corunna, and Moore could prepare for a fighting withdrawal to his ships.

He did not have the full strength of the British expeditionary force which had gone into Spain. During the retreat he had sent off General 'Black Bob' Craufurd with the Light

Division to march west to Vigo, where they embarked. This left Moore's forces at Corunna as 15,000 infantry (all the surviving cavalry and artillery had been embarked as soon as the transports arrived, apart from nine light guns to bolster the infantry). By the 16th Soult had three infantry divisions in line, with a fourth still on the march. He had set up a formidable battery of 24 heavy guns, and his eight cavalry regiments were poised to strike at the British rear once Moore's line had been driven in by frontal attack. All in all, the French outnumbered the British by slightly over 1,000 — but the French force was a balanced one. Moore would have to fight with infantry alone.

Soult's dispositions were sound, and he also held all the cards with regard to terrain and high ground. But he had never encountered anything like the steadiness of British infantry, which not only failed to break when attacked by the French infantry but soaked up the cannon-fire from the French battery as well. There was another factor, a moral one: after their frustrating and agonizing campaign the British rankers wanted nothing better than a stand-up fight. There are many eye-witness accounts of how Moore's heartsick and leg-weary troops revived like magic on hearing that they were going to get the chance to hit back.

This pugnacity was something Soult had not bargained for. He had been secretly hoping that a little pressure would make the British panic and run for their ships. Another unwelcome surprise was Moore's careful deployment of two reserve divisions which counter-attacked at exactly the right moment and forced back Soult's agonizing forces. The heartened British would certainly have pushed forward and taken the French battery but for the confusion caused by the wounding of Moore and Baird. Sir John Hope, who eventually took over, was quite content with the fact that the direct threat to Corunna had been averted for the time being. He dropped the idea of a further advance and ordered a staged withdrawal to the ships. But before the last embarkations were completed, Moore was dead.

In later years the Duke of Wellington commented that the trouble with the French Marshals was that they planned all their operations like a splendid set of ornamental harness, which was all very well until something snapped and ruined the whole thing. He himself, he said, preferred to use rope: if something snapped he would tie a knot and go on from there. Soult at Corunna was a fair enough example. His plan was put out of joint by the enemy standing up to his attack and actually counter-attacking — a strap in the harness had gone, and Soult was unable to recast his plans accordingly.

At the time, however, the tactical implications of the battle of Corunna seemed less important than the fact that the British had been flung right out of Spain. Napoleon once more ordered an all-out propaganda campaign to get the most out of the event, showing up the cowardly British mercenaries leaving their betrayed Spanish allies in the lurch. There was a very good reason for all this drum-beating: his plan for an all-in-one conquest of the Peninsula had been spoiled. The French mass at Madrid, which had been beautifully placed to radiate west into Portugal and south into Andalusia, had been abruptly siphoned off into the mountains of north-western Spain by Moore's raid. This meant that the Peninsular War would certainly continue throughout 1809, although it seemed unlikely that the British would put in another appearance after Corunna.

Worse still — from the point of view of the French Marshals on the spot — it would continue without the crack troops which Napoleon had hurled against Madrid in November 1808. Another full-blooded Napoleonic campaign was in the making, this time against the Austrians. For the first time the Peninsular Marshals were about to experience the bitterness of being expected to finish off the job with what they had while the Emperor's attention — and his best troops — were engaged elsewhere.

Joseph Bonaparte, Napoleon's elder brother and puppet-king of Spain

Comte Pierre Dupont de L'Etang, one of the leading generals who failed to reach the ranks of the Marshalate. His surrender at Bailen earned him the title of *'le capitulard'*

Jean-Andoche Junot ('*La Tempête*'), who led the first Imperial French army into the Peninsula but who also never became a Marshal

Charles-Pierre-François Augereau, the rough diamond of the Marshalate. His service in the Peninsula was limited to the secondary theatre of Catalonia

Jean-Baptiste Bessières, who served in two campaigns in Spain but whose contribution remained slight

Jean Lannes, one of the best fighting generals Napoleon ever had. He was the first of the Marshals to be killed on campaign (in Austria in 1809)

François-Joseph Lefebvre, whose blunders caused Napoleon to recall him in 1809 with the verdict: 'He cannot grasp the meaning of his orders'

Etienne-Jacques-Joseph-Alexandre Macdonald, the son of a Scots Jacobite. He succeeded Augereau as commander in Catalonia but failed likewise to pacify the province

Bon-Adrien-Jannot de Moncey, stolid, unimaginative, and largely ineffectual. His later intervention in Spain in 1823 was to be infinitely more successful

Joachim Murat, the flamboyant cavalry commander who supervised the repression of the *Dos de Mayo* rising in Madrid and who quitted Spain before seeing what he had started

Jean-Baptiste Jourdan, Joseph Bonaparte's Chief-of-Staff in 1809–09 and
1812–13 and perhaps the least effective of the 'full-time' Peninsular Marshals

Claude-Victor Perrin (better known as Victor), indomitably mediocre. He was the Marshal of schoolboy legend—the drummer-boy with the Marshal's baton in his knapsack

Edouard Mortier, the most likeable of all the Marshals and the perfect subordinate

Michel Ney, 'the bravest of the brave' who proved too impatient to adapt easily to the failures of others

Louis-Gabriel Suchet, the only one of Napoleon's generals to earn his baton in the Peninsula and the only one to succeed in pacifying and administering rebellious Spanish territory

Auguste-Frédéric-Louis Viesse de Marmont, whose impressive record in the Peninsula was cut short by a wound received at Salamanca

André Massena, cynical, taciturn, and cunning, the best field commander on the French side, and the man who pushed Wellington as he had never been pushed before

Nicolas Jean-de-Dieu Soult. His faults were legion—avarice, selfishness, *folie de grandeur*—but he possessed, as Napoleon recognized, the best strategic brain in the Peninsula

YEAR OF RIVALRIES

While Soult was tackling Moore at Corunna on 16 January, 1809, Napoleon was still in Spain. From his headquarters at Valladolid he was churning out a torrent of orders which were intended to clean up the 'Spanish business' while he was away.

But the Emperor began with a fundamental and disastrous mistake which froze all hopes of effective action in the Peninsular theatre, and which was a direct by-product of his favourite technique of 'divide and rule' to make certain of his own ascendancy. King Joseph was graciously restored to the throne of Spain after a stage-managed petition from a group of Madrid worthies (such as could be found). King Joseph was given supreme command of the Army in Spain. But King Joseph, not being a commander of any prominence at all, was also given the assurance that detailed orders would still be sent direct to the corps commanders from Imperial Headquarters. It was one of the worst command set-ups ever created, and it was all Napoleon's work.

The 1809 campaign in the Peninsula started with the disgrace of one of the Marshals. Lefebvre had been ordered to set out on a round trip from Talavera, smash the Spanish levies in Estremadura on the central Tagus, and return to his base. But the dog-like blundering which had caused Lefebvre to spare Blake's army from destruction in November 1807, led him this time to march north into Old Castile and end up at Avila instead of Talavera. He was removed from the command of the IV Corps on the personal orders of Napoleon; 'he cannot grasp the meaning of his orders,' lamented the Emperor.

The other Marshals might have been excused for at least questioning theirs. Soult was given an extremely ambitious programme. He was to head south, marching directly on Lisbon via Vigo and Oporto, and he was given a hair-raising timetable — Oporto by 5 February, Lisbon by 16 February. Ney was to overrun Asturias and garrison Galicia, nailing down north-western Spain. Victor was to stay on the Tagus until Soult told him that Oporto had fallen, and then move down to Merida on the Guadiana. From Lisbon, Soult would reinforce Victor with a division or two, and after taking Badajoz Victor would head south to take Seville, Cadiz, and Gibraltar. Further to the east, up on the Ebro, Lannes was to take Saragossa and sweep through Valencia and Murcia to reinforce Victor; and Saint-Cyr would clear Catalonia. Lapisse was posted at Salamanca with his division to act as a link between Victor and Soult during the latter's march on Lisbon. And General Sebastiani, who took over IV Corps from Lefebvre, was to stay on the Tagus to cover the southward approaches to Madrid.

Now the fact that this basic plan was too complicated — and certainly far too ambitious as far as the schedule was concerned — should not have mattered. A really sound, controlling mind in Madrid could have adapted the essentials of the plan to suit the circumstances. But Joseph's chief-of-staff was Marshal Jourdan, one of the ex-Republican 'old-timer' Marshals, who had been given no independent field command since his resounding defeat at Stockach in 1799. Jourdan was aware that the Emperor was asking for the moon, but he was not the man to put things right, although he got on well enough with King Joseph. Nor were any of the veteran corps commanders of the *Grande Armée* disposed to accept orders from Jourdan, even assuming that any of them made sense. Thus Napoleon's basic error of a split command for the Peninsular theatre was compounded by the appointment of unpopular nonentities as its leaders.

Given this situation it was only too likely that the neat co-ordination envisaged by Napoleon for the 1809 campaign would break down into individual efforts. But the actual situation in every sector of the Peninsula made it a complete certainty.

On the Ebro the siege of Saragossa, stoutly defended by Palafox, was still pursuing its appalling course. The rout at Tudela on 23 November did not affect the determination of the people of Aragon's capital to stand another siege. The first, in summer 1808, had given the Spanish people a legend as strong as that of Bailen (though the chaos and military incompetence which the British found during Moore's foray into Spain caused many Britsh officers to disbelieve the story of Saragossa). But the second siege was far worse. It was, quite simply, the Stalingrad of the Peninsular War.

A swift assault on Saragossa after the victory at Tudela would probably have done the trick. But Saragossa had been entrusted to Moncey, and Moncey was one of the most hesitant and slow-moving of all the Marshals. By the time that the city was properly invested – over a month after Tudela – the people of Saragossa had responded magnificently to the urgings of Palafox and had made it virtually impregnable to direct assault. Mortier and Moncey, later joined by Junot's forces, contined to paw at the outer defences throughout the last days of December, but no more. And the city's example kept Aragon alive with armed *guerrilleros*. There could be no question of subduing the province – let alone using it as a base for a drive into southern Spain – until Saragossa's resistance was broken. And in the third week of January 1809 the French forces around the city were taken over by one of the toughest and most fiery of Napoleon's Marshals: Jean Lannes, the victor of Tudela.

Lannes took command on 22 January. He had to succeed where his predecessors had failed, with 22,000 moderately demoralized French troops pitted against 50,000 desperate

Spaniards determined to fight to the last in the name of Nuestra Señora de Pilar, the city's patron saint. Lannes made one bloody attempt to break the shell of the strongpoints which the Saragossans had created among their numerous convents and churches — and then he settled down to the exhausting and soul-destroying task of destroying the city with mine and bomb, wall by wall, house by house, block by block.

The horrid work began. The Saragossans fought back more fiercely than ever as they realized the inevitable destruction crawling in on them. It took a month of indescribable house-to-house fighting, the ferocity of which had never been experienced by the most hardened veteran in the *Grande Armée*. Lannes himself, one of the most ferocious fighting men the French Army has ever known, was shaken; he wrote of the fighting in Saragossa as *'une guerre qui fait horreur'*. Typhus broke out in the city. By 20 February the death-toll was 600 to 700 per day. Palafox knew that he must surrender, although there were still many hard-core defiants who cursed him as a traitor for his decision. Armistice preliminaries were concluded on the 20th, but three days passed before the Spanish leaders were tracked down and handed over to the French as required. Palafox himself was treated not as a captured general but as a war criminal. Napoleon branded him personally responsible for the carnage at Saragossa, and Palafox was consigned to the French 'VIP' prison at Vincennes.

The French made their official entry into Saragossa on 24 February. It was a smashed-open charnel-house of dead and dying, which after the eight weeks of the siege looked as though it had been hit by an earthquake. One-third of the city had been totally destroyed. The total death-toll of the Spanish troops and civilians of all ages was finally put at around 54,000. The French losses came to around 4,000 dead.

It was Lannes' last contribution to the course of the Peninsular War. Within weeks he was withdrawn from Spain to join the main body of the *Grande Armée* in its new campaign against Austria. Mortally wounded at Essling on 22 May, he took a week to die after losing a leg – the first of the Marshals to be killed on campaign.

Contrary to all expectations it was not the French who made the running in the first quarter of 1809, but the Spaniards. Napoleon's apparent belief that his recapture of Madrid had dispelled all organized resistance was soon proved wrong. In the first week of January a new insurgent army under the Duke of Infantado moved against Madrid. It was seen off in short order by Victor, who won an easy victory at Ucles on the 13th, but two more Spanish armies materialized in February. The first, the Army of Andalusia, was beaten at Ciudad Real by Sebastiani on 27 March. The second and most important was the Army of Estremadura under Gregorio de la Cuesta. (His forces should have been dispersed by Lefebvre; the latter's failure to do so had caused his replacement by Sebastiani.) Cuesta had learned little since his defeats in the previous summer. He made an attack on the Tagus crossing at Almaraz which laid him wide open to a counter-attack from Victor, who may not have been a brilliant general but knew a good thing when he saw it. Victor's corps chased Cuesta from the Tagus to the Guadiana, caught his army, and routed it at Medellin on 28 March, the day after Sebastiani's win at Ciudad Real. These new Spanish defeats left the southern approaches to Madrid still securely in French hands. The notable characteristic of this phase of the war was the speed in which loose-knit, local patriot armies were formed in the provinces and loosely hung onto the sagging backbone of the regular units to hand. Their trouble, however, was that it was still commonly believed that any such improvised hotch-potch could score a Bailen of its own.

Soult was the prime mover in the French offensive plan for 1809, but he took a long time to get moving. Four days after the fight at Corunna he had entered the port, and he consolidated his hold on north-western Spain by occupying Ferrol on 27 January. This was a sound enough move: it meant that the British would have to send any further aid via Lisbon alone. But there could be no question of Soult making any rapid move down into northern Portugal. Galicia was still in open revolt, and the insurgents were stiffened by the remnants of de la Romana's army which had survived the Corunna campaign. Soult's corps had considerable trouble in crossing the Minho river — marking the Portuguese frontier near the coast — and for a while he withdrew northwards to Orense.

One gets a good idea of the appalling delays in the transmission of news — and of the chronic wishful-thinking in high places — by taking a look at the manner in which King Joseph followed the progress of 'his' armies. When Joseph finally got the news of Soult's withdrawal to Orense, the King made a sweeping re-adjustment to the timetable. He now set the Marshal's estimated time of arrival in Lisbon at 15 March. In fact, Soult did not even reach the Douro until 29 March, when he took Oporto.

The invasion of Portugal was well behind schedule, but at last it was under way. Or so it seemed. Soult did not press on beyond the Douro. He had lost touch with Ney's forces in Galicia and was out on a limb; his troops had been tired by the marching and counter-marching which had taken them from Corunna to Douro, and needed a rest.

But now a surprising new development began to lower the morale of Soult's officers still further. The Marshal got a bad attack of title-fever. Northern Portugal was his. With a bit of luck he might end up as prince or even king of 'Northern Lusitania'. There had been odder territorial arrangements made since Napoleon had become the arbiter of Europe, after all. And so it was that while he lingered at Oporto Soult made strenuous efforts to placate the local Portuguese, and organize a deputation of Portuguese quislings who would, when the right time came, petition the Marshal to become their ruler.

If Soult's plans had progressed much further than they did, he would almost certainly have been weeded out by a furious

Napoleon and would have ended his days as a permanently-disgraced Marshal . From this he was saved by his own sluggishness, which resulted in a trouncing defeat at the hands of the British and their Portuguese allies.

The trouble was that although the Corunna campaign had expelled the British from Spain, it had not expelled them from the Peninsula. There were still some 10,000 of them based on Lisbon. How long they would stay there, however, was a matter for doubt. The British commander, Sir John Craddock, regarded the situation with undisguised gloom, and was certain that Lisbon would have to be evacuated sooner or later. But as often happens the man on the spot was out of touch with the overall situation.

For a new coalition was forming against Napoleon, with Austria's bid to break the French domination of central Europe at its core. The key battles would be fought out in the Danube valley — and the British Government knew that the Peninsular theatre, even after the disaster at Corunna, would be invaluable in tying down French troops which would otherwise be thrown against the Austrians.

Battered and incredibly down-at-heel, with a tradition of strategic incompetence and tactical defeat second to none, the Spanish armies had still not been eliminated, and until they had been the French field armies in Spain would have to stay where they were. But the British were now aiming to bring the Portuguese into play as well as the Spaniards. After consultation with the Regency Government of Portugal, a British general was sent out to take what remained of the Portuguese Army in hand.

His name was Major-General William Carr Beresford, and he landed at Lisbon on 25 March. With a small team of British NCOs and officers and the Portuguese rank of Marshal, he flung himself into the task of making the Portuguese regular army units fit to stand up to the French. Beresford, a superb organizer, did for the Portuguese Army what the German adviser Liman von Sanders did for the

Turkish Army before 1914. What was more important, his new Portuguese forces improved so much that they became fit to stand in the line with the British regular forces, giving the British field commander the chance to pick his fights on comparatively equal terms.

The new British commander was Sir Arthur Wellesley, the victor of Vimiero, who was the only one of the three generals responsible for the Convention of Cintra to be cleared by the subsequent Committee of Enquiry. He had unravelled the basic equation of the Peninsular War: continued Spanish resistance meant that the French could not conquer Portugal and take Lisbon with their current forces in Spain. He had learned much from the Vimiero campaign — as much about the performance of the British troops as about the French — and he had ideas on the prosecution of the Peninsular campaign which he meant to try out. These boiled down to assessing the most immediate threat to Lisbon and eliminating it as quickly and as cheaply as possible.

When Wellesley reached Lisbon on 22 April, there was little doubt as to which was the most immediate threat. It was posed by Soult's corps up on the Douro; and Wellesley immediately began to lay his plans for the neutralization (and if possible decisive defeat) of Soult.

Wellesley started by taking the title of Marshal-General of Portugal, making it clear that Beresford's command would be subordinate to his own. Since his own arrival in Lisbon Beresford had managed to train about 5,000 Portuguese which Wellesley considered acceptable, although the latter was moved to scathing comments on the state of the Portuguese Army in general. He left the bulk of the Portuguese, 7,000 strong, with 4,500 British troops to hold the eastern approaches to Lisbon against any possible moves by Victor. With a main body of 16,000 British, Wellesley himself headed north to tackle Soult at Oporto, sending Beresford and the Portuguese towards Lamego to block the French line of retreat eastwards along the Douro.

After concentrating his forces at Coimbra, four days'

march south of Oporto, Wellesley moved out for the decisive clash on 7 May.

It was one of the most extraordinary lapses in Soult's career. He was not even taken by surprise, for there was a spirited fight south of the river on 11 May near Grijon and the French had time to destroy their pontoon bridges. At dawn on the 12th Wellesley was given every facility short of a guided tour to mark down a totally unoccupied sector of the far bank, commandeer three handy wine barges, and shoot half a regiment across before Soult woke up to what was afoot. All French counter-attacks against the bridgehead were beaten off with the help of the artillery fire from the British bank of the Douro, and Wellesley pushed his main forces across. Soult's splendid position had been well and truly punctured; the citizens of Oporto rose enthusiastically to help the British and Soult's hold on the city was broken. The French broke and fled in great disorder with hundreds of prisoners falling to the exultant British, who lost only 23 killed and 98 wounded.

Although Soult's corps had been bounced out of Oporto in double-quick time, it was no part of Wellesley's plan to hunt it down to destruction. He wanted to get his army back to the Tagus, join hands with the Spaniards, and try accounts with Victor, and so the follow-up to the crossing of the Douro consisted merely of seeing the French safely out of northern Portugal. Soult's retreat was precipitate enough. Abandoning all guns and baggage, he ran for Galicia and a link-up with Ney. It was a nine-day ordeal which raised Soult's total losses to the neighbourhood of 4,000.

The British crossing of the Douro and Soult's flight from northern Portugal back to Spain were the prelude to a chaotic series of events on the French side. Fortunately for them, however, the situation was just as bad in the Allied camp. True to their tradition of recalcitrant incompetence the Spaniards now did everything they could to wreck Wellesley's plans for a piecemeal whittling at the French concentrations.

They were, however, to fail, and the result was Wellesley's next victory at Talavera, which raised him to the peerage as Vicount Wellington – but Talavera soon proved a hollow victory. Its immediate sequel was the French conquest of the south of Spain, taking them to the gates of Cadiz. This period – May 1809-February 1810 – lowered the Allies' fortunes in the Peninsular War to their lowest ebb since Napoleon's invasion of Spain in November 1808. Moreover, it was the prelude to what the British had always feared most: a French invasion of Portugal in force, with Spain temporarily quiescent.

But when Wellesley gave up the pursuit of Soult in May and turned south to return to the Tagus, this dramatic reversal of fortune hardly seemed likely. The insubordination and furious rivalry of the Marshals was rapidly coming to the boil. Nothing, it seemed, was going to make them work together.

When Soult quitted Galicia to conquer Portugal Ney had remained, constantly receiving orders from Napoleon to hand over the administration of the province to the local Spaniards, move inland from Corunna and Ferrol, and conquer Asturias. This, of course, was farcical, as Ney well knew. The hatred of the Galicians towards King Joseph's regime was fanatical. But he did try to subdue Asturias. In early May he brought in Kellermann from Leon and Bonet from Santander and pulled off a neat converging attack on Oviedo, the Asturian capital, inflicting a fresh defeat on de la Romana's military ragamuffins in the process. But while the French moved on Oviedo the Spaniards broke out again in Galicia, while Santander was captured from the French to the east. Back went the French forces – Bonet to retake Santander, Kellermann to Leon, and Ney to Galicia.

Immediately after this episode, infuriating for Ney, Soult's routed II Corps arrived in Ney's territory after its retreat from Portugal, totally dependent upon Ney's VI Corps for help and supplies. On a purely human level Ney can be excused for feeling that he was being made to do all the work for no thanks. But as a military commander he should have been able to fight down these feelings in the knowledge that others were pulling their weight in the same team. As he knew well, there was no team, and for Ney, the fiery individualist, it was all too much. A violent spate of blood-feuding broke out between Soult and Ney, which got so bad that their staff officers began duelling; and on one occasion Ney himself drew steel on Soult before the two were hastily parted.

Now this was a sufficiently appalling situation in itself but it led directly to the permanent abandonment of one of the occupied provinces of Bonapartist Spain. Ney and Soult buried the hatchet so far as to agree on a joint venture in Galicia, to crush the insurgents whose rising had brought Ney back from Oviedo in early May. Soult, however, once the troops were on the move, decided to go down into Leon without telling Ney, and did so. Ney marched dutifully in the opposite direction — but when he heard what Soult had done he reacted with a fit of blind rage and evacuated Galicia himself. His VI Corps left a trail of twenty-six blazing towns and villages as it marched out of the province: a permanent disgrace on Ney, and on the French Army as a whole. No military purpose whatsoever was served by this brutality. It was an act of pure, vindictive spite.

In Madrid, King Joseph was constantly being mortified by the orders coming in from Napoleon. On 1 July he heard that Ney and Mortier were to be placed under Soult's command for a renewed invasion of Portugal. The weaknesses of such an arrangement were obvious — Ney and Soult had already deluged Joseph with complaints about each other and the hapless King had commented: 'I do not think that it will be possible for them to act together.' After the Galicia affair, it was a masterly understatement. But what made Joseph really unhappy, of course, was that an independent command for Soult (or anyone else, for that matter) would make his own position as nominal commander-in-chief openly ludicrous. He already knew that Victor and Sebastiani, to the south-west and south of Madrid, regarded themselves as independent professionals who should not take orders from an amateur. But Joseph also knew that any complaint he ventured to make to Napoleon about the military set-up in Spain never got a reply. The full emptiness of Joseph's power was shown when he ordered Mortier to make a third with the other two corps around Madrid. Soult, acting – quite correctly – on Napoleon's orders, countermanded Joseph's order and brought Mortier back into his own territory.

Joseph believed that the British were bound to follow up their success at Oporto and move into Leon. To scotch this, he wanted to strike first by taking Ciudad Rodrigo, which with Almeida guarded the northern approaches to Portugal. Wellesley, on the other hand, was convinced that the French troops on the Tagus must head directly west in a march on Lisbon. Accordingly, his counter-plan was to join up with the Spanish Army of Estramadura (Cuesta) and the Army of the Centre (Venegas) and launch a spoiling attack on Victor's corps at Talavera.

Wellesley knew that he was being sent reinforcements from England: Light Brigade Corunna veterans and the crack Royal Artillery Chestnut Troop. While these were on their way he planned to join with Cuesta's 33,000 Spaniards and move directly against Victor, who was to be cut off from Madrid by Venegas. On 27 June he moved east from Abrantès and arrived at Plasencia on 8 July. But here, yet again, the terrible problem of getting co-operation out of the Spaniards raised its head.

Wellesley's main problem was not the French but Cuesta, who disagreed with the British general's plan. There was no encircling move to cut Victor off from Madrid. Instead there ensued three weeks of stop-go incompetence which took the Allies as far as Talavera on the 22nd, saw the Spaniards blunder on towards Madrid, enabled Victor and Sebastiani to unite their corps – and exposed the Allied armies to an attack by 46,000 Frenchmen.

King Joseph himself was riding with the French army, sensing that the time had come for him to claim a legitimate victory in battle, but the dominant commander was Victor. On the 26th Victor won an easy success over Cuesta's men at Torrijos, driving them back on Talavera. Wellesley now had to get Cuesta to agree to placing his forces in the defensive position north of the town which Wellesley had selected. This had its front along the Portina brook, its left anchored on the heights of the Cerro de Medellin, and its right on the town of Talavera itself. He gave the Spaniards the easiest job: to defend Talavera with their 30,000 men while the 30,000-odd British and German troops held the rest of the line.

Thanks to Cuesta, the Allies were now in an extremely bad position. All the cards had been handed to the French. And Soult was determined to use the opportunity to avenge his humiliation at Oporto. On hearing that the British were moving up the Tagus towards Madrid, he proposed a strike at the British base at Plasencia which would cut them off from Portugal. Mortier and Soult, heading south from Salamanca, would then be attacking the Allies' rear with 50,000 troops while Victor and Sebastiani attacked in front with 46,000. It was an excellent reaction to an unforeseen course of events, which certainly compares favourably with Napoleon's own redeployment and advance against Moore the previous December. It also shows how sound was the professional mind of Soult, for all his recent chain of setbacks and his deep-rooted personal ambitions.

Such a threat was obvious to Wellesley and he had asked Cuesta to see to it. A strong force holding the Baños Pass, commanding the Salamanca-Plasencia road, would do the trick, and Cuesta had assured Wellesley that the Spaniards would handle the job. What Wellesley did not know was that Cuesta only sent a couple of battalions to the Baños Pass, and the French soon discovered the fact. And so it was that the overall situation of the Allied armies at Talavera was as tense as it could be. Their position was strong, certainly, but all Victor and Sebastiani had to do was to wait until Soult and

Mortier took Plasencia, which would catch the British and Spanish armies in a trap of overpowering strength.

The reason why this failed to come about was Victor's insistence on an immediate attack on Talavera, which ended in a clear-cut defeat for King Joseph's army on 28 June. It is hard to blame Victor for forcing the pace. Of all the generals in attendance on the King, it was Victor who had the biggest personal score of victories over the Spaniards, which he had just increased by his trouncing of Cuesta at Torrijos on the 26th. Quite clearly, however, he also wanted to establish a firm moral ascendancy over King Joseph by winning a battle all by himself under that synthetic monarch's nose.

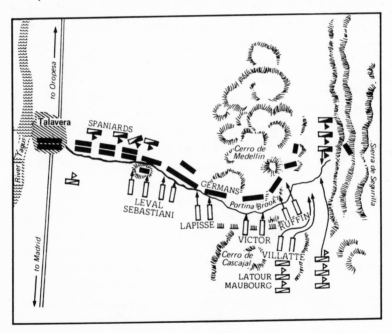

The battle of Talavera, 28 July 1809

On the 27th Victor advanced towards Talavera across the Alberche river and made contact with the Allied forces, which were still taking their places in the line. In a spirited action Lapisse's division surprised the British rearguard and inflicted 400 casualties on it. One of Victor's light cavalry brigades, probing towards Talavera itself, panicked 2,000 Spanish troops. Victor was so encouraged by all this that he sent in a division to take the heights of the Cerro de Medellin in a night attack, but this failed. Victor's natural reaction was to inform Joseph that he would launch a general attack against the Allied line at dawn on the 28th.

This was, quite clearly, jumping the gun, for the 28th was the day in which the first French troops were due to arrive before Plasencia, and full co-operation between the four French corps would not be possible. But King Joseph let Victor have his way. Headstrong and opinionated though Victor might be, the events of the last 48 hours showed that there was a lot to be said for his methods. The engagements of the 27th had also suggested that the Anglo-Spanish force was eminently beatable. Above all Joseph knew that if Victor were reined in at this stage he would promptly complain to the Emperor that an easy victory had been thrown away by the caution of the King of Spain.

Victor's haste was his undoing, as had been the case with Junot at Vimiero. The British left flank was eminently vulnerable: a stretch of low ground permitted a flanking movement against the British line up on the ridge. A general frontal assault against the British line would suffer more heavily, but Wellesley's forces were strung out two deep over some 1½ miles and looked temptingly weak. Victor, however, chose to open proceedings with an attack by a single division – Ruffin's division, which had already suffered some 400 casualties during its attack the previous night. Ruffin's men advanced under cover of smoke from the muzzles of over fifty French guns, which opened fire at 0500 hours on the morning of the 28th. As the French infantry cleared the smoke and drove uphill towards the crest of the Cerro de Medellin, Sir Rowland Hill's division went into action, focusing its musketry fire-power on Ruffin's masses, which outnumbered their British opposite numbers by about a thousand. It was Vimiero all over again as the French staggered to a halt and recoiled downhill towards their start-line on the east side of the Portina brook.

For several hours after the defeat of Ruffin there was a tense silence. Both sides collected their dead, fraternized across the Portina brook, and cooked scratch breakfasts from what rations they had (thanks to Spanish lack of co-operation the British had been on half-rations for days). But up at the French HQ on the Cerro de Cascajal, looking across at the Cerro de Medellin, the debate was whether to renew the attack or to wait for Soult to close the trap. King Joseph was now worrying about a possible threat to Madrid from Venegas, whose forces had finally put in an appearance near Toledo and Aranjuez. Jourdan criticized Victor for even thinking of launching frontal attacks against the British position, pointing out that it was now too late to flank the British as Wellesley had placed cavalry on the low ground. But Victor insisted that a mass attack on the British-held heights by I and IV Corps could not fail.

Victor's moral hold over King Joseph has already been described, but now the King clutched at the military argument (one, he felt, that would certainly sound good in a report to Napoleon) that a crushing victory of the British would release forces for the elimination of Venegas, and of all danger to Madrid. So Victor got his way.

From the early afternoon Victor's attack raged all along the British line, heralded by a bombardment of the eighty guns of I and IV Corps. The greatest success was won by Sebastiani and Lapisse, who broke through the British centre. A simultaneous attack against the Cerro de Medellin by Ruffin would have prevented Wellesley from plugging the gap with reserves and driving back the French, but Victor had decided to try a probe around the British left with the divisions of Villatte and Ruffin. While Wellesley made good the repairs to his centre, his cavalry counter-attacked Ruffin and Villatte with all the boisterous, slap-dash élan which was to infuriate him right down to Waterloo. By the late afternoon 41,000 French troops had been committed and the attack was obviously getting nowhere. King Joseph was becoming increasingly apprehensive. He refused Victor's demand for the last free division, Dessolles's. And as darkness crept in the French retired to the Portina, with the Allies still holding their position.

Victor had made a thorough mess of this latter stage of the battle, his first against British troops, and had got a bloody nose in consequence. The French had lost 7,628 men, a casualty list of one in six which they could well have afforded — if they had won. With no alternative but to renew the battle on the following day, Victor pounced on the King's refusal to give him Desolles' division as a face-saver and began to withdraw I Corps to the Alberche river during the night of 28-29 July. Seething with recriminations (Sebastiani in particular was furious with the decision to give up), the rest of the French divisions followed.

Wellesley's army may have been victorious, but it was exhausted for the time being. Where the French had lost one man in six, the British had lost one in four: 5,363 all told. What was worse, they were down to one-third rations now. They stayed where they were until 1 August, when Wellesley finally heard of the threat to Plasencia in his rear: Mortier's troops, leading Soult's triple drive on Plasencia, had taken the Banõs Pass. By 3 August Wellesley was back at Oropesa, where he heard that Plasencia had fallen to Mortier the day before. It now became a race between Soult and Ney, whose combined forces numbered 50,000, and Wellesley, who had been reinforced by Craufurd's Light Brigade and whose army was now 18,000 strong.

With Plasencia gone, Wellesley could only cross the Tagus and secure his retreat-line to Portugal along the south bank of the river. He could only make the crossing at Arzobispo, as the Almaraz bridge was down and the French were too close to the ford there. At this point Cuesta futilely announced that he was not afraid to stand and fight. After a blazing row, Wellesley told him bluntly that the British were going to leave him, and sent off Craufurd's Light Brigade to block the ford at Almaraz from the southern bank. They got there on the 6th – barely in time to foil Ney's attempt to seize the crossing.

Soult, Mortier, and Ney had put in an impressive performance, however, racing their corps down from Salamanca and even further north in little over a week. But it was clear that now the British had won the race for the Tagus crossing they would be able to retire towards Trujillo, Medellin, Badajoz, and the Portuguese frontier. Soult therefore fell upon Cuesta, driving him back from the Tagus in a tough fight at Arzobispo on 8 August. Sebastiani had chased Venegas away from the south-eastern approaches to Madrid by the middle of August. And on the 21st Wellesley decided to retreat to the Portuguese frontier and the Badajoz-Elvas region, shrugging off the bitter protests of the Seville Junta. His army had lost a third of the men which had marched into Spain, and he was going to fall back on his supply bases to get it back in fighting trim again.

Thus by the end of August 1809 another British intervention in Spain had been foiled and the Pensinsular Marshals had inflicted fresh defeats on the Spaniards. Madrid was safe, and once again the French corps were strung round King Joseph's capital in a great arc. But there was too much grit in the works on the French side, and another outbreak of disputed authority was the inevitable result.

It was precipitated by King Joseph, who refused to admit that his easy victory had evaporated on him. Stupidly (if pathetically) he sent off a despatch to Napoleon announcing a victory. It was headed 'In bivouac at Talavera' and used blatantly untrue or misleading phrases such as 'The British 30th Dragoon Regiment [non-existent] was taken', 'I regret that we did not capture the whole British Army',etc., etc. Jourdan, in his own report, sang much the same song. But neither of them had remembered that Napoleon got his best intelligence from British newspapers; and when he read the official British reports of the action at Talavera he was furious with the mendacious rubbish sent to him by King

Joseph and Jourdan. Napoleon not only rebuked his brother in the severest terms for sending him 'republican romances fit only for schoolboys': Jourdan was returned to France on sick leave and replaced as chief-of-staff by Soult, of all the Peninsular Marshals the man whom Joseph most disliked and distrusted, on 16 September.

In the weeks after the Talavera campaign there were two changes of command on the French side. Of these, naturally, Soult's replacement of Jourdan was the most important. King Joseph, however, wanted to get rid of Victor (which contrasted oddly with his Talavera despatch, in which Victor had necessarily been described as having done well). Joseph told Victor that he could go to France on leave, and asked Ney to take over I Corps. Victor turned down this 'offer', and Ney refused to do anything without a clear-cut order from the Emperor. In the end, on 4 October, Ney got one: to return to France for some much-needed leave himself. General Marchand took over VI Corps in Ney's absence.

When Cuesta had told Wellesley that the Spaniards would go it alone if necessary, he had meant what he said. In the autumn of 1809 new Spanish armies appeared on the scene. In October the Duke del Parque marched on Salamanca with 21,500 men. Marchand, who had only taken command of VI Corps a fortnight before, marched out of Salamanca to challenge del Parque with 13,200 men and got himself beaten at Tamanes on 18 October – the first French defeat at the hands of a Spanish army since Bailen. Marchand was forced to evacuate Salamanca, which del Parque entered in triumph on 25 October. Soult reacted promptly, replacing Marchand with Kellermann and sending 8,000 reinforcements to his command, and Kellermann proved his worth yet again by recovering Salamanca in two weeks and restoring the situation in Leon.

But del Parque's army was not alone. The Seville Junta had raised Venegas's former command to nearly 60,000 men by transferring forces from the Army of Estremadura and by raising fresh ones. Cuesta had had a paralytic stroke in

August and the command of this new army had been entrusted to General Carlos Areizaga.

At the beginning of November Areizaga prepared for a surprise dash on Madrid from the Sierra Morena, regardless of the fact that del Parque's northern army had been formed to act in concert with his movements. More by luck than by good judgment Areizaga headed his army straight through the defensive perimeter of corps around Madrid. By 8 November his foremost cavalry units were threatening Aranjuez. But instead of continuing his rush on Madrid, Areizaga dallied at La Guadia for ten days — ample time for Soult to concentrate the IV and V Corps and march against him. The result was the battle of Ocana on 19 November, one of the most ruinous battles fought by the Spaniards in the entire Peninsular War, which added mightily to Soult's stature. In return for 2,000 casualties the French accounted for around 4,000 Spaniards and rounded up 14,000 prisoners. On the 28th the French triumph was clinched when Kellermann smashed del Parque at Alba de Tormes. It was the end of the Spanish hopes for a concerted offensive against the French in 1809. All that remained now were the 10,000-odd men of the truncated Army of Estremadura near Almaraz — and the British in Portugal.

In the meantime a self-contained drama was working itself out in Catalonia, hundreds of miles away from the scene of the principal action. Ever since Napoleon's counter-offensive of November 1808, the walled city of Gerona had held out for King Ferdinand VII. It survived General Saint-Cyr's overrunning of Catalonia with the French VII Corps, and, inspired by the example of Saragossa, refused to surrender.

Gerona was no more siege-proof that Saragossa; the truth was that the siege was conducted with extraordinary laxness by Saint-Cyr, who was succeeded by Marshal Augereau on 1 June. But Augereau did not want to take command of his old corps. He contracted a diplomatic attack of gout and took himself off on a prolonged cure. Saint-Cyr accepted the situation until October, when he resigned his command, wrote to congratulate Augereau on his recovery, and returned to France. The whole business was an astonishing example of what the Army generals of the Napoleonic Empire could get away with when they put their minds to it. Saint-Cyr went on to become a Marshal in the Russian campaign of 1812.

Augereau was therefore compelled to grasp the nettle of Gerona at last. He settled down to the siege in earnest, hanging local *guerrilleros* and writing reams of splendidly windy proclamations to the city of Gerona and the Catalans in general. Gerona, last bastion of serious Spanish resistance in north-eastern Spain, fell on 10 December, 1809. Its Governor, the iron-willed Mariano Alvarez de Castro, was inhumanly treated by the French on Napoleon's orders and died in prison. But he and the Geronese had been true to the spirit of Palafox and the Saragossans. More to the point, the eight-month siege had whittled down the strength of the French VII Corps by some 14,000 men, and had tied down thousands more Frenchmen in communications duties.

Now the French commanders in Spain made a crucial decision: to invade and conquer Andalusia, Spain's southern province, without first eliminating the British in Portugal. It was a decision which looked obvious when drawn in on a map, but as far as strategy was concerned the conquest of Andalusia would have to be total. There must be no prolonged sieges, no French troops tied down in static garrison or communications duties. And if there was one lesson which the French in the Peninsula should have learned by November 1809, it was that this was impossible.

King Joseph urged the Andalusian venture and Soult was the man who should have talked him out of it. After Talavera Soult had pressed for an immediate invasion of Portugal, but had been ordered to wait by Napoleon. Certainly there were reasons for adding Andalusia to Bonapartist Spain: it was the richest province in the kingdom, and King Joseph's exchequer needed the money, being totally bankrupt. There were strategic reasons, too: if Cadiz and Gibraltar could be taken the entire situation in the western Mediterranean could be changed dramatically. The British Navy would be shut out of the Mediterranean and the Bourbons of Naples, Britain's last allies east of the straits, would no longer be able to hold out in Sicily.

But it was selfish reasoning which prompted the invasion of Andalusia and gave the British in Portugal a breathing-space. King Joseph wanted to prevent Napoleon from taking personal charge of the Peninsular theatre. On 14 October Austria, beaten at Wagram on 6 July, had finally knuckled under to humiliating peace terms and a return to the fetters of Napoleon's Continental System. It seemed more than likely that the Emperor would take the opportunity of crushing resistance in the Peninsula and running the place as a French colony, whereas Joseph really saw himself as the King of a country which was allied to France and yet which had rights of its own for which he, Joseph, was responsible.

Soult, too, was motivated by personal interest. As long as the Peninsular campaign continued in its present form, he would retain an autonomous command. And this, quite bluntly, meant not only power but loot. Soult was already notorious as one of the most avaricious of all the Marshals; in the overview he shared that distinction with Massena. It was obvious that there would be plenty of treasures in the south to add to his extensive art collection.

Certainly Napoleon should have vetoed the Andalusian expedition and ordered that Portugal be made the top priority. But once again poor brother Joseph in Spain was duelling with phantoms. After Wagram and the neutralization of Austria, Napoleon was far more concerned with establishing his dynasty. This meant arranging a divorce from the barren Empress Josephine and checking the princesses of the imperial houses of Europe for their eligibility. While all this was going on Napoleon did not want to know about the

Peninsula. It was as simple as that. He was so disinterested in the whole affair during the winter of 1809-10 that King Joseph and Soult virtually got the imperial approval in default of an answer.

Throughout the last days of 1809 the French commanders in Spain were sending out concentration orders to the corps which would carry out the invasion and conquest of Andalusia. By 11 January, 1810, headquarters had moved down from Madrid to Ciudad Real on the Guadiana and the preparations were all but complete. The expeditionary force would total 68,000 veterans. Soult would be in overall command over Victor and Sebastiani; Mortier's V Corps would also take part, its task being to slam the door on the British in Portugal by taking Badajoz.

The Spanish forces along the Sierra Morena, only 25,000 strong and still headed by Areizaga, who had been thrashed at Ocaña, never had a chance. The French drove south and south-west in four separate columns, in a trouble-free advance. All key passes over the Sierra Morena had been taken by 21 January, the day Joseph entered Bailen. Sebastiani took Jaén on the 22nd and moved on to Granada, while Victor entered Cordoba on the 24th. On the 29th the Junta at Seville, hopelessly discredited after the defeats of the previous year, panicked and fled to Cadiz and Gibraltar. On 1 February King Joseph and Victor entered Seville, the ancient capital of Andalusia, in triumph.

It was the last triumph of the campaign.

The Spanish General Albuquerque of the Army of Estremadura, watching everything go to pieces, had come to a courageous decision. He could not save Seville; he could not help Areizaga. But one thing he still had time to do, and that was to help defend Cadiz. On 4 February Albuquerque entered Cadiz with 12,000 soldiers, the makings of a full-strength garrison; and by the time Victor's plenipotentiaries rode up to the city 48 hours later, demanding instant surrender, it was too late. Cadiz was going to fight.

A new spirit had arisen on the Spanish side, symbolized by

a new Council of Regency, dominated by Castaños, the hero of Bailen. (This was an attempt to restore some measure of respectability to the Spanish cause, respectability which the regional insurgent Juntas – the brains, be it remembered, behind the Spanish defeats of 1808-9 – had notably failed to retain.) This Council, together with the heartening presence of Albuquerque's troops, intended that contrary to Soult's confident forecast to King Joseph on 30 January Cadiz would not fall as the inevitable result of the fall of Seville. Moreover, the British sent help from Portugal: 3,500 British and Portuguese troops were landed in Cadiz on 10 February.

Cadiz, on its narrow peninsula, was impregnable to anything but a prolonged and intricate siege; but with complete command of the coastal approaches to the port the Allies could make besieging Cadiz as unprofitable as dipping up water in a bottomless bucket. But Talavera had shown that Victor was not very good at assessing what was an impossible task and what was not, and by 20 February he was preparing for a full-dress siege. A powerful siege force dug in around Cadiz – it had to be a powerful one to stop the British using the port as an offensive base, like Lisbon – was the one thing the French could not afford. And the siege of Cadiz, which represented the high-water mark of the French hold on the Peninsula, was destined to last for nearly two and a half years.

None of the real significance of the siege of Cadiz was apparent to the feckless King Joseph, who spent February-March 1810 riding around Andalusia, basking in the glow of what seemed to be a bloodless conquest and writing happily about the joyous reception he was getting from 'his' loyal and loving subjects.

He was soon to be totally disillusioned.

CHAPTER SEVEN

TORRES VEDRAS

Puppet rulers, no matter how base their motives for accepting power may be, always have a slightly pathetic appearance because of the basic dependence of their position. King Joseph of Spain was no exception – but his situation was far more unhappy. He really believed that, given the chance, he could rule Spain as an independent, happy, and prosperous ally of Napoleon's France.

Years later, writing his testament on St Helena, Napoleon made the preposterous claim that this condition was what he had really wanted for the whole of Europe. The fact that his armies had kept Europe at war for some twelve years was not his fault, of course. His noble ideals had been sabotaged by perfidious Albion, the forces of counter-Revolution, treacherous and incompetent generals and officials, and just about everybody but himself.

No admirer of the Emperor can deny the fact that Napoleon, like Hitler, was a master of the big lie. The two men were very alike when it came to lofty statements about fighting for a new and better Europe. Another parallel with Hitler is that Napoleon had always been quite clear what he was really after: 'My policy is France before all.' A slightly less well-known *obiter dictum* of the Emperor is equally typical of Napoleon the man and his ruling technique: 'When I need a man I am not squeamish: I'd kiss his backside.'

At no time, therefore, did King Joseph's pathetic dreams of being cherished by posterity as Joseph the Good of Spain, father of his country, archetypal enlightened monarch, and so on, have a chance. And on 8 February, 1810, as Marshal Victor's I Corps was sitting down to besiege Cadiz, Napoleon issued an Imperial decree which made a formal mockery of King Joseph's hopes. Catalonia, Aragon, Navarre, and the Biscay provinces were declared military governments, entirely free of the jurisdiction of King Joseph's government in Madrid. It was the first stage in moulding the administration of Spain into the form Napoleon wanted: a conquered country, a milch-cow for France, and a source of revenue, material, and men for the Empire in general.

Poor Joseph's ephemeral sense of triumph at the annexation of Andalusia evaporated overnight. He sent message after message to Napoleon. What sort of a King of Spain was he supposed to be? Who was to be the boss – he, Joseph, or the Marshals and the generals? By the summer of 1810 the position had become brutally clear. Napoleon was going to put all Spain under military governments and reduce Joseph to the effective status of a provincial prefect, with his military resources limited to his royal guard and his jurisdiction to the environs of Madrid.

On 17 April Joseph published a decree of his own, solemnly dividing Spain into thirty-eight prefectures on the best French model. But this was made totally meaningless by the previous establishment of the military governments, and worse was to come. On the very day of Joseph's decree, Napoleon appointed Marshal Massena to the command of the new 'Army of Portugal', which was made up of VI Corps (Ney), II Corps (Reynier), and VIII Corps (Junot). This army, too, was to be an autonomous command, and Massena would have total responsibility for the province of Leon and the Salamanca region. In the following months even more military satraps were set up: south to Plasencia and east to Valladolid and Burgos, effectively parcelling out the northern half of Joseph's kingdom for military rule. The climax came on 14 July, when Soult was appointed to the command of the 'Army of the South' in Andalusia: I Corps (Victor), IV

Corps (Sebastiani), and V Corps (Mortier). Joseph's one claim to having achieved something since his return to Madrid, the acquisition of Andalusia, had been taken away from him. Economically his position would be hopeless without the wealth of Andalusia. And as if to add insult to injury Soult was also given Dessolles' division, which had been part of Joseph's Madrid garrison until then.

It was total humiliation for King Joseph, and it virtually meant *carte blanche* for the military. Three examples of how the Peninsular Marshals chose to behave when given a free hand in this manner may be cited. Soult made a useful fortune for himself by selling off all the British merchandise which had been captured in Andalusia – an obvious source of revenue which Napoleon had deliberately forbidden Joseph to exploit. Up in Valladolid General Kellermann was doing a roaring trade in selling ransoms for Spanish prisoners being marched through his territory on their way to prisoner-of-war camps in France. (It was very efficently done, with publicly-displayed posters.) And Ney went so far as to march into Avila (an area which had never given any trouble since the French occupation) and plunder the local tax returns to pay his troops, provoking another howl of protest from King Joseph to the Emperor. Napoleon's reply was not very comforting. He assured Joseph that Avila did indeed lie within his jurisdiction. But Ney got off scot free without even an official reprimand from Imperial Headquarters, let alone any order to hand back the money.

None of this was helped by the fact that the new commander of the Army of Portugal was known throughout the French Army as a notorious peculator and miser: André Massena. Since 1805 his career had been a chequered one, with periods of semi-official disgrace caused by his shameless avarice; but Napoleon never forgot the paramount talents of this great general. In 1809 Massena had helped win the murderous battle of Wagram for Napoleon. He was now a prince. He was also, quite clearly, the leading Marshal of the *Grande Armée* in 1810; and this was why he was entrusted with the Army of Portugal, the powerful new weapon forged for the conquest of Portugal and the expulsion of the British.

Of Massena Napoleon wrote: 'He is a good soldier, but is entirely dominated by his love of money.' The latter was true enough, as far as it went; but a lot of the blame should be laid at Napoleon's door for insisting that his armies should largely support themselves – *'la guerre doit nourrir la guerre.* Napoleon, shrewd judge of men that he was, should also have taken a lot more trouble in winning Massena's confidence. Massena was a tricky character: taciturn, acid, and withdrawn. Part of the trouble, of course, was undeclared jealousy for his formidable list of achievements in the field which none of the other Marshals could match, and which, when examined in detail, showed quite as much skill as Napoleon himself. At Toulon in 1793 Napoleon may have stolen all the limelight, but Massena was the man to whom it was due. Since then Massena had saved the day repeatedly – at Rivoli in 1797, in the defence of Zürich in 1799, and in the siege of Genoa in 1800.

These were indeed gruelling and thankless tasks, but the first campaign of the *Grande Armée* in 1805 had promptly saddled Massena with another. With the 40,000-odd effectives of the Army of Italy, he was expected to take the offensive against the formidable Archduke Charles of Austria, who had twice the strength of the Army of Italy. Massena nevertheless managed to pin down the Archduke and fight him to a draw at Caldiero, by which time Napoleon and the bulk of the *Grande Armée* had sealed the fate of General Mack in Ulm on the Danube and were marching on Vienna. Certainly Massena had done all that could have been expected in Italy, and more; but all he got from Napoleon was a thinly-veiled rebuke for not having won a decisive victory.

The year of Jena and Auerstädt, 1806, saw Massena forced to step down to the level of a corps commander and lead the newly-formed VIII Corps to conquer southern Italy for Joseph, the new King of Naples, whom he loathed. This time

Massena had the opportunity of fighting a tough siege from the outside, at Gaeta, a key port which the British were assisting the Bourbons of Naples to defend. While the siege was still in progress General Reynier, commanding one of Massena's divisions, got himself thrashed by the British at Maida. Gaeta fell to the French on 19 July after a five-month siege. Massena then had to spend four thoroughly unpleasant months fighting partisans in Calabria, quarrelling repeatedly with King Joseph in the process. On 15 December he wrote to Joseph asking to be allowed to resign his command, and to Napoleon asking for a corps command with the *Grande Armée* in Germany. It was during this depressing period that Massena was forced to disgorge the 3 million or so francs which he had made by selling trade licences in southern Italy, the proceeds being secretly paid into a Livorno bank.

Massena's ensuing spell of service with the *Grande Armée* during the Friedland campaign added little to his laurels on the battlefield and permanently damaged his health. He took over V Corps while Lannes was on sick leave after Eylau, but did not see action at Friedland at all: his task was to shield the right flank of the *Grande Armée*. Like the other corps commanders, however, he was awarded a profitable slice of 'liberated' Poland: an estate worth £34,000 per year, plus an additional gratuity of £16,000. Apart from the money, however, Massena took nothing home from Poland but a permanent and enfeebling lung ailment which weakened his constitution greatly.

He was, however, allowed the year 1808 to spend away from the Army, and on 19 March he was proclaimed Duke of Rivoli – a permanent if belated tribute to his victory there in 1797. But in September 1808 Massena suffered yet again at the Emperor's hands when Napoleon accidentally shot him in the left eye on a shooting party. Napoleon promptly blamed Berthier, who had become enough of a courtier to take it gracefully. Massena lost the eye, however, and one can only wonder what went through his mind when he painfully read he following piece of effrontery from Napoleon: 'I have heard of your unfortunate accident with the deepest regret. After having passed unscathed through so many dangers, it was rough luck to be wounded at a shooting party . . .'

One-eyed though he now was, the new Duke of Rivoli was given a leading role in the crucial campaign against the Austrians in 1809. Massena was put in command of the strong new IV Corps of five divisions – four of infantry and one of cavalry – which was the backbone of the allied German contingents of the new 'Army of Germany'. He distinguished himself in the four-day battle of Eckmuhl (20-23 April), which opened the road to Vienna. The Austrian capital was entered on 11 May, but a decisive action with the main Austrian field army – 80,000 men under Massena's old opponent, the Archduke Charles – had yet to be fought.

All Napoleon knew was that the Archduke's army was on the north bank of the Danube, and he planned to cross and seek it out. The island of Lobau, which in 1809 virtually spanned the Danube five miles east of Vienna, was chosen as the crossing-place. But an incredible blunder by Napoleon nearly resulted in total disaster. On 20 May Massena's four divisions crossed the northern branch of the Danube and occupied the villages of Aspern and Essling – and on the following day the Archduke swooped down on Massena's 29,000 with 80,000 Austrians.

After two days of desperate fighting for Aspern and Essling, Napoleon accepted the fact that he was not going to convert this terrifying situation into a victory, and ordered a retreat to Lobau. In a brilliant fighting withdrawal Massena's corps, supported by that of Lannes (this was the fight in which Lannes was mortally wounded), pulled back to the island. It was a clear-cut tactical defeat for the *Grande Armée*, with the French losing 44,100 killed, wounded, and missing and the Austrians only 23,340.

A month of intense preparation followed. On Massena's advice Napoleon had decided to hold Lobau as a base for a new crossing. Massena's corps garrisoned the island, and he was put in charge of preparing all the details of the next attempt. A mutual cease-fire settled along the Danube, during which Napoleon, Massena, and an ADC would disguise themselves as a party of sergeants going for a swim, and spy out the land for the best sites for the new bridges.

By the end of June 1809 fresh drafts and reinforcements had poured into the *Ile Napoléon*, as Lobau was now known to the army, and 150,000 Frenchmen were preparing to tackle the crossing again. There was no mistake this time. On the night of 4-5 July the whole of the *Grande Armée* surged across the Danube and swung north to engage the Austrians. The result was the carnage of Wagram, one of the hardest-fought victories ever achieved by the *Grande Armée*. In it, Massena commanded his corps from a coach-and-four, having hurt his leg in a riding accident just before the crossing. His corps, strung out on the French left flank, held out valiantly until Napoleon's main attack went in on the right and centre and forced the Austrians to withdraw.

This incident gave place to a story about Massena which has been described as malicious, but which rings horribly true. Massena was driven about the battlefield by his civilian driver and footman, and was said after the battle to have been too mean to grant them both annuities as a reward for their bravery under fire. He decided on a niggardly flat payment, only to be shamed out of it by the Emperor slyly expressing approval of the 'annuities' he had paid. Whether or not this did actually happen, Massena came out of the Wagram campaign as the most prominent Marshal involved; and on 21 January, 1810, Napoleon proclaimed him Prince of Essling.

As commander of the Army of Portugal in the Peninsula, Massena had an obvious brief: to put down Portugal and expel the British. The French had tried twice now — three times, if Napoleon's arrested venture is counted — and it was becoming obvious that one certain key to military success in the Peninsula was concentrated force. Hence Massena's three-corps command, which would certainly be the strongest French force to attempt the subjugation of Portugal.

Impressive as it was, it should have been stronger. The manpower of the Army of Portugal, discounting troops earmarked for garrison duties, was around 65,000, and this force had been assembled with the idea that a two-to-one superiority over the British Army should avoid any mistakes this time. But Napoleon and Massena had no idea of the dramatic changes which had taken place in Portugal since the Talavera campaign — changes which had effectively increased the striking power of the British by nearly a hundred per cent.

'I have fished in many troubled waters, but Spanish troubled waters I will never fish in again.' So said Sir Arthur Wellesley after the heartbreaking experience of trying to work with the Spaniards in the Talavera campaign, which had nevertheless gained him the title of Viscount Wellington. Despite the 'croakers', the professional grumblers and pessimists against whom Wellington fought a ceaseless war of his own, he was determined to play the game out; and he was going to do it in Portugal, not Spain, letting the French come to him where he could fight them on ground of his choosing.

Wellington's forces were much stronger than they had been in 1809. In addition to his basic force of 33,000 British and German troops, Wellington could now call upon 20,000 regulars of the Portuguese Army, well armed and equipped, whose training at the hands of Beresford and his small team had worked wonders. This gave Wellington a mobile army of 53,000; and he could now leave several vital but troop-consuming garrison duties to units of the Portuguese militia, which was some 30,000 strong.

Yet to outsiders there seemed no reason why the new French concentrations should not act together and use their over-powering strength to roll right over the British and Portuguese. What would happen if Soult and Massena should join forces? A single French corps striking westwards towards Lisbon while Massena came down from the north could spell disaster. But Wellington knew better; and in a letter to his brother on 10 June he put his finger squarely on the weaknesses of the French — weaknesses which spelt nothing but opportunities for him. *'This is not the way in which they have conquered Europe. There is something discordant in all the French arrangements for Spain. Joseph divides his Kingdom into* prefétures, *while Napoleon parcels it out into governments; Joseph makes a great military expedition into the south of Spain and undertakes the siege of Cadiz, while Napoleon places all the troops and half the kingdom under the command of Massena and calls it the Army of Portugal . . .'* [Author's italics]

It was a perfect diagnosis, and a far more brilliant analysis of 'the other side of the hill' than Napoleon and his Marshals ever made of him.

There was not only something discordant in all the French arrangements for Spain: there was downright depression, rivalry, and hostility among the commanders of the Army of Portugal. It was largely Massena's fault. He had a reputation second to none as a military commander, which was why Napoleon had given him the job. But a commander's first task on taking up a totally new command must be to inspire confidence in every man who will be working with him; and when Massena arrived in Spain and told his staff that he was getting old, he was tired, he was ill, that he was obeying the Emperor's order virtually under protest, and that 'no man has two lives to live on this earth — the soldier least of all,' it caused profound depression among all and sundry. 'God! How he has changed,' noted General Foy, who had fought under Massena ten years before at Zürich. 'This is not the old Massena, the man with the flashing eyes, the expressive face, the alert figure . . . he is only 52, but he looks as if he were 60.'

There was another problem, caused directly by the Prince of Essling's sex life. Massena had always been a great success with women — but it was going too far when he took his latest girl friend on campaign with him dressed in the uniform of a hussar, and treated her like an *aide-de-camp*. She was in fact the sister of one of Massena's full-time ADCs – and the wife of an officer, Leberton. This minor scandal blew up into a full-scale social uproar because Junot had brought his wife, the Duchesse d'Abrantès, to GHQ at Valladolid, and Massena was tactless enough to present his Madame Leberton to her. The Duchesse responded by turning her back and executing a classic First Empire Parisian cut, refusing to sit at the same table. At a later meeting Ney followed this lead. He did not refuse to sit at the same table as Massena's lady; he merely refused to say a word to her. It should be remembered that this was not solely on moral grounds. Ney was not merely a happily-married man in private life: as the next senior Marshal he had been hoping for the command himself, and in fact he and Massena clashed from the start.

The first major row between Ney and Massena broke out over the problem posed by the twin northern padlocks to Portugal: the fortresses of Ciudad Rodrigo and Almeida. Ney wanted to mask them with a division and launch a full-dress attack into Portugal. Massena, however, was perfectly happy to follow Napoleon's orders and take his time, and he ordered Ney to take Rodrigo first. The result was a formal siege which lasted twenty-four days, with the Spanish General Andrés Herrasti and his garrison of 5,000 holding out nobly until 9 July.

Ney directed the siege of Rodrigo from Salamanca, leaving his trusted sapper commander, Major Conche, to get on with the job. But the irascible Marshal was infuriated when one of Junot's staff officers, Lieutenant-Colonel Valazé, turned up at his HQ with a letter from Massena stating that Valazé was to take over the siege. Ney boiled over. He sent Valazé back to Valladolid with a flea in his ear and the sneering message: 'I don't want the Duc d'Abrantès to bother me with his protégés. If they are so good, let him keep them for himself.' Massena, equally furious, sent Valazé straight back to Ney, whose reply was to sit down and write a red-hot letter to his commander-in-chief – a letter which stands in a class of its own as a piece of unbearable insolence:

'*Monsier le Maréchal*,' Ney began, 'I am a Duke and a Marshal of the Empire like you; as for the title of Prince of Essling, it is of no importance outside the Tuileries. You tell me that you are commander-in-chief of the Army of Portugal. I know it only too well. So when you tell Michel Ney to lead his troops against the enemy you will see how he will obey you . . . I esteem you, and you know it. You esteem me, and I know it. But why the devil sow discord between us over a mere whim? After all, how on earth do you know whether your little man can throw a bomb better than my old veteran, who is, I assure you, a reliable fellow. They say your man dances prettily; all the better for him; but this does not mean that he can make those mad Spaniards dance, and that is what we want.'

When Valazé arrived back yet again with this astonishing letter, Massena broke out in Junot's presence with: 'So I am only a fake commander-in-chief! I mean that this young man shall conduct the siege, and by the devil in hell Monsieur Ney shall bow the knee before my will, or my name is not Massena!' He gave Ney the straight alternative between doing what he was told or resigning his command. Grudgingly, Ney backed down and Valazé duly took over the siege operations around Rodrigo. (Not that this made much difference; most of the work had already been done.) It had been a rousing clash of wills over an extremely trivial subject; but this is certainly one of the most dramatic altercations in the story of the Peninsular Marshals.

The next objective was Rodrigo's twin across the Portuguese frontier: Almeida. The British troops deployed as a frontier defence force were Craufurd's Light Division; and a combination of Ney's pugnacity and Craufurd's reluctance to retreat brought them to the brink of being cut off and destroyed. As it was, Craufurd's men just managed to get across the Coa river in time. Ney kept up the pressure with repeated attacks until Craufurd fell back another ten miles. By the end of July Almeida was at the mercy of the French.

Unlike Rodrigo, Almeida had an important role in Wellington's plans. He had put 4,500 Portuguese troops into the place – regulars and militiamen – under a British general, Brigadier Cox. Almeida itself was an extremely solid fortress, sited on a granite plateau which made the digging of siege trenches an unenviable task; it was well stocked with provisions, and Wellington hoped that it could be held at least until the bad weather of autumn set in to embarrass the French further.

As at Rodrigo, the task of taking the fortress fell to Ney. He drew his siege lines round Almeida on 15 August, but it took another ten days to bring up the siege guns and get them properly sited. (This shows the chronic shortage of transport – draught animals and vehicles – which both sides had to cope with in the Peninsular theatre.) The battle for Almeida began at dawn on 26 August with a massive bombardment from Ney's siege guns – and it lasted effectively a mere fourteen hours. Really bad safety precautions caused a powder barrel to explode at the open door of the main magazine, and 70 tons of gunpowder went up with a terrifying explosion – 'like a volcano erupting,' recalled one of Ney's awed staff officers in the French lines. Almeida was defenceless, and Cox was forced to surrender on the night of the 27th. The road to central Portugal – and Lisbon – was open to Massena's army. By 15 September Reynier's II Corps had joined up with the corps of Junot, Ney, and General Montbrun's Reserve Cavalry; and the Army of Portugal, 65,000 strong and fully concentrated at last, was ready for the march on Lisbon.

But which road would it take? Incredibly – after three years of planning for the subjugation of the country – the French had no detailed maps of Portugal at all. And instead of taking the best roads to Coimbra known to the French, Massena decided on a circuitous route through Viseu – 'one of the worst roads in Portugal,' as Wellington noted with mingled astonishment and satisfaction.

Viseu was reached on the 19th, but instead of pressing on towards Coimbra Massena stayed put for a full six days. We have two reasons for this otherwise puzzling halt, both of them more than likely. The first is the official one sent in despatches to Napoleon: the delay was necessary to bring up the guns and baggage train. Considering the terrible road Massena had selected, this was almost certainly true. The second reason, however, is put forward by one of Massena's own ADCs, Baron Marcellin de Marbot, the source of many anecdotes about the Marshal, most of them malicious, all of them convincing. Marbot blames the six-day wait at Viseu on Massena's concern with finding suitable lodgings for 'Madame X' – Henriette Leberton, who had been brought along by the Marshal for the advance on Lisbon.

Whatever the reason, the six-day respite offered by the French halt at Viseu was just what Wellington needed. He had certainly been puzzled by Massena's opening moves, but he had never underestimated his opponent, rebuking a group of wise-cracking officers with a cutting 'Gentlemen, we are in the presence of one of the first soldiers of Europe.' Wellington had been worried by the weight of Ney's attacks on the Coa and severely disappointed by the rapid surrender of Almeida. But Massena's delay at Viseu enabled Wellington to fall back to the superb defensive position which he had marked down as ideal for blocking the Coimbra road: the hog's back ridge of the Serra do Bussaco, where he intended to stand and fight.

As Wellington's Anglo-Portuguese army fell back on Bussaco and the French pursued, the first of Wellington's 'secret weapons' for the defence of Portugal came into play. This consisted of the use of the *Ordenança* – the Portuguese home guard call-up mechanism dating back to the Middle Ages – and 'scorched earth' policy. Wellington had got the Portuguese Regency Government to approve the total evacuation of the population, livestock, all food and forage stocks, and transport from the path of the French advance. What the people could not remove they were to destroy. Thus instead of supplying themselves off the fruits of the Portuguese harvest – the main reason for the leisurely, deliberate pace of the invasion – the French advanced, as Massena sourly commented, into a desert. And as they advanced the Portuguese militiamen and *Ordenança* closed in behind them, cutting off all communications with Spain.

By nightfall on the 15th the French outposts had made contact with Wellington's army, which was now in position along the Bussaco ridge. Rather like Rommel with his Italo-German *Panzerarmee* at Alamein, the British general had 'corseted' his Portuguese units with British troops. Wellington's total strength was 50,000 men. He was not trying to hold the entire ridge: just the sectors which the French could not afford *not* to attack if they wanted to drive him out of the position.

The handling of this problem by Reynier, Ney, and Junot under the lack-lustre chairmanship of Massena was one big disaster from start to finish. Reynier and Ney closed up to the Bussaco position without making the slightest attempt to seek a way round the flanks. They both interpreted the troops they could see up on the ridge as a rearguard, and pressed for an immediate attack. This was turned down by Massena, and quite rightly – but not because he interpreted matters in a different light from what he could see through his telescope. He and 'Madame X' were eight miles to the rear; and once again he wasted precious time before drifting up to the front late in the afternoon of the 26th and calling a conference of his commanders.

It is worth pointing out that on the eve of this battle Massena was the first French commander-in-chief to have the opportunity of seeking the advice of generals who had had the bitter experience of attacking British troops in position. These were Junot (at Vimiero, in 1808) and Reynier (at Alexandria during the Egyptian expedition, and at Maida in 1806). Even Ney had had a brush with Moore's rearguard during the retreat to Corunna. Ney has often been dismissed as an unthinking advocate of the heads-down attack. But at this conference he argued against an attack on the ridge on the 17th. He wanted Massena to accept the fact that a surprise attack was now out of the question, pull back, and make sure of Oporto before resuming the advance on Coimbra and Lisbon. Junot backed him up, and so did the artillery commander, General Eblé, who made the point that the Bussaco ridge was too high to be swept by the French guns. Reynier, however, pressed for a strong frontal assault on the British positions for the following day. With this sharply-differing advice at his disposal, it was up to Massena to decide.

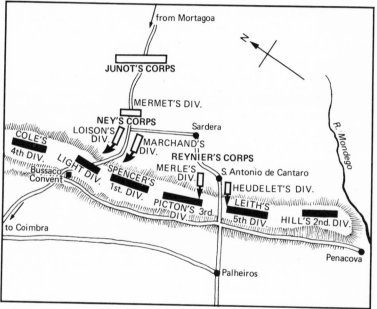

The battle of Bussaco, 27 September 1810

He did not take long to administer another snub to Ney and order a frontal assault. Reynier would attack the British right; Ney would tackle the strongest part of the British line, the left flank blocking the Coimbra road. Junot and the VIII Corps would he held in reserve, together with Montbrun's cavalry. It was an astonishing decision. The strength of Wellington's position was obvious to everyone. The French would be attacking an enemy who would be fully prepared. Nothing at all had been done to out-manoeuvre the British,

although both geography and Massena's unchallenged superiority of cavalry would have made this perfectly possible.
And the Prince of Essling, having put his signature to this
thoroughly unimaginative sheaf of orders, rode back the eight
miles to his Headquarters and 'Madame X' for the night. The
attack was scheduled for dawn on he morrow.

At dawn on the 17th Reynier's columns rolled forward to
the attack. They had numbers on their side, certainly, but the
sweating French troops took over an hour to struggle up to
the crest of the ridge. When they reached the top they
immediately came under scourging fire and spirited bayonet
attacks, although the weight of numbers was on their side.
Reynier's men, however, were not attacking the British right
flank but the centre; and a decisive flank attack now struck
them, launched by General Leith's division. After repeated
attempts to crown the ridge Reynier's corps recoiled with the
extremely heavy casualty-list of nearly 3,200.

Ney carried out his part to the letter, waiting until he saw
that Reynier's leading troops had got to the top of the ridge
before sending VI Corps forward against Bussaco itself. But
this was the key sector of the Anglo-Portuguese line, with
carefully-sited guns and troops waiting to catch the advancing
French in enfilade. While Reynier's attack was being hurled
back in its track, Ney's leading formations were coming under
a devastating fire. Both divisions of VI Corps were thrown
back, and Ney refused to inflict more punishment on them
by ordering further attacks.

Massena's clumsy, head-on butt at Wellington's line had
been decisively repelled, and he knew it. He therefore made
the decision not to commit Junot's VIII Corps but – at last
– to manoeuvre the British out of their position. As soon as
Montbrun's cavalry patrols went out a way round was
discovered: a rough track across the pass at Boialvo, leading
round the Anglo-Portuguese position towards Coimbra. Massena immediately ordered the Army of Portugal to take this
track – as Wellington knew it must. Coolly and efficiently,
the Bussaco position was evacuated. The retreat on Coimbra

and Lisbon had begun.

The battle of Bussaco had cost the Army of Portugal 4,486 casualties. They were totally unnecessary: the whole affair had been one of the most depressing performances which Massena had ever put up. On the Allied side, the Portuguese troops had responded magnificently to their baptism of fire and had been instrumental in repelling Ney's attacks. Anglo-Portuguese casualties were only 1,252, and these were exactly — and significantly — divided between the British troops and the Portuguese. Thus Bussaco was a fine tribute not only to Wellington's brilliance in fighting defensive battles, but also to Beresford's invaluable work in training up the Portuguese Army until its troops were fit to take on the veterans of the *Grande Armée*.

Coimbra fell to the French on 1 October. Massena wanted the city as a base in central Portugal, but this did not save the place from being thoroughly sacked first. Junot's corps was foremost in the plundering, in which many important supplies were senselessly destroyed. The capture of Coimbra led to another collision between Massena and Ney. Some of the most valuable items of loot which fell to the Army of Portugal were the telescopes from the observatory, and Massena sent a particularly fine specimen to Ney. The latter, however, sent the telescope back to Massena with the information that Marshal Ney was not a receiver of stolen goods.

It took time for the French to recover themselves after the sack of Coimbra, and the march on Lisbon was not resumed until 5 October. Massena decided that he could not afford to leave a full-size garrison in Coimbra, and left his 3,500 sick and wounded there. Within twenty-four hours of the French rearguard leaving the city, Coimbra was retaken by the Portuguese militia brigade led by Colonel Nicholas Trant. (He was one of those enigmatic figures who crop up time and again in military history — a total individualist, a 'private army' leader and an extremely tough and nasty fighter.) Trant saw to it that all the French wounded were carted off to Oporto, and then settled down to use Coimbra as a base for strangling Massena's communications with Spain. The recapture of Coimbra not only shot a bolt behind the backs of the French as they forged on towards Lisbon: it was a stunning blow to their morale. They did not know that now Almeida, too, had been sealed off by the *Ordenança* and militiamen of the Douro.

The tide turned between 11 October and 14 October.

From the 11th, reports came down the line from Montbrun's cavalry outposts that a range of hills lay between the Army of Portugal and Lisbon, and that there was no way through. The British had flooded streams, built entanglements across valleys, blasted artificial scarps and built formidable chains of forts across the stubby peninsula between the Tagus and the sea. A full-scale break-through would have to be made, and the prospects did not look good. On the 14th Massena came up to see for himself and found that the reports were true. The road to Lisbon was blocked by the Lines of Torres Vedras.

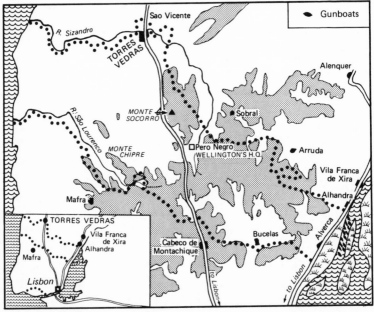

The Lines of Torres Vedras

The existence of the Lines was almost as much of a surprise to Wellington's own army as it was to the French. Wellington had ordered their preparation after Talavera, and the work had gone forward in conditions of strict secrecy. The idea was to create a defensible barrier across the Lisbon peninsula which could be held to cover an embarkation of the British Army, should this finally prove necessary. The Lines themselves were the supreme achievement of Wellington's Chief Engineer, Lieutenant-Colonel Richard Fletcher. He made use of the contours of the hills and valleys to the north of Lisbon to create two belts of mutually-supporting strongpoints, all of them well armed with artillery, none of which could be surprised or stormed without inflicting heavy losses on the attacker. Behind the two main lines at Torres Vedras lay a third and final defensive perimeter around the embarkation beach at São Julião da Barra. But this did not mean that Wellington's troops marched into the Lines and went into garrison service. The forts were manned by the Portuguese militiamen, leaving the regular forces free to manoeuvre, to move instantly to any sector of the Lines where danger threatened. Not that this seemed likely. It was only too clear to Massena that the Lines posed an impossible problem. Even Ney flatly refused to attack them. Any retreat from the Lines would be tantamount to an admission of failure. The sole alternative was to stay in position in front of the Lines and pray that the British would venture out.

Massena's decision to hang on created one of the most extraordinary situations in military history. On the face of it the British were holding behind their fortifications and the French were besieging them. But once again the basic facts of geography transformed the military scene. With their backs to the sea it was the British who were receiving uninterrupted supplies and reinforcements. With their communications to Spain severed and the surrounding country swept bare of anything like the amount of food and forage needed to sustain their army, it was the French who now had to endure all the privations of a siege.

Massena knew that the situation could yet be retrieved if Soult's Army of the South would lend a hand. But such a basic strategic decision could only be made by Napoleon, as there was no supreme commander in Spain with the authority to co-ordinate the movements of the armies. Massena therefore sent off General Foy with a personal message to the Emperor, escorted by an infantry battalion and a full squadron of cavalry to make sure he got through. But it took Foy from 29 October to 21 November to get from the Tagus estuary to Paris, and he did not get back to Massena's HQ until 5 February.

One month of skirmishes in front of the Line convinced Massena that as it was to be a waiting game his army must have a secure base of its own. On 14 November he began to withdraw the Army of Portugal up the Tagus towards Santarem, where he prepared to dig in with his left flank anchored on the river. Plans were drawn up to build a pontoon bridge which would enable the army to cross into the province of Alemtajo. The move had been neatly completed by 21 November. 'The French have a position at Santarem,' wrote Wellington, 'compared with which Bussaco is nothing.' Tactically, it was stalemate – but the withdrawal had made no improvement whatsoever to Massena's chronic supply problem.

With this stalemate on the lower Tagus the only hope for a French success lay in a relief operation by the Army of the South. The main reason why this did not come off was an extremely vague series of non-orders from Napoleon. He did little more than suggest that Mortier's V Corps should move to the mouth of the Tagus – and Soult rejected the idea out of hand. Soult's counter-proposal was that the Army of the South should concentrate on taking Badajoz, which he duly besieged on 26 January, 1811.

Throughout the terrible winter of 1810-11 one thing alone kept the Army of Portugal in position: the will of Massena, the man who had held on in equally impossible situations at Zürich and Genoa. By January 1811 his original strength of

65,000 had withered to a mere 47,000 through sickness, starvation, and desertion. Still hoping for a relief column, he ordered the bridge to be moved twenty-five miles upstream to Punhete on the Zezere, a fast-running tributary of the Tagus, which extended the available foraging area and eked out the life-span of the Army of Portugal a little longer. But by the time General Foy returned from his mission to Napoleon in Paris, on 5 February, even Massena had had to accept the in-evitable. The Army of Portugal could hold on no longer. He had to choose between falling back to the Mondego valley and breaking out to the south-east to join Soult. The Em-peror's message brought him little cheer. Massena was re-buked for throwing away a fine chance at Bussaco and told that unspecified help was on its way from Soult — but he was given the option of a temporary shift to the Mondego if he should consider this really desirable.

On 1 March, 1811, Massena gave the order for a retreat to the Mondego. It was high time, for Wellington's army had been raised to a strength of 60,000 men and the latter was preparing to sally out of the Lines and fall on the enfeebled French in their position. Massena's decision to pull out was one of the most timely he ever made, for his troops were down to only fifty rounds of ammunition per man. The retreat began on the night of 5-6 March, and, like the with-drawal from the Lines to Santarem, it was carried out with stealth and skill.

But the full significance of the retreat could not be disguised. The third and greatest of the French attempts to conquer Portugal had failed disastrously. Now it remained to be seen whether Massena could hold on to central and northern Portugal — or, failing that, keep the advancing British out of Spain itself.

CHAPTER EIGHT

'IF BONEY HAD BEEN THERE...'

No general, stated the elder Moltke, can be assessed as a great commander who has not had to conduct a retreat. Moltke might have added that following up a retreating enemy is hardly less of a problem for any military commander, who had to advance further and further from his base while his opponent falls back on his own. Certainly this was the case in the Peninsula during the spring of 1811. Massena's retreat from Torres Vedras and Santarem only meant fresh head-aches for Wellington.

One of the biggest problems was Soult and his Army of the South. Wellington was not worried about any serious threat to Lisbon itself, for he did not believe that Soult would try to break through to the Tagus estuary. But there was no avoiding the fact that the vital fortress of Badajoz was in trouble. Mortier and his V Corps had drawn their ring round Badajoz on 26 January, and with Massena still holding on at Santarem Wellington could not spare a man to march to the aid of Badajoz. All he could do was position Marshal Beresford with 10,000 men south of the Tagus to block any serious thrust which Soult might dare to make past Badajoz. But it was equally clear that Soult had troubles of his own. He was pinned down by the need to maintain Victor's siege of Cadiz — and it was Cadiz which offered the best chances of striking back at Soult and the Army of the South.

When he made his decision to move against Badajoz, Soult was forced to draw heavily on the manpower of Victor's I

Corps, with the result that by mid-January 1811 Victor was maintaining the siege of Cadiz with some 19,000 French troops against 25,000 Spanish, Portuguese, and British. Major-General Thomas Graham, the British commander in Cadiz, did not miss this obvious chance. He submitted plans for an amphibious operation to break the siege of Cadiz, while at the same time Andalusia was to be raised against the French. This must force Soult to drop his plans for the capture of Badajoz. But at this point the French were helped, yet again, by the suicide tactics of the Spaniards in the field.

There were in fact two Spanish field armies in the frontier region dividing Estremadura from Portugal, and as far as Badajoz was concerned the most important was that commanded by General Mendizabal. This worthy, like most other Spanish generals apart from Castaños and de la Romana, was totally unaware of the paramount importance of keeping his army in being as a fighting force until adequate help could come to its aid. He started by throwing 4,000 men of his army down the drain by adding them to the garrison of Olivenza (a hopelessly run-down link in the chain of fortresses around Badajoz) which fell to Soult in less than a week. Mendizabal then went on to make a thorough job of destroying his own army by getting himself routed by Mortier on the Gebora river on 19 February. At that moment nothing could have suited the French better. Their investment of Badajoz was now secure.

Two days later, however, the Allied break-out force embarked at Cadiz to tackle Victor. It was basically a bi-national affair: 9,500 Spaniards and 4,900 British, with 300 Portuguese thrown in. But it was crippled by the Spanish commander, General Manuel La Pena, and the absence of local co-operation in the country south of Cadiz. The Allies landed at Algeciras on 23 February amid total apathy, and Graham was forced to use blackmail to get La Pena on the move towards the French lines around Cadiz. (This was quite simple: he threatened to march the British contingent the other way, add to it the Gibraltar garrison, and leave La Pena on his own.) By 3 March La Pena and Graham were closing up to the Santi Petri river and the next phase should have been a concerted break-out across the Santi Petri by General Zayas and the Çadiz garrison. Zayas, however, ruined everything by striking too soon, enabling Victor to hurl him back into Cadiz and turn against the Allied relief force with his full strength.

The clash came on 5 March, and it was a head-on, bloody business. The battlefield was the Chiclana plain and its dominating feature: the Torre Barossa ridge. Both sides recognized the importance of the latter, but thanks to La Pena's inertia the French were allowed to gain possession first. Graham was forced to redress the balance on his own with frontal attacks against greatly superior numbers, and to a large extent it was bayonet against bullet and grape. The battle of Barossa lasted just under two hours. It saw the French pushed bodily off the ridge at bayonet-point and it cost them six guns, a regimental eagle, one divisional commander — General Ruffin, who was wounded and captured by the British — and 2,000 dead. The British losses were only slightly less — but for Victor, Barossa was a far more serious defeat than Talavera had been in 1809. If La Pena and his 9,500 had deigned to co-operate and the Allies had followed up the success won by Graham's men, Victor would have had to abandon the siege of Cadiz. What actually happened was that Graham and La Pena withdrew into Cadiz amid mutual recriminations, and Victor, thoroughly chastened, resumed the siege.

The news of the Allied move against Victor reached Soult at Badajoz before the grim details of the battle of Barossa, but it was bad enough. Soult knew that his Army of the South simply did not have the strength to garrison the key cities of Andalusia, maintain a full-dress siege at Badajoz, and wage a separate field campaign around Cadiz. On 9 March he did the only thing he could do: he called on the Spanish governor of Badajoz to surrender the place. It was pure bluff: Soult could not have stayed outside Badajoz if the demand had been rejected. But within twenty-four hours the Spanish garrison marched out of Badajoz in surrender. It was a timely stroke of luck for Soult, who left a garrison in Badajoz and hastened back to Seville.

Even without the immobilization of Soult, Massena's Army of Portugal would have been unable to stay where it was. By 5 March, the day of Barossa, it had scoured the surrounding country into a desert in its desperate search for provisions and could remain no longer. Victor's defeat at Barossa coincided exactly with the start of Massena's retreat to the Mondego. And between Victor and Massena was the main body of Soult's army, for the moment unable to give anything like substantial help to either of them.

When he had confronted Wellington across the Lines of Torres Vedras Massena, as we have seen, had been in the position of a besieger besieged. And when he decided to retreat he found himself in an even more uncomfortable situation. First, he would have to fight his way out. And second, he had been given reinforcements which he could not use.

On 30 August of the previous year Napoleon had made another of his misinformed and confusing interventions in the Peninsular War by setting up a new unit in Spain: IX Corps, commanded by General Count Drouet d'Erlon. It was 12,000 strong, based on Valladolid, and intended to safeguard Massena's communications with Spain. D'Erlon, however, was not under Massena's orders. He had an independent brief, summed up by Napoleon's bland statement: 'I do not intend IX Corps to get involved in Portugal unless the British are still holding out.' There was no way in which Napoleon could know that when he dictated that particular gem on 3 November it was no longer a question of the British managing to hold out in Portugal, but the French. But it was clear that one part of d'Erlon's original brief would have to be modified. He could not, as originally envisaged, reopen Massena's lifeline without entering Portugal, and Napoleon granted the use of one of IX Corps' divisions for the job.

Even this was insufficient. By 26 December d'Erlon's whole corps was in Portugal and contact with Massena had been duly re-established. Massena was naturally infuriated that all he was going to get was one division, and on loan at that; but d'Erlon did agree to stay on at Leiria for the time being. And so it was that when Massena issued his orders for the retreat of the Army of Portugal in early March, d'Erlon's corps went along with it in what might best be described as a freelance capacity, with one of its divisions (Conroux's) operating with Ney's VI Corps.

True to his orders 'not to get engaged in Portugal', d'Erlon had not done what would have been most useful to Massena: chase Trant's ruffian force out of Coimbra and clear what had been Massena's original line of advance into the country. D'Erlon had got through to the Army of Portugal along the Celorico-Ponte da Mucela-Miranda do Corvo road. Massena hoped to retreat with his main body through Pombal and Redinha, sending Montbrun's cavalry on ahead to clear Coimbra, while Ney's reinforced VI Corps acted as rearguard.

Ney's first successful rearguard action against Wellington's pursuing army was fought at Pombal on 10 March; but no sooner was it over than d'Erlon announced that he wanted Conroux's division back according to the basic premise of his orders from the Emperor. Massena begged him to reconsider, but d'Erlon was adamant and Ney was forced to fall back from Pombal. He had to fight again on the 12th, at Redinha — and in the meantime Montbrun and the cavalry had decided that it would be impossible to recapture Coimbra. Massena was therefore compelled to change his plan and take the Ponte da Mucela road.

13 March was one of the most eventful days of the whole eventful retreat. Ney made an unexpectedly speedy withdrawal from Condeixa, a move which exposed Massena's own HQ at Fonte Coberta to near capture by a sudden cavalry raid. The Prince of Essling, his staff, and the ever-present 'Madame X' had to make a lightning getaway at full gallop, and the result was another blazing row between

Ney and his commander-in-chief. Massena was convinced that Ney had endangered him deliberately; Ney, it is said, reacted to a rumour that Massena had been captured with an exultant 'Taken, is he? So much the better! The army is saved!' This is one of the many anecdotes which is usually labelled 'probably apocryphal'. Like most of the ones about the Marshals, however, it rings true. It is especially typical of the mood of contemptuous defiance which was gradually overtaking the hot-headed commander of VI Corps.

Ney, of course, as rearguard commander, was having to do all the fighting; and it is significant that his worst outbursts were made when this was the case. On 14-15 March there were stiff rearguard actions at Casal Novo, Miranda do Corvo, and Foz de Arouce – but after the 15th there was a lull. Wellington was forced to halt until his supply-train could be pushed forward sufficiently for the pursuit to be continued. By 22 March the Army of Portugal was in the Celorico-Gordo area, regrouping after a sixteen-day retreat. Harking back to Moltke's comment about generalship and coping with retreats, one must conclude that Massena had extricated himself extremely well from his previously impossible situation. He was now only thirty-five miles from the frontier and his main depots in Spain were within easy reach.

But on that day, 22 March, he astonished and appalled his corps commanders by announcing that the retreat on Almeida and Ciudad Rodrigo would not continue. Instead the Army of Portugal would now regain the strategic initiative by striking south through Coria, Plasencia, and Alcantara into Estremadura. Napoleon himself could not have conceived of a better plan for turning the tables; but the plain truth that such a move was quite beyond the exhausted and emaciated troops who had survived the winter in the Portuguese desert, followed immediately by the rigours of the retreat.

Ney refused point-blank. He came up with a number of excellent reasons for falling back on Almeida. When these were turned down he stated – verbally and in writing – that

VI Corps, at any rate, would not be accompanying the Army of Portugal. It was the supreme crisis in the long and stormy relationship between Ney and Massena, and the latter could take no more. Ney was formally relieved of the command of VI Corps and General Loison was appointed provisional commander – but it was a hollow triumph. Massena had 'pulled his rank' over a junior Marshal attached to his command. But he could not prevent d'Erlon from citing his own direct orders from the Emperor and setting off for Ciudad Rodrigo.

Massena's dismissal of Ney was a significant event in itself. Ney had led the VI Corps from the day when it was training for the invasion on England in 1805. Together they had been instrumental in winning battle after battle which had set the seal on Napoleon's mastery of Europe. Some have argued that it would have been best if he had been killed at Friedland in 1807, where he had won one of his greatest triumphs.

For Ney, the invasion of Russia, his title 'Prince of the Moskowa' (as the French always called the battle of Borodino) and the terrible retreat from Moscow still lay ahead after the Peninsula. So did the exhausting efforts to ward off defeat in 1813-14, the social humiliations of court life under the restored Bourbons, and the agonizing decision to rejoin Napoleon in 1815 – the decision which brought him before a Royalist firing-squad after Waterloo. In the Peninsula, like most of the other Marshals, Ney's performance was mediocre to poor. He had made an honest effort to apply familiar principles of war to a theatre of war which rejected the lot. And his 'prima donna' outbursts of contempt and defiance were definitely provoked by the obviously futile and anarchic command structure which Napoleon had imposed on the French corps in the Peninsula.

Massena had got rid of Ney, but his troubles were not yet over. He would soon be obstructed by yet another of the Emperor's changes in the high command of Spain. Bessières, the idol of the Guard, was back, this time with the grandiloquent title of Commander-in-Chief, 'Army of the North'.

Bessières, it will be recalled, had commanded the Reserve Cavalry of the *Grande Armée* during Napoleon's descent on Madrid and pursuit of Moore. After Napoleon's return to Paris in January 1809, Bessières was named military commander of the northern provinces of Spain, a post which he held till March. Recalled to Germany for the campaign against Austria, he led the Reserve Cavalry at Aspern-Essling (after which Napoleon created him Duke of Istria) and at Wagram. In the latter battle Bessières was nearly killed when a bullet smashed into the pistol on his hip and hurled him senseless off his horse.

After the drama of the campaign on the Danube Bessières enjoyed one month of peace before being appointed to the command of the Army of the North in the Low Countries. Here his task was an easy one. In 1809 the British had landed on the island of Walcheren. Thanks to the 'after-you-no-after-you' relationship between the two new British commanders, Chatham and Strachan, the Walcheren expedition (almost exactly like the Helder expedition in 1799) never got further than its first base. Bernadotte, the first French commander in the area, had plenty of time to flood the land approaches to Antwerp; he then left the initiative to the British — and to the natural effects of malarial fever, typhus, and dysentery. The latter savaged the British force on Walcheren far more than any defeat in the field could have done, and the outcome was yet another ignominious re-embarkation. At this point (11 September) Bernadotte was replaced by Bessières, who had the idea of re-occupying Walcheren and the town of Flushing. After this easy clearing-up operation in the Scheldt estuary Bessières returned to Paris and the command of the Imperial Guard.

In March 1810 Bessières was given his last major job before being appointed to command the Army of the North in Spain. As Military Commander and Governor of Strasbourg he was responsible for seeing that the ceremonial welcome of Napoleon's new Empress, the Austrian Archduchess Marie-Louise, went off smoothly. This is a reminder that Bessières had always been one of the 'inner circle' Marshals. In his normal command with the Reserve Cavalry or the Imperial Guard he was always in close proximity to the Emperor, obviously; but Bessières, although as brave as the next man when under fire, was definitely more of a courtier than a soldier. His achievements in the field came nowhere when compared with those of Massena, Davout, Lannes, or Ney. Bessières was generally liked, but there was always a strong under-current of resentment against the favour which the Emperor showed him. And this resentment showed itself very clearly after the retreat of the Army of Portugal from Santarem to the Spanish frontier, when Massena and Bessières had to work together.

For a while, however, a direct confrontation with Bessières was postponed by Massena, having got rid of arch trouble-maker Ney, going ahead with his plan for a sweep to the south. D'Erlon's corps had already set off for Ciudad Rodrigo, and so it was with only the three original corps that the Army of Portugal moved off towards Belmonte and Sabugal on 24 March. The whole affair turned out a fiasco which only exhausted the Army of Portugal further. The terrain to be traversed was appalling, with passable roads and local supplies both virtually non-existent. The infantry became separated from the artillery and the three corps straggled some fifteen miles apart. In five days Massena's army had become a shambles and he was forced to give up. On the 29th he ordered a concentration along the upper Coa river.

But now Wellington was back in the game. Massena's fruitless route-march through the mountains had given the Anglo-Portuguese army time to come up, and Wellington was one jump ahead of Massena again. He planned to deal a heavy blow across the Coa at Reynier's corps, near Sabugal. This move caught Massena (ten miles away, with Junot's corps at

Alfaiates) completely by surprise. On 3 April Wellington's attack went in, and Reynier's corps had to fight for its life. It was only saved by bad reconnaissance on the British side, the results of which gave the French just enough time to get out. But the Army of Portugal was forced back from the Coa, and on the night of the 3rd Massena gave the order for a retreat into Spain. Wellington's follow-up was cunningly aimed, cutting off the French garrison in Almeida from the main body of the Army of Portugal. The latter fell back towards Salamanca, leaving only the Almeida garrison as an outpost of French power in Portugal. And on 10 April Wellington broadcast the fact by issuing a formal announcement to the Portuguese nation that the liberation of the country was complete.

It sounded good, but it was not quite true. Both sides knew very well that as long as the French held on in Almeida the Portuguese war must continue. Massena resolved to waste no time in launching an expedition to relieve Almeida – and he began a fusillade of dispatches to Bessières, requesting adequate reinforcements for the venture which he hoped to launch on 26 April.

Thanks to the drafts of recruits which he found waiting on the other side of the Portuguese frontier, Massena had adequate infantry replacements. His main worry concerned cavalry, artillery teams, and provisions – and Bessières was simply unable to produce them out of a hat. Bessières was no quartermaster. On the other hand, he had no scruples in writing catty notes to Berthier in Paris about the demoralized and generally run-down state of Massena's army. Massena was forced to postpone his relief operation twice – and even then he had to blackmail Bessières into concrete action by arguing that further inaction must only lead to the loss not only of Almeida but of Rodrigo as well. Massena managed to regain the use of IX Corps. Supplies reached Rodrigo, and a trickle of the full reinforcements demanded by Massena. And on 1 May Bessières himself turned up to accompany the expedition (prompting Massena's comment 'I could have done with more men and less Bessières.') On the afternoon of the 2nd, Massena set out for the relief of Almeida. His army had been raised to an overall strength of 42,000 infantry, 3,500 cavalry, and 42 guns.

Wellington had never had to fight a battle like this one. Both physical and political maps are needed to understand his position, for it was right on the frontier, extending north to south along a front of some eight miles, and – as usual with Wellington – capitalizing on every geographical advantage there was. For a start, he had to make sure that Brennier's forces in Almeida would not cause trouble. This was straightforward enough: an Anglo-Portuguese detachment (a Portuguese brigade and a British battalion) commanded by General Pack would suffice. The direct road route from Ciudad Rodrigo was safe enough, too, for it was guarded by the gorge of the Dos Casas river and an artificial strongpoint: Fort Concepcion. This sector was held by Erskine's 5th Division. Wellington's centre stretched over five miles along the high ground running down to the Dos Casas valley. It was a sound defensive position against which no serious attack was likely, and its defence was entrusted to Campbell's 6th Division. By far the most crucial sector of Wellington's position, however, was the right, for it was here that local geography turned against him. A second road leading to Almeida crosses the Dos Casas at the village of Fuentes de Oñoro, and to the south and south-west of the village the heights fell away. Thus a powerful French assault, shrewdly aimed, could very well turn Wellington's right, cutting him off from his line of retreat to the Coa, and even destroy his whole army.

For this reason the guts of Wellington's defence were at Fuentes de Oñoro. Here he had no less than four divisions: 1st Division (Spencer), 3rd Division (Picton), 7th Division (Houston) and the Light Division (whose commander, Craufurd, was hurrying back to the front after a recent trip to England). Out on the far right was Cotton's under-strength Cavalry Division. Spencer and Picton between them had put five battalions into Fuentes de Oñoro itself. In English Civil

War terms this latter force was a 'forlorne hope', an outlying force stationed in front of the main position, intended to absorb the first crunch of the enemy's attack. In addition Wellington could call on the doubtful support of the *guerrillero* leader Don Julian Sanchez, whose band had occupied Nave de Haver, another five miles south of Fuentes de Oñoro.

With Almeida at stake, Wellington could take no other measures to meet Massena's advance. It was a strong position with a weak spot but he knew what the weak spot was, and had deployed his forces to cover it if necessary. But after the help it had received from Bessières and the Army of the North, Massena's army had the advantage in numbers. Wellington had 35,150 infantry, 1,850 cavalry, and 48 guns, as opposed to Massena's 41,500 infantry, 3,500 cavalry, and 42 guns.

Massena's second move against Portugal was a far more precipitate affair than his invasion in the previous year. He wanted a sudden-death campaign, and this was to prove his undoing. He pushed Reynier's II Corps out on the right towards Fort Concepcion. Junot's VIII Corps faced the British centre, but it was a corps in name only, consisting of a single division (Solignac's). Junot's other division, Clausel's, had been cannibalized to bring the other divisions of the Army of Portugal up to strength. Loison and d'Erlon, with VI and IX Corps, covered by Montbrun's powerful cavalry division, formed Massena's left.

In his haste to come to grips with Wellington, Massena made a fatal mistake which cost him the chance of making any surprise move against Wellington's vulnerable right flank. As at Bussaco, the leading French columns were thrown into a heads-down charge at the nearest but strongest sector of the British position: Fuentes de Oñoro itself. (This mistake, incidentally, is one common to many great generals. Like most mistakes in war, if successful it is called daring or brilliant. Rommel, for instance, made several incredibly unimaginative attacks against formidable defensive positions

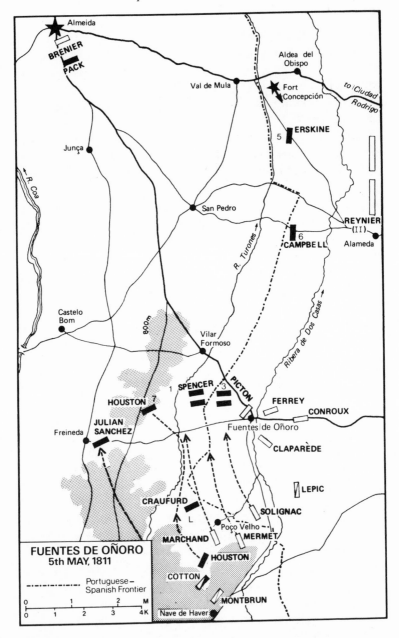

Almeida

BRENIER

PACK

Val de Mula

Aldea del Obispo

to Ciudad Rodrigo

Fort Concepción

Junça

5 **ERSKINE**

San Pedro

R. Coa

R. Turones

6 **CAMPBELL**

REYNIER (II)

Alameda

Castelo Bom

800m

Vilar Formoso

Ribera de Dos Casas

1 **SPENCER** 3 **PICTON**

FERREY

CONROUX

HOUSTON 7

JULIAN SANCHEZ

Freineda

Fuentes de Oñoro

CLAPARÈDE

LEPIC

CRAUFURD L

SOLIGNAC

Poço Velho

MARCHAND

MERMET

HOUSTON

COTTON

MONTBRUN

Nave de Haver

FUENTES DE OÑORO
5th MAY, 1811

—·—·— Portuguese–Spanish Frontier

0   1   2   M
0   1   2   3   4K

in North Africa, with heavy results for the Afrika Korps each time.) At Fuentes de Oñoro in 1811, Massena, for once, was at the front when the two armies came in sight of each other. After a lightning scan of the British line through his telescope he ordered the leading division of VI Corps to go in and take Fuentes de Oñoro. Spirited counter-attacks drove the French back, and the British were still in position when night fell on 3 May.

Massena's clumsy if powerful 'straight left' had failed to budge the British, and he resolved to try a 'left hook' around their position. This time he was more deliberate, taking the whole of the 4th to lay his plans. He split VI Corps, one of whose divisions was to 'pin' the British in Fuentes de Oñoro while the other two shifted further south to take the village of Poco Velho and flank Wellington's line. Junot's single division was pulled in from the French centre to back them up. This turning movement would be spearheaded by Montbrun's cavalry. A feint attack by Reynier's II Corps at the other end of the line would, Massena hoped, stretch the British reserves to breaking-point.

It was a sound piece of improvisation, but it assumed that the British would do nothing to prevent themselves from being flanked. Once again, Wellington stole a march on his opponent. While Massena was sending out the orders for his master-plan, scheduled for the 5th, Wellington, on the 4th, pushed Houston's 7th Division down to Poco Velho. Two cavalry squadrons went down to Nave de Haver to stiffen the *guerrilleros* there. Spencer and Picton, with Craufurd in reserve, swung south to link Houston with Fuentes de Oñoro. The British centre and left divisions remained in position.

Massena's attack went in at dawn on 5 May. First blood went to the French with the capture of Poco Velho by Solignac's division, but the greatly outnumbered British cavalry charged in to help the hard-pressed infantry; and a prolonged and messy cavalry battle ensued which slowed up Montbrun's wheeling move. All this gave Wellington time to swing back his right-wing divisions, still hinged on Fuentes de

Oñoro, through ninety degrees, which he had to do to save Houston's division from being cut off. This retirement to the north was superbly covered by the Light Division, which formed square and fell back slowly, repelling charge after charge by Montbrun's cavalry.

Despite the setbacks with which they had met, the fortune of the battle was swinging decisively in favour of the French. All Wellington could do now was hold on where he was: he had no mobile reserves with which to cover his line of retreat to the Coa, which was now wide open. Massena knew this very well and he prepared to send in a decisive stroke against the vulnerable British flank. He would attack again with General Lepic's magnificent brigade of Imperial Guards cavalry, which was part of the reinforcements placed at the disposal of the Army of Portugal by Bessières.

But at this moment, with decisive victory in his grasp, Massena was undone by the inbred rivalry which bedevilled the operations of the Peninsular Marshals. Lepic sent word that his men were under the orders of Bessières, not of Massena, and that he would not move. Massena, infuriated, was unable to get in touch with Bessières, and the supreme opportunity was lost.

Massena therefore changed his plan again, this time relying on a concerted assault by Loison, Junot, and d'Erlon — six divisions in all — to cave in Wellington's position. But this never came off. Instead there was ding-dong fighting for Fuentes de Oñoro, d'Erlon's main target. D'Erlon's grenadiers stormed through the village shortly after noon but were flung out again by a counter-attack spearheaded by the Connaught Rangers — one of the toughest and nastiest outfits in Wellington's army. The French offensive broke up into a series of half-hearted and piecemeal attacks which the British repelled with ease.

By mid-afternoon, however, Massena was ready for yet another throw, once more against the open right flank of the British. But this attack never got started. The reason was simple: lack of ammunition. Bessières' failure to arrange adequate teams of horses for the supply-train meant that the Army of Portugal was now down to four rounds per man with no more to come. Massena was forced to postpone his new attack until the morning of the 6th, planning to rush up fresh ammunition supplies during the night. But everything was ruined for Massena when Bessières decided that he could not have his precious waggons careering about in the night and refused to co-operate. The French and British bivouacked where they were during the night of 5-6 May — but when morning came Massena came to the bitter conclusion that a renewal of the attack with what ammunition he had was out of the question. As at Torres Vedras, however, he decided to stay where he was, and smuggled a message through the British line for the Almeida garrison to break out as best it could.

He still held out for victory — but now he faced open obstruction from his corps commanders, who argued that the acute supply problem must enforce a withdrawal. On the 7th Massena accepted the inevitable and ordered a retreat on the Agueda, returning himself to Ciudad Rodrigo. And it was there, on the 10th, that a letter reached him from Berthier in Paris. It spelt out his dismissal from the Army of Portugal in the harshest terms and nominated his replacement: Marmont, who had only taken command of the VI Corps three days before. Massena was to return to Paris at once.

Massena's dismissal was the brutal end to a heart-breaking chapter of accidents. When he took on the job of conquering Portugal the previous year he had instantly discovered the extent to which the problems of campaigning in the Peninsula had been underestimated by Napoleon. Massena had nevertheless put up an amazing performance. Wellington's 'scorched earth' policy had failed to destroy either Massena's army or his determination to keep fighting. Right down the line Massena had had to struggle with unruly or independent subordinates — Ney, d'Erlon, Lepic — and the refusal of his colleague Bessières to give sufficient aid. He had made tactical and strategic mistakes, and had paid heavily for them — but he had extended Wellington and his army as never before. Of Fuentes de Oñoro itself Wellington wrote soberly: 'If Boney had been there we would have been beaten'. If Massena's corps commanders and subordinate generals had done their job, Wellington would have been. Seldom has any general ever had to fight a battle under such frustrating conditions as Massena had to.

Massena' s disgrace was not followed — as it should have been — by the appointment of a single French commander-in-chief for the Peninsular theatre. Instead the Army of Portugal was given to the young, energetic, and supremely confident Auguste-Frédéric-Louis Viesse de Marmont, the 'whizz-kid' of the *Grande Armée*, who flung himself into his new task with gusto.

Marmont was one of the oldest colleagues of the Emperor and one of the youngest generals in the French Army. He was born at Chatillon-sur-Seine on 20 July, 1774, and became a *sous-lieutenant* in the Regular Army Chartres garrison in 1790. In March 1792 he went to the Artillery School at Chalons and emerged in September as a lieutenant in Napoleon's former unit — the La Fère Artillery Regiment. He was at the siege of Toulon in 1793, after which, now a captain, he served for a year with the Rhine Army before becoming one of Napoleon's ADCs in February 1796. Marmont served right through the Italian campaign and got his brigade. Italy was followed by Egypt, and the favourable impression he had made on Napoleon was clearly shown by Marmont's inclusion as one of the chosen few taken with Napoleon on his blockade-running dash back to France.

During the Marengo campaign of 1800 Marmont commanded the artillery of the Reserve Army. After Marengo, Napoleon put him in charge of the artillery of the Army of Italy, made him *général de division* in September 1800 and Inspector-General of Artillery two years later. It was in the latter post that Marmont's most impressive talent — his capacity for organization and reform — was first given full rein. Excellent though the artillery of the Gribeauval era had been the basics were improved upon by Marmont — fewer wheel sizes, standardization of tools and spare parts, selection of the 6-pounder as the basic calibre, and so on. Marmont was thus a key man in the forming of the *Grande Armée* and was effectively rewarded with the command of II Corps in 1805. He was the only man of the seven corps commanders of 1805 who had not been made a Marshal the year before.

Marmont's role in the Ulm/Austerlitz campaign was a secondary one after the initial triumph at Ulm. His II Corps had the job of holding down Carinthia in co-operation with Ney, while the main business was done by the main body of the *Grande Armée* in Bohemia. Napoleon then transferred Marmont to the I Corps of the Army of Italy; but it was on 7 July, 1806, that Marmont was given the command that might have been made for him. He was appointed Commander-in-Chief and Governor-General of Dalmatia, the new French province across the Adriatic which had been wrested from Austria after Austerlitz. It was a corps command; he was completely on his own; he had much fighting to do, and the whole province was his to administer and rule. He did magnificently.

First of all Marmont had to cope with the problem of a Russian amphibious force which was operating off the Dalmatian coast. He freed the key port of Ragusa from the blockade imposed by Admiral Sinyavin, and decisively beat the expedition force at Castelnuovo. Having seen off the Russians in short order, Marmont settled down to put his province in order. He built hundreds of miles of roads through the inhospitable terrain of Dalmatia, founded *lycées* at Ragusa, Zara, and Sebenico, and thoroughly earned his title of Duke of Ragusa, awarded on 15 April, 1808.

Marmont's Dalmatian idyll was brought abruptly to a close with Napoleon's Danube campaign of 1809. After the near disaster of Aspern-Essling, Napoleon scoured Europe for fresh troops and brought up Marmont's corps from Dalmatia to join the bulk of the *Grande Armée* at Lobau on the

Danube. At Wagram Marmont's corps formed Napoleon's main reserve, and Marmont, following up the victory, clinched the French triumph by winning a subsequent engagement at Znaim on 9 July. For his role in the Wagram campaign Marmont was finally given his Marshal's baton on 12 July, returning to Dalmatia in October. There he reduced the Croats to submission before being assigned to the Peninsula as Ney's replacement as commander of VI Corps on 9 April, 1811. It was an appointment that was rapidly superseded by Napoleon's outburst of dissatisfaction with Massena; and within three days of his arrival at the front the young Marshal-Duke of Ragusa had become Commander-in-Chief of the Army of Portugal – his first army command.

Marmont was given little time to settle into his new job. The failure of Massena's attempt to relieve Almeida coincided with a dramatic switch of the centre of gravity of the Peninsular War from the Almeida-Rodrigo area to that of Badajoz. While Massena and Wellington had been manoeuvring for the capture of Almeida a similar contest was afoot down in the south, where Soult and Beresford, duelling for Badajoz, had fought an extremely gory battle at Albuera which reflected little credit on either of them.

Soult's unexpected capture of Badajoz on 10 March, coinciding as it did with the northward retreat of Massena's army, had thrown Wellington's plans right out of gear. Now the southern gateway into Portugal was back in French hands, and Wellington was faced with the problem of recovering three of the vital frontier fortresses – Almeida, Ciudad Rodrigo, *and* Badajoz – before any future ventures in Spain could be countenanced. Wellington reacted with a momentous gamble. He divided his army, the larger portion, under his own command, to follow up Massena and a second, under Beresford, to re-take Badajoz before Soult stiffened its defences and made a major siege essential. This was why Wellington was in such a tense situation when he had to stand and fight at Fuentes de Oñoro, for 22,000 of his troops had been detached under Beresford to tackle Badajoz.

Beresford, being a superb administrator and trainer of troops but a relatively inexperienced field tactician, thoroughly mismanaged his assignment. He started well enough, bouncing Mortier out of Campo Mayor on 25 March and chasing the retreating French as far as Badajoz itself. But he allowed Mortier's siege train – which for a while was completely at his mercy – escape intact, and the one thing his force needed was heavy siege guns. So, for that matter, did Wellington's. The British force in the Peninsula (like the Afrika Korps in its early days in 1941) was regarded at home as purely defensive. Siege equipment and its provision were supposed to be the concern of the Spaniards and Portuguese. In Beresford's case this was particularly unfortunate because Soult had put a brilliant fortress commander into Badajoz: General Armand Philippon, who set about restoring the defences of the place with near diabolical energy. By the time Beresford's army lumbered up to Badajoz in the third week of April the French could regard any attacks on the fortress with equanimity.

Beresford finally invested Badajoz on 5 May, the second day of fighting at Fuentes de Oñoro, and work began on the siege trenches three days later. But little or no impression had been made by 12 May, when the news reached Beresford that Soult was on his way to Seville to raise the siege.

Unlike Wellington at Fuentes de Oñoro, Beresford had a decisive advantage in numbers when he prepared to give battle, on the ridge at Albuera which guarded the road from Seville to Badajoz. Beresford had some 15,000 Spanish troops at his disposal, some of whom actually turned up on time and did as they were told (thanks to Castaños, who had placed himself under Beresford's command). This gave Beresford some 37,000 men against Soult's 24,000. Beresford drew up his forces along the Albuera ridge in such a way that any orthodox French attack which came charging along the road, head-on against his position, could be contained with ease.

Unfortunately for Beresford, Soult refused to oblige. He

not only upset the form-book by delivering one of the most imaginative and skilful attacks ever seen in the whole Peninsular War: he did it while the later Spanish arrivals were still taking up their position on Beresford's right flank, and he almost won the battle before a shot was fired.

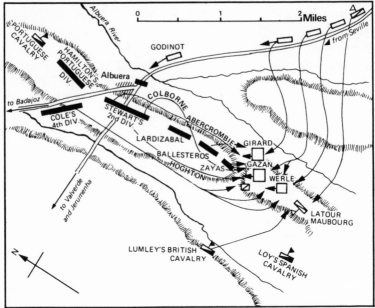

The battle of Albuera, 16 May 1811

What happened at Albuera is best explained by looking at the map above. While Godinot's division sparred away in front of Albuera itself, Soult laid five-sixths of his army right across the disorganized flank of the Allied Army, attacking the latter at right-angles. The attack went in at dawn on 16 May and threw the Spanish troops into hopeless confusion. To their credit the Spaniards fought doggedly as the advancing French divisions crumpled them up, but they were about as much practical use to the British as the Genoese cross-bowmen had been to the French knights at Crécy in 1346. They got in the way, forcing the British to shift for themselves. Incredibly, the British responded by attacking.

That complete disaster was averted by the British was the work of Major-General William Stewart, commanding the three brigades of the 2nd Division. An impetuous, battlefield hot-head, he threw his forces into piecemeal attacks that only succeeded by their sheer audacity – but at a fearful cost. To find anything like a comparison for the counter-attack of the 2nd Division at Albuera one must think of the Light Brigade at Balaclava, of Pickett's charge at Gettysburg, and then pile on the casualty figures as extras. Those British regiments engaged which had only 50 per cent losses could count themselves fortunate. For the British Army, Albuera was the battle where the 57th (Middlesex) Regiment earned its grisly soubriquet 'The Diehards' from the dying cry of its mortally wounded Colonel: 'Die hard, 57th, die hard!'

Die hard they did. There were some 10,500 British troops at Albuera, of whom 4,689 went down – but they took 7,000 Frenchmen with them. And the result of these appalling, reckless counter-attacks was exactly the same as that of Moore's counter-attack against Soult at Corunna in January 1809. Soult's plan was derailed, his easy victory vanished, he lost heart and drew off, this time puffing with resentment in terms which have created yet another legend for the worshippers of the 'Thin Red Line'. 'They could not be persuaded that they were beaten. They were completely beaten, the day was mine, and they did not know it and would not run.'

Here again was proof of the essential soundness of Wellington's diagnosis of Soult: he was first-class at getting his men onto the battlefield, but he did not seem to know what to do with them once he had got them there. Soult never forgot Albuera – but nor did Wellington. He dare not. Taking one look at the 'butcher's bill' sent him by Beresford after the battle, Wellington said: 'This won't do; it will drive the people in England mad. Write me down a victory.' And as such Albuera was duly announced in England. Napoleon and his Marshals were not the only ones capable of slick public relations work when unpalatable facts had to be related to the public.

Victory or not, the actual aftermath of Albuera worked, for a short while, in favour of the Allies. Wellington was freed to resume the siege of Badajoz. This meant starting from scratch, for the wily Philippon had seized the opportunity of sallying out from the fortress and making a thorough job of flattening the British siege works. But then the unbelievable happened. For the first time in the Peninsular War, two French Marshals actually co-operated with each other and forced Wellington completely off balance.

For this all credit was due to Marmont, who raced the full strength of the Army of Portugal down to join Soult. On 18 June Wellington was forced to raise the siege of Badajoz again. With 60,000 Frenchmen concentrated for the purpose there was nothing he could do with his own army of 50,000. Soult and Marmont reinforced the Badajoz garrison, topped up its ammunition and food supplies, and left d'Erlon's corps, 15,000 strong, to shield the fortress.

Thus by midsummer 1811 Wellington's army had been forced to fight two exhausting battles and was no closer to taking either Ciudad Rodrigo or Badajoz. Even the recovery of Almeida in the north had been a hollow victory, for Brennier's garrison had sneaked through the British lines on the night of 10-11 May and had reached Ciudad Rodrigo in safety. But there was another side to it. The French were no closer to conquering Portugal than they had been before the formation of Massena's Army of Portugal the year before. They were still besieging Cadiz, they still had to hold Rodrigo and Badajoz and they still had to hold down Spain. Even without the prodigious demands of manpower which Napoleon was about to make on the French armies in Spain, they lacked the resources to do all these jobs at once.

Midsummer 1811. Deadlock for the moment — with time working against the Peninsular Marshals. . .

CHAPTER NINE

CIUDAD RODRIGO:
THE TURNING-POINT

In the summer of 1811 the uneasy deadlock on the Spanish-Portuguese fronter was broken by a brisk little bubble of success for the French, 300 miles away in Catalonia. There General Suchet earned his Marshal's baton by capturing Tarragona on 28 June. It was practically the only solid achievement in the field which the French had scored during the frustrating first half of 1811 — but it had fatal results.

What happened, briefly, was this. Napoleon seized on Suchet's victory at Tarragona, ordering the reduction of the whole of eastern Spain. The Peninsular Marshals, in trying to carry out the Emperor's orders, were forced to expose Ciudad Rodrigo and Badajoz, and by mid-April 1812 both fortresses had been taken by Wellington. Such was the disastrous aftermath of the rise to fame of Suchet, of whom it was said that if there had been two of him, Napoleon would have conquered Spain.

Louis Gabriel Suchet, the only one of Napoleon's generals who earned his Marshal's baton in the Peninsula, was born at Lyons on 2 March, 1770. He first appeared on the military scene as a National Guards cavalryman in 1791, and rose rapidly through the *cursus honorum* of democratic elections which speeded the careers of so many officers in the Revolutionary Wars. On 20 September, 1793, he was elected lieutenant-colonel of the 4th *Bataillon de Volontaires de l'Ardèche*, which he led during the siege of Toulon. There he did well, capturing the British General O'Hara in a skirmish in December. Suchet was then transferred to the Army of Italy and soldiered through Napoleon's first campaign in Massena's division. Switzerland was his next service area, where he got his brigade on 23 March, 1798.

Suchet's next promotion could well have been fatal for him. He returned to the Army of Italy as provisional chief-of-staff and fought under General Joubert in the disastrous campaign against Suvorov which culminated in the rout of the French at Novi. Suvorov's landslide advance after his conquest of northern Italy was halted by Massena's successful defence of Zürich, by which time Suchet had enjoyed a brief spell as provisional commander of the Army of Italy after Joubert's death at Novi.

During the Marengo-Hohenlinden campaign of 1800 Suchet commanded the left wing of the Army of Italy, under Massena. Here he put up a most indifferent performance, failing to execute Massena's orders with sufficient speed and generally being instrumental in getting Massena blockaded in Genoa. Suchet himself fell back to the west amid a flurry of defeats at the hands of the Austrians, but he managed to hold the line of the Var river. During the mopping-up phase after Marengo Suchet acquitted himself sufficiently well to be appointed first Governor of Padua in January 1801 and then Inspector-General of Infantry in July of that year. He retained this post during the crucial training-period of the *Grand Armée* after the Peace of Amiens.

During the operational debut of the *Grande Armée*, the Ulm/Austerlitz campaign, Suchet served as a divisional commander, first with Soult's IV Corps and then with the V Corps of Lannes. He did well at Ulm, at Hollabrünn (the fight against Prince Bagration which is highlighted as 'Schön Grabern' in Tolstoy's *War and Peace*), and at Austerlitz. By the time of the battle of Jena, 14 October, 1806, Suchet had been advanced to the command of the 1st Division in Lannes' corps. It is interesting that his letting-down of Massena during the 1800 Genoa campaign does not seem to have affected his chances when Massena took over V Corps from Lannes in early 1807. By the summer of 1808 Suchet had risen to the same prominence as Dupont before the latter's dispatch to the Peninsula and the disaster of Bailen: a proven and able divisional commander, ripe for corps or even army command, a Count of the Empire, and evidently a man to watch. Unlike Dupont, however, Suchet's introduction to the Peninsular theatre was made as the commander of the 1st Division of Mortier's V Corps, during the *Grande Armée's* Spanish campaign of December 1808-January 1809.

After the initial battles and manoeuvring which carried Napoleon into Madrid, Suchet found himself with an independent role. Based on Calatayud, he had the job of keeping open the lines of communication between Madrid and the French forces besieging Saragossa. On 5 April, 1809, he was given III Corps and the effective governorship of Aragon. Like Marmont in Dalmatia, Suchet proved that he had a flair for civilian administration. All the records of the Peninsular War underline Suchet as being far ahead of his colleagues in the uncongenial and tricky job of reconciling the locals to the Bonapartist regime. He was a stickler for law and order, and above all for the discipline of his own troops. He made no heavy-handed financial exactions at the expense of the Spanish civilians, among whom he encouraged the development of trade, public works, wider employment, and the improvement of social services. But at the same time he had his share of fighting to do against the Aragonese insurgents led by Blake, whom he beat at Maria on 15 June and Belchite on 18 June.

Suchet also tried loyally to work in harmony with King Joseph – another fact which sets Suchet aside as a somewhat unusual character. In return, Joseph was grateful for Suchet's attitude. At the height of the great row between Soult and Ney in the north-east, Joseph wrote to Napoleon: 'Your Majesty will have seen, from the good services rendered by Generals Suchet and Sebastiani, how advantageous it would be if I had fewer Marshals here and more generals like those two, who take notice of my orders and who can pacify their provinces by their good conduct and by the discipline they impose on their troops.' But as we have seen this was no part of the Imperial Plan for Spain; and it goes without saying that this was yet another of Joseph's letters of complaint which Napoleon left unanswered.

Basically, however, Suchet was in precisely the same case as all the other French commanders in the Peninsula: he had far too much on his plate and was expected to be everywhere at once. In addition to his main brief, the policing of Aragon, he was called upon to co-operate with Augereau's forces in Catalonia (which were primarily concerned with keeping open the lines of communication with France across the eastern end of the Pyrenees), and operate against the insurgents in Valencia as well. Ever since the great Spanish insurrection of 1808 Valencia had been a thorn in the side of the French. Suchet tried to take the town in March 1810 but failed like Moncey before him. He then decided to concentrate on clearing the lower Ebro valley, and set about reducing all the focal points of resistance in the area. He took Lerida in May 1810 and Mequinenza in June, forcing back the hard-core rebels into the Tortosa-Tarragona region near the coast. Tortosa fell to him on 2 January, 1811, and in May he moved in for the kill by besieging Tarragona, which he took on 28 June. It was an extremely patient, efficient solution to a difficult local problem, and if Suchet had been given the chance to apply his methods to the newly-acquired area of control the north-eastern approaches to Madrid would certainly have been made completely secure for the French.

Napoleon, however, casting his dilatory eye on the progress of Suchet's operations, saw things differently. He had already transformed Suchet's corps into the 'Army of Aragon' and ordered that it be reinforced to 44,000 strong. He now decreed that it be used to eliminate Spanish resistance in Valencia — a venture which was as strategically dangerous as Soult's move south into Andalusia the year before. Where Napoleon really went wrong was in ordering the eager and dutiful Marmont to deplete the Army of Portugal to help Suchet. It was this that gave Wellington the chance to break the deadlock on the frontier.

Before telling the story of this ill-advised move against Valencia, mention must be made of the many incidental changes to the muster-roll of the Peninsular Marshals. First among these was Augereau. That aggressive, malingering, rough diamond of the Marshalate had finally been withdrawn from the command of the Army of Catalonia (much to his relief) in April 1810. He had been replaced by one of the most unusual and talented of the Marshals, a man who never really gets his fair share of the limelight compared to Massena, Ney, Soult, Lannes, and all the other stars: Marshal Macdonald, Duke of Taranto.

Etienne-Jacques-Joseph-Alexandre Macdonald was the son of a Scots Jacobite who settled in France after the 'Forty-Five. The future Marshal was born some twenty years after Culloden on 17 November, 1765, at Sedan. He joined the French Army in 1784, his regiment – appropriately enough – the *Légion Irlandaise*. After a year with the *Légion de Maillebois* in Dutch service he returned to France, joined Dillon's regiment of infantry, and had risen to *sous-lieutenant* by the time Louis XVI summon the States-General in 1789. Dillon's regiment (re-classified the 87th Infantry Regiment in 1791) first tasted action under Dumouriez's command in the following year. So it was that Macdonald's service in the Revolutionary Wars started well and truly in the thick of things: the great sweep of the French Revolutionary army across Belgium and Holland. Macdonald was in fact to spend the next five years in this northern sector, and his promotion was swift. He got his division in November 1794, exercised effective corps command in the Army of the North in 1796-97, and had a taste of army command for just over a week in January, 1798, in Holland.

Macdonald was then transferred to Italy, to serve with the French troops stitching together the patchwork of brand-new republics set up after Napoleon's Italian victories of 1796-97.

In this theatre – like Suchet – Macdonald had his army future thrown in jeopardy by the great Allied come-back led by Suvorov in 1799. Macdonald, commanding the Army of Naples, was driven out of southern. Italy. Wounded at Modena on 12 June, he was then thrashed in a two-day battle on the Trebbia river (17-19 June), and was permitted to return to France for convalescent leave in the following month.

Macdonald's next assignment, however, was even more dangerous. It put him in the wrong political camp. After the establishment of the Consulate with the coup d'état of 18th *Brumaire*, Macdonald was sent to the Rhine Army under Moreau, Napoleon's most prominent rival. In the Marengo-Hohenlinden campaign of 1800 Macdonald more than atoned for his defeats in the previous year. Stationed in the Grisons district of Switzerland to cover Moreau's right flank, Macdonald pulled off a feat which puts the physical difficulties of Napoleon's over-publicized crossing of the St Bernard Pass to shame. Unlike Napoleon, who crossed the Alps in the early summer, Macdonald flogged his army across the Splügen Pass in mid-winter, occupied Trent, and effectively disposed of the last remnants of Austrian resistance south of the Alps.

At this stage of his career Macdonald, like many other French generals (Ney for instance), was way outside the 'inner circle' of generals who backed Napoleon or who had always been closely associated with him. Unlike Ney, however, Macdonald was not deliberately drawn into the 'inner circle'. On the contrary: he was marked down as an adherent of Moreau, and was officially disgraced for defending Moreau when the latter was forced to flee the country in 1804. Macdonald spent the next five years in disgrace, what was more, until the suddenly-increasing demand for generals returned him to service with the Army of Italy (under Napoleon's stepson, the Viceroy Prince Eugène) in April 1809.

During the great panic after Aspern-Essling, when the *Grande Armée* was licking its wounds on the island of Lobau, four divisions of the Army of Italy were brought north to the Danube as reinforcements. Those four divisions were commanded by Macdonald, and it fell to their lot to strike the decisive blow at Wagram on 6 July. Four months of brilliant service cancelled five years of disgrace at a stroke. Macdonald's black mark as a Moreau-supporter was erased: he was now the man who had won the battle of Wagram, and for that he became Marshal Macdonald, Duke of Taranto, with all the trappings. For Macdonald, who always took things as they came (above all changes of political regime, to which he was particularly adaptable), his sudden elevation was doubtless a transformation devoutly to be wished. It certainly ranks as one of the oddest feats of alchemy in the story of the First Empire.

After Wagram, Macdonald joined the list of the Peninsular Marshals when he took over the Army of Catalonia from Augereau in April 1810. It was a thankless job, as Augereau had already found. The Catalonian patriots were extremely formidable enemies (one of their bands went so far as to cross the Pyrenees and rough up a French canton, sending Napoleon into one of his celebrated fits of rage when he heard about it). Macdonald's performance in the Peninsula was not impressive. He was there for sixteen months, during which he did nothing to pacify Catalonia. He dutifully marched hither and thither, launching punitive raids on *guerrillero* strongholds, and generally keeping the pot of mutual hatred on the boil. When Macdonald was recalled to France in September 1811, Catalonia was added to Suchet's charge, but it was too late. For one thing, Suchet's main concern now lay with Valencia; for another, even Suchet's flair for smoothing down belligerent Spanish patriots would never have had a chance against the Catalonians after the successes which they had achieved.

Bessières was recalled to France shortly after Macdonald, on 25 September. As far as the French cause in the Peninsula was concerned, it was not much of a loss. Bessières was woefully lacking in the manifold talents which that extremely unpleasant war theatre demanded. He had made a thorough mess of things as commander of the Army of the North and had let Massena down badly at Fuentes de Oñoro, the battle which could have reversed the French setback in Portugal suffered during the Torres Vedras campaign. But it is not fair to write him off as a complete ass. He saw the basic problems clearly enough; in a letter to Berthier on 6 June, 1811, he wrote: 'We are grasping at dreams. Cadiz and Badajoz swallow up everything we have – Cadiz because we cannot take it, Badajoz because it needs an army to support it.' Bessières was not far off the mark. Within six months of his recall the French forces covering the Portuguese frontier would be sufficiently weakened to put both Ciudad Rodrigo and Badajoz in mortal danger.

Mortier had gone home in May. He is one of the most *simpatico* of all the Marshals, a man who never came out with any melodramatic statements such as Ney's 'The wine is drawn and we must drink it,' or 'Tell His Majesty that here we don't share glory with anyone.' Mortier got on with his job without playing to the gallery. He never tried to stand on his own dignity but did what he was told – and in the Peninsula Napoleon could have done with a lot more like him. In private life Mortier stands out as the warm-hearted, boozy Marshal who liked to shoot out the candles with his pistol after dinner. The famous snide comment about Mortier was 'A big mortar (*mortier*) has a short range.' In the Peninsula he was most notable as Soult's understudy, playing no small part in making possible the French recapture of Badajoz in early 1811.

Junot, the might-have-been Marshal, left the Peninsula for the last time a month after Mortier: June 1811. His defeat at Vimiero in 1808, and its humiliating aftermath the Convention of Cintra, had not resulted in official disgrace. Despite Junot's consistent string of failures Napoleon obstinately retained him as a corps commander in the Peninsula. After his recall in 1811 only two more years of life were left to Junot. In the first he had to go through the appalling strain of the 1812 Russian campaign; in the second he went mad when Governor of Venice and took to wandering round the streets, naked apart from his epaulettes and his sword. Junot's death in July 1813 was a tragic one, the result of crazed, self-inflicted mutilation.

All these departures were countered by the return to Madrid on 8 July of Marshal Jourdan, King Joseph's former adviser. Jourdan came back as Governor of Madrid, but in October 1811 was given the post of chief-of-staff to the King. However, it was in the summer of 1811 that the numerical strength of the French forces in Spain reached its peak. On paper — as ever — things did not look too bad. The French had six armies — North, Centre, Andalusia, Portugal, Aragon, and Catalonia — with which to contain Wellington and hold down the Spaniards. They had 354,461 men with which to do it, plus another 8,000 in reserve at Bayonne. But these two observations were completely nullified by reality. For a start, the total number of French troops sick, missing, or detached was 63,000 — exactly the figure of Wellington's army. The majority of the remainder were tied down with garrison duty.

This was why, after the siege of Badajoz had been raised in June, the powerful concentration of force created by Marmont's southward march with the Army of Portugal could only be temporary. The French mass on the Guadiana was dragged apart by the compelling tension of too much space and too few troops elsewhere.

But Suchet's Valencian expedition, which got under way in mid-September, was different. It was an attempt to exploit a local success by extending the area of French control. Suchet, as ever, proceeded with methodical care. With his 26,000 men he was not going to take any chances against the Spanish Army of Valencia and the oft-defeated but indomitable General Blake. Murviedro was occupied on 27 September and Blake was beaten again at Puebla de Benaguasil on 1 October. Then came an unforeseen hitch. Sagunto, like so many other Spanish fortresses, decided to hold out, and a formal siege was necessitated which lasted until 25 October. The immediate sequel was the cutting-off and siege of Valencia itself, before which Suchet had failed in March 1810 and Moncey in June 1808. Valencia held out stubbornly, but finally capitulated on 9 January, 1812. Valencia had been added to the Spanish territory under French occupation and the French forces in the Peninsula had – finally – been stretched too far.

In July, with Badajoz safe, Marmont moved north to make sure of Rodrigo and Wellington went with him. Marmont joined forces with General Dorsenne, who had taken over the Army of the North from Bessières, and planned a revictual-ling operation for Rodrigo. At Tamames on 23 September the two commanders concentrated nearly 60,000 men, and effectively prevented Wellington from making any surprise moves against Rodrigo.

Two days later there was a spirited battle at El Bodon, six miles south of Rodrigo. Marmont had sent out a cavalry reconnaissance-in-force under Montbrun to find out what Wellington was up to. His troopers caught the British outposts and forced an engagement before Wellington could concentrate, and for a while it was touch and go. But as had happened at Fuentes de Oñoro, British infantry drill proved superior to the magnificent French cavalry. Wellington was able to withdraw to his planned position before Sabugal, and Marmont refused to be drawn into attacking it.

The frontier stalemate must have continued had not Napoleon, as 1811 drew to a close, withdrawn 27,000 crack troops from the Peninsula, ordered Marmont to send 16,000 men from the Army of Portugal to assist Suchet, and generally created a situation entirely favourable to Welling-ton, whose army had been reinforced to a strength of 60,000 – and equipped, at last, with a siege train. Marmont was in the act of transferring his depleted army to the Valladolid region when the news came in that Wellington had opened the siege of Rodrigo on 8 January.

This was no leisurely, methodical, step-by-step siege. Wellington, like a surgeon operating in the pre-anaesthetic age, had to get it over at top speed. He was developing a lot of respect for Marmont and knew that the young Marshal would concentrate every available man against him as soon as he could. Marmont did everything he could, speeding recall orders to the forces already on the march — but he never had a chance. Wellington's siege guns had made two breaches by the morning of the 19th and he attacked that evening without giving the French garrison time to make the breaches impassable. In a wild, storming attack Rodrigo fell to the British. The northern gate into Bonapartist Spain had been beaten in.

Far more important was the fact that Marmont could do absolutely nothing to get Rodrigo back, because the entire siege train of the Army of Portugal had been in the fortress when it fell. With hideous clarity he saw what would happen next: it had to be the turn of Badajoz. Only another lightning link-up with Soult could avert total disaster.

But once again Napoleon had other ideas.

CHAPTER TEN

FROM BADAJOZ
TO SALAMANCA

When he got the news that Ciudad Rodrigo had fallen, Marmont saw at once what was coming next. To him, on the spot, it was obvious: 'Everything seems to show that Lord Wellington intends to besiege Badajoz,' he wrote to Paris, 'and I need to be able to go to its help.' Marmont had done precisely that in the previous summer, and Badajoz had been saved. Now, with Rodrigo in Wellington's pocket, it was more vital than ever for the French to hold on to Badajoz. But Napoleon, in his wisdom, thought otherwise and ordered otherwise, and the long-term results of the orders he now sent Marmont included the loss not only of Badajoz but of the whole of Andalusia – and Madrid itself.

Soult, not Marmont, was the man responsible for Badajoz, decreed Napoleon. It would have been better if he had sent a duplicate of this to Soult, who believed the opposite. Marmont's job, continued the directive from Imperial Head-quarters, had been to defend Almeida and Rodrigo, which he had failed to do, and not worry his head about what was going on elsewhere. Now he must concentrate the Army of Portugal at Salamanca and threaten northern Portugal. Wellington would be mad even to consider moving against Badajoz if Marmont did this. In fact, however, the Salamanca region was as bare as an overgrazed paddock and could not support the Army of Portugal, as Marmont very properly pointed out, 'for a fortnight'. To crown everything Napoleon ordered Marmont to invade Portugal, retake Almeida (if not

Rodrigo as well) and position himself where he could threaten Lisbon if Wellington threatened Badajoz. Presumably Napoleon saw all this as a long-overdue basic strategy lesson for a subordinate who was getting a bit above himself. Certainly what he spelt out to Marmont was a queen-for-a-queen situation: the recovery of Rodrigo, Almeida, and northern Portugal for the (unlikely) loss of Badajoz.

As a whole, the new product of Napoleon's imagination amounts to one of the most damning pieces of evidence of his most serious failing as a Great Captain: that of 'making pictures'. None of the new orders made any sense. There was no point in Marmont's shadow-boxing against either Rodrigo or Almeida without siege guns. Nor could he supply the Amry of Portugal either in the Salamanca region or in northern Portugal itself. Much more to the point, Soult did not, as Napoleon airily stated, have 80,000 men with more to come from Suchet in Valencia if required. The forces of both Soult and Suchet were strung out like the knots in an overstressed seine net and were just about as mobile. Nor was it any comfort to Marmont that over 10,000 of the French troops in the south had been weeded out from the Army of Portugal itself. . .

In short, Wellington himself could not have drafted orders better calculated to pin down the Peninsular Marshals while he came down on Badajoz like a ton of bricks.

As at Rodrigo, Wellington planned to take Badajoz with a swift, decisive stroke, and he wasted no time in getting down to the task. Rodrigo had fallen on 19 January. Within five weeks the Allied Army was heading south, on the march for Badajoz. By 16 March it had concentrated at Elvas – one day's march from Badajoz itself, which was invested on that day. First siege works were opened on the 17th, and were driven forward with furious speed in appalling weather for the next seven days.

General Philippon, Governor and garrison commander of Badajoz, had created the most formidable obstacle that

Wellington's men had yet had to tackle. All the classic devices of fortification – glacis, counter-scarp, and ditch – had been put to rights after years of Spanish neglect. The old walls and turrets had been renovated and the fortress guns were cunningly sited for the most deadly enfilade fire. Along the ramparts were massed the oil-soaked 'carcasses' – inflammable bundles which, in the years before searchlight and flare, were lit and dropped over the walls to illuminate the attackers for the garrison's musket and cannon fire.

Like most fortresses, however, the dictates of local geography meant that Badajoz had its weak spot. South-east of the main city wall the approaches to the chief defences were commanded by Fort Picurina. As long as the French held Picurina, the British would not be able to bombard direct but must choose other, more difficult sectors for the main point of their attack. (By a curious coincidence the weak spot in the defences of 'Fortress Tobruk' in the Second World War was also the south-east corner of the perimeter.) Picurina was therefore marked down as the first objective of the siege, and when it was stormed on the night of 25 March the British siege guns could commence their work of opening up practicable breaches in Badajoz's main defences. By 6 April three breaches had been made – but Philippon's men had converted them into death-traps. The approaches to the breaches were covered by defence batteries, trenches, mines, iron harrows, and loose boards studded with vicious spikes. The grimmest obstacle of the lot awaited the British in the main breach: a mighty wooden beam, through which had been driven scores of razor-sharp sword-blades and bayonets to make a bristling, gleaming, and deadly hedgehog obstruction.

Wellington knew that this would be a tough assignment. The precipitous height of the walls made the besieger's other main standby – escalade, or the good old-fashioned scaling ladder – vitually impossible. He planned a two-division rush at the breaches, banking on the fighting fury which had taken Rodrigo to carry the day at Badajoz. Escalade parties would do what they could to pin down the French in the city castle and the San Vincente bastion. As darkness fell on 6 April Wellington's army braced itself for the assault. H-Hour was set for 10 p.m. And right from the start, it was slaughter.

The attack on Badajoz has been superbly described by Napier. As the first attackers went in they were spotted, illuminated by fireballs thrown from the walls, and flayed by the French guns. The breaches became blood-swamped infernos of writhing wounded and shattered dead, choked with waves of fanatics struggling a few steps further forward until they dropped in their turn. Terrible scenes occurred in the main breach, where dying men struggled to tear out the sword-blades with their bare hands and others forced their comrades onto the blades to try to get themselves over. It was appalling, futile, and relentless. No Japanese *kamikaze* attack or *banzai* charge was ever pressed home with such utter sacrifice. And it failed. After two hours Wellington had to call off the attack on the breaches – unaware that the diversionary attacks had done the job for him.

Suffering heavy losses in its turn, Picton's 3rd Division had in fact managed to storm the castle, swarming up the shuddering, blood-soaked ladders and overcoming the French defenders on the ramparts by sheer weight of numbers. And on the far side of the town a detachment of Leith's 5th Division had taken San Vincente, sweeping the ramparts and swarming down into the street to take the astonished defenders of the breaches in the rear. Philippon's men had fought superbly. They had held the breaches with complete success – but their morale collapsed when these terrifying enemies came raging into the town at their backs. The sequel was as horrible as the attack. Strained far beyond the normal limits of sanity by fighting madness the victorious troops went raving mad. For two days they surged through the town in an orgy of drink, rape, and destruction until Wellington finally restored order by setting up gallows in the square. The survivors of Philippon's garrison went into captivity but they had cost Wellington some 4,670 men – of whom 3,713 had fallen in the assault on the breaches.

With the capture of Ciudad Rodrigo the strategic deadlock in the Peninsula had been broken. With the capture of Badajoz the initiative passed to Wellington and stayed there. Now that the Spanish-Portuguese frontier was secure at last he could devote himself to the only offensive policy open to him: taking on the scattered French armies piecemeal, and beating them piecemeal. Wellington had to do this because in the spring of 1812 there were 250,000 French troops in the Peninsula to his 65,000. He had seen for himself, however, that the forbidding balance-sheet of manpower was meaningless because of the failure of the Peninsular Marshals to co-operate. After taking Badajoz he therefore marked down his next victim: Marmont.

Marmont, for all his protesting, had dutifully tried to carry out Napoleon's orders. As Wellington's siege guns began the final bombardment of the walls of Badajoz in the last week of March, Marmont crossed the frontier with the Army of Portugal. It was an utterly futile affair; a shadow blockade was imposed on Almeida, while the main body pushed sixty miles into the country looking for someone to fight, and finding nothing but Portuguese militia. The whole abortive venture was called off on 14 April when the news of Badajoz came up from the south; and by the 23rd the Army of Portugal was back in Spain, having accomplished precisely nothing.

One thing – and one thing alone – could still have saved the day for the French: that Napoleon should come to Spain himself and take over personal control until the English had been decisively beaten. But ever since January 1809 he had been repeatedly distracted, and his sense of priorities distorted. In 1809 there had been echoes of sedition in Paris, plus the desperate Wagram campaign against the Austrians. These had been succeeded by Napoleon's obsession with finding a suitably blue-blooded and fertile bride who could give him sons, and his quite genuine infatuation with Marie-Louise of Austria. That particular distraction effectively took his mind off the Peninsular campaigns of 1810. In 1811 came all the tension, fuss, and crisis surrounding the birth of Napoleon's son and heir, Napoleon II, King of Rome. And in 1812 came the biggest obsession of all: Russia. With first his imagination, and later his armies, advancing further and further to the east, the likelihood of Napoleon taking time out to unravel the Spanish tangle receded yet again.This helps explain the extraordinarily casual — and as often as not downright disastrous — way in which Napoleon regarded the Peninsular theatre. And one of its manifestations was the sudden appointment in the middle of March 1812 of King Joseph as supreme commander of the French armies in Spain, with Marshal Jourdan as chief-of-staff. Again, this shows how inconsistent Napoleon always was: how good commanders like Dupont and Massena could be disgraced, and how self-proven failures like Junot, Joseph, and Jourdan were not only retained but even given additional responsibility.

It was the nearest Napoleon had ever come to centralizing the muddled pattern of command in the Peninsula, but in practice Joseph got the shadow of power without the substance (the story of his life, in fact). It was the old story. The French Army professionals would not take orders from Jourdan, let alone Joseph. Instead they preferred to 'work to rule', following the vague directives laid down for them in their personal orders from the Emperor, and claiming that these orders superseded anything Joseph might care to say. This even applied to Suchet, normally the most dutiful commander. The smaller units in the north — the Army of the North (still under Dorsenne but about to be taken over by General Cafarelli) and a new hybrid called the Army of the Ebro under General Reille — were similarly recalcitrant. It goes without saying that Soult simply withdrew all his forces from picket duty along the Seville-Madrid road, thus effectively sealing himself off in his vice-royalty of Andalusia. Power-mania had seized Soult again, much worse than it had in Portugal in 1809. He put on all the airs and graces of a reigning prince, and a petulant, arrogant one at that. It was thoroughly bad for the Imperial cause in Spain. Soult had been a law unto himself for too long and his behaviour was soon to verge on open mutiny. 'He can only be communicated with with the greatest difficulties,' went a bleat from Madrid. 'We do not even know whether he has received the news that the Emperor has put him under the King's command.'

The Army of the Centre (the only one really under Joseph's command) was the weakest of the lot: 18,500 men. It should have been the strongest, able to detach corps or divisions as required to reinforce the Armies of the North, of Portugal, of the South, of Valencia, Catalonia, Aragon, and the Ebro. In fact the Army of the Centre's main task was safeguarding Madrid. Thus Joseph and Jourdan had no central reserve, and would get no more troops – Napoleon airily told Joseph that 'The forces which His Majesty [i.e. Napoleon himself] has put under your orders will permit you to do what is necessary.' And this meant that Joseph and Jourdan awaited the events of the summer of 1812 with nothing but apprehension. All they could do was pray that Soult and Marmont, whose armies must hold the front line of Bonapartist Spain, would keep in touch and do what they could to keep Wellington out of Spain.

But preventing Soult and Marmont from keeping in touch was the first thing the British attended to. On 19 May the extreme right-wing corps of Wellington's army under General Hill pounced eastwards and cut the last bridge across the Tagus held by the French downstream of Toledo, at Almaraz. The result was that all communications between Soult and Marmont would virtually have to be routed through Madrid. Marmont would not, therefore, get any rapid help from the Army of the South if he should suddenly find himself in trouble. And this was assuming that Soult would have sent it anyway – he still blamed Marmont for the loss of Badajoz. On being ordered to send d'Erlon's corps, 12,000 strong, to help Marmont if necessary, Soult demurred. He needed every man he had. If he transferred d'Erlon, Andalusia would have to be evacuated. And then, in the first week of June, Hill made another raid, this time into Andalusia itself, causing Soult to yell for more troops merely to save the province. It was neat timing, for Wellington moved out towards Salamanca on 13 June with the main force of the Allied Army. As a result Joseph and Jourdan in Madrid had the unenviable task of trying to decide whether Wellington was going to attack Marmont or Soult, and which of the two Marshals was crying wolf.

By dint of strenuous efforts Marmont had managed to concentrate 40,000 men at Fuentesauco, twenty-odd miles north of Salamanca, by 19 June. To do this he had had to tear up Napoleon's orders to occupy Asturias and maintain all existing garrison dispositions. He still needed time for his last forces to join up, however, and knew that Salamanca was Wellington's for the taking until they did. Nevertheless he had set up three strongpoints to command the Tormes river at Salamanca, withdrawing his main body from the city; and although Wellington duly entered Salamanca in triumph on 17 June, he had to reduce these strongpoints before moving on to try accounts with Marmont's army. When this was finally done on 27 June, Marmont decided to pull back to the Douro and dig in between Tordesillas-Toro-Zamora. Here his last reinforcements joined up – the most important being Bonet's division from Asturias – and by 10 July he had 43,000 men and 78 guns present under arms.

It was a fine achievement, all the more impressive because it meant that the rival armies were almost exactly equal. On a head-count Wellington had the better of it with 48,000 men – but of these 3,000 were Spanish and 18,000 Portuguese. Nor did Wellington have all his British troops with him: Hill's corps was still down in Estremadura. Wellington and Marmont, therefore, were well matched as they faced each other across the Douro between 2-15 July.

As expected, no help would be forthcoming from other quarters. Cafarelli had told Marmont that the Army of the

North had nothing to spare. This was fair enough: it had always been under-strength anyway. Suchet, too, could not help. He was obsessed with the possibility of a British amphibious landing on the east coast of Spain and wanted all his forces on call to cope with such a landing. (Suchet was quite right to take this line. The expedition had been preparing in Sicily for weeks but had been held up by the incompetence of the British commander, Bentinck). The real trouble was Soult. Once Joseph had found that Hill's corps had not joined up with Wellington, he and Jourdan agreed that Marmont must be given every chance to destroy Wellington's incomplete force and ordered Soult to send d'Erlon's corps north across the Tagus with all dispatch. On 30 June Joseph wrote to Soult: 'If you have formally forbidden Count d'Erlon to cross the Tagus you have given him orders which contradict those I have given you,' and threatened Soult with instant dismissal if this really was the case. Soult's megalomania is proven by the attitude he took to this message. He did what Napoleon would have done, and ignored it. Marmont remained unsupported on the Douro.

On the same day, 30 June, Joseph wrote in similar vein to Marmont, pointing out that it seemed that Wellington only had 18,000 British troops with him, and why was Marmont not attacking? Marmont was puzzled by this message when it finally arrived on 12 July, but he needed no further urging, and his army re-crossed the Douro on the 15th.

Now there ensued the most fascinating six days of the entire Peninsular War: pure manoeuvre, with Wellington and Marmont watching each other like hawks for the first sign of an opening. Marmont held the initiative right from the start, and fenced Wellington back towards his start-line with a brilliant succession of feints and thrusts —first at Wellington's left, then at his right. On the 18th the two armies were so close that they marched in sight of each other all day. By the 21st they were back on the Tormes which was crossed with the French slightly in the lead, Marmont crossing at noon and Wellington in the evening. Marmont was now less than ten miles from Salamanca and Wellington knew that he must fall right back to Ciudad Rodrigo if the French kept up this pace. Captured despatches had told him that Joseph had completely denuded the area of the Army of the Centre and was hastening north with a relief corps of nearly 14,000 men. Rather than risk being caught between Joseph and Marmont he was prepared to pull right back into Portugal and wait until the scales tilted again before trying another foray into Spain.

Then, on the morning of the 22nd, it happened. Marmont, cracking on the pace in an all-out effort to slice across Wellington's communications, failed to notice that the Allied withdrawal had stopped at the small village of Los Arapiles, some six miles south of Salamanca. Once again Marmont cut at Wellington's right flank, with his pursuing divisions strung out in a lengthening crescent. But the Allied forces had swung to the south. The French were not enveloping Wellington's flank, but marching directly across his front.

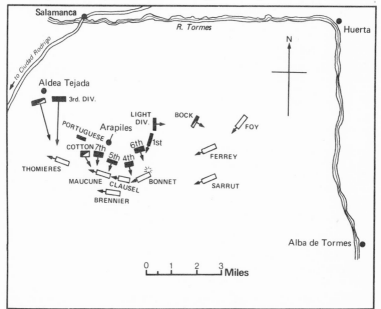

The battle of Salamanca, 22 July 1812

Had the pace of the French advance been more deliberate things might have turned out very differently. As it was, Marmont's leading division, that of Thomières, had drawn steadily ahead of its fellows until a gap of nearly one mile had opened in the French line. It was exactly the sort of chance that Wellington had been waiting for, and he seized it with both hands.

Ably backed up by d'Urban's Portuguese cavalry, Picton's 3rd Division fell upon Thomières' division like the wrath of God and smashed it to pieces, while further back the 4th and 5th Divisions charged the nearest French division, Maucune's. Overwhelmed by the weight of the British counter-stroke, Maucune's men were cut down as they fled by a superb charge by Sir Stapleton Cotton's cavalry brigade, which not only completed the ruin of Maucune's division but shattered Brenier's as well. In something under forty minutes one-third of the Army of Portugal had been destroyed as a fighting force. Far more important, the French were temporarily leaderless. Galloping up the line to take the situation in hand, Marmont had been hacked down by a British shell, with his right arm broken and two bad wounds in his side. It was some time before General Clausel took over the command.

By this time the French resistance was stiffening. The British and Portuguese troops who attacked the next two French divisions, those of Clausel and Bonet, found them much tougher to crack. The Allied attack failed and Clausel and Bonet counter-attacked. But Wellington, as ever, had kept his reserves well in hand, and now they went in to finish the job. Twenty more minutes sufficed to force back the divisions of Clausel and Bonet to join the retreat of the survivors from the three leading French divisions. But for all the magnificent dash and courage with which Wellington's men went into action at Salamanca, they could not break the last three divisions of the Army of Portugal. Ferrey and Sarrut formed line and covered the retreat of the four defeated divisions and withdrew from the battlefield in splendid order, while General Foy's untouched division took over the duty of rearguard.

For Marmont, invalided home, it was a tragic end to a brilliantly-opened campaign. One mistake had been enough to undo him. Every general in the Army of Portugal, and in the entire Peninsula, was shaken by the terrible lesson of Salamanca. A belief had grown up that although Wellington was undoubtedly formidable when holding a chosen defensive position, he was not really a man who reacted with anything like the speed he showed at Salamanca. General Foy later wrote: 'Hitherto we had been aware of his prudence, his eye for choosing a position, and his skill in using it. At Salamanca he has shown himself a great and able master of manoeuvre. He kept his dispositions concealed for almost the whole day; he waited until we were committed to our movement before he developed his own.'

Wellington was robbed of complete victory by Spanish negligence. He had seen to it that the ford across the Tormes at Huerta, by which Marmont had crossed on the 21st, was made secure by the Light Division. But he never dreamed that the Spanish commander at Alba de Tormes, eight miles to the south-east of the battlefield, would evacuate the town and leave Clausel's beaten fugitives a clear road across the river to safety.

It fell to General Fabrier to set off on an epic ride across France, Germany, Poland, and White Russia to take the news of the defeat at Salamanca to the Emperor. Fabrier finally caught up with the *Grande Armée* on 6 September and was just in time to join in the battle of Borodino on the following day. . .

Brilliantly covered by Foy's rearguard, Clausel's army straggled eastwards: across the Douro, evacuating Valladolid, finally halting at Palencia. When Joseph heard the appalling news he swung his relieving forces eastward, too, and made for Segovia, where he arrived on 28 July. The following day he sent a fateful message to Soult: ' . . . I give you my formal order to evacuate Andalusia and march to Toledo with all your forces. This is the only way to restore the situation . . .

no other course is open to us.'

Wellington pushed on in cautious pursuit of the Army of Portugal until he was quite sure that, unlike Massena the previous year, Clausel would not recoil against him. He then planned a descent on the south to settle the Army of the Centre before Joseph added to his forces. After entering Valladolid in triumph – the second major Spanish city to be liberated in the 1812 Peninsular campaign – he headed south across the Guadarramas, his sights set on Madrid itself. Once again panic reigned in King Joseph's capital, with court officials and collaborating Spaniards running for their lives before Wellington's advance. Joseph had no hope of saving Madrid. Contenting himself with savaging d'Urban's Portuguese cavalry brigade (which had pushed too far forward) on 11 August, he ordered the evacuation of his capital, which Wellington entered amid scenes of joyous hysteria on the 12th.

Once again King Joseph of All The Spains was a fugitive. With the Army of the Centre he headed for Valencia, planning to consolidate the defence of what remained of his kingdom there. He was still confident that if he could join forces with Suchet and Soult and reopen communications with the Army of Portugal, all would be well. But within a week of his arrival at Valencia on 31 August Joseph was infuriated to hear that his hopes had come to nothing. Soult had disobeyed orders once more and was refusing to move.

CHAPTER ELEVEN

THE LAST ACT

Nicholas Jean-de-Dieu Soult is certainly among the most difficult of all the Marshals to assess. He was inordinately vain and ambitious. He could be utterly selfish. He was suspicious of any potential rival and was a practised back-stabber. Time and again these damning weaknesses jeopardized the entire French hold on the Peninsula. But under his petulant, conceited facade there was bedrock. Soult was a professional. And although he sulked and stormed like a spoilt child at the very idea of giving up 'his' province of Andalusia, his professional instincts won the day in the end. With Wellington on the loose in Castile and Leon there was nothing for it but to pull out of Andalusia and concentrate against him, and Soult knew it.

But he spent the second half of August and the whole of September making as big a scene as possible about the evacuation. In so doing Soult went even further than Ney had done during his last row with Massena in the spring of 1811. Ney had taken indignant insubordination across the border-line into attempted mutiny. Soult pushed it into downright treason.

What happened was this. Joseph had reached Valencia on 31 August, and he waited there for a week in growing impatience to hear what Soult was up to. On 8 September, Joseph heard all he wanted and more. He had finally received a letter from Soult which was a masterpiece of impertinence, pouring scorn on the idea of evacuating Andalusia and containing the imperious sentence: 'There is only one way to re-establish the situation: let Your Majesty come to Andalusia, bring all the troops of the Army of the Centre and such of the Armies of Portugal and Aragon within the reach of orders.' But much worse was to come. On the night of 8 September Marshal Suchet was handed a letter from Soult to the War Ministry in Paris (the ship carrying it had been forced to run from British cruisers instead of making a French port direct), and Suchet passed it to Joseph.

The contents were dynamite. Soult had dared to state that he had reason to believe that Joseph was pressing for the evacuation of Andalusia in order to arrange an undercover deal with the Spaniards. Joseph, naturally, was incensed. This was the last straw, and he packed off Colonel Deprez with a letter to Napoleon demanding that Soult be relieved of his command and court-martialled. But Soult was saved by time and distance. For a start, it took Deprez until the 21st to reach the War Ministry in Paris, his first destination along the long road east to Napoleon's headquarters in Moscow.

The War Minister, General Henri Jacques Clarke, was no fool and he knew very well that Soult's behaviour was impossible. But he knew something else that was impossible. Sacking a full-blown Marshal was an act which could only be done by Napoleon himself, and so poor Deprez was politely speeded on his way to Moscow. By the time he got there it was 18 October, the day before the great retreat began; and it was not surprising that Napoleon's reaction to more tidings of woe from the Peninsula was, to say the least, brusque. Soult was wrong this time, but basically he was quite right to keep an eye on Joseph. Certainly Soult could not be spared from Spain. He must work more closely with Joseph. Having dashed off a brief note to this effect, Napoleon returned to the more pressing matter of the retreat from Moscow.

Napoleon could not know that by this date, 19 October, the French squabbles in Spain had been resolved (albeit temporarily) for over a fortnight. On 12 August, the very day that Soult wrote his bombshell letter of accusation, the self-styled ruler of Andalusia had set the evacuation of the province in motion. The outlying garrisons went first; Niebla on the 12th, Ronda and Medina Sidonia on the 15th. And on 24 August, 1812, the long siege of Cadiz was raised at last — the siege which had been imposed in February 1810, and which had been running down like an unwound clock since the departure of Victor on 9 February, 1812. (Victor's complete inability to take Cadiz had been consistently demonstrated for twenty-four months — but at least he could claim the credit for having prevented the British from using Cadiz as a second Lisbon.) By the last week of August the concentration of the Army of the South was gaining momentum. Soult pulled out of Seville on the night of 26-27 August. He was heading for Cordoba, as was d'Erlon's corps which Soult had ordered in from its beat in Estremadura. D'Erlon and Soult duly made rendezvous at Cordoba on the 30th, making up a formidable concentration of 45,000 men. After a pause in Granada, which was evacuated on 16 September, the Army of the South set off to link up with the Army of Valencia. By the end of the month this had been done, and on 3 October Soult and Joseph met in a tense interview to try to reconcile their differences.

This conference showed Joseph at his best. It started with a *tête-à-tête* between the King and his back-stabbing Marshal in which Joseph made it clear that as far as he was concerned, bygones were bygones. He then called in Jourdan and Suchet and the foursome got down to business.

It was too good to last, of course. Suchet complained loudly about the behaviour of Soult's men in his, Suchet's, territory, and asked for 5,000 men from Soult's army to reinforce his own. Soult was prepared to see him damned first. He hedged, telling Joseph that he would be making a written report on what he thought best. Joseph countered by asking for written reports from all three Marshals present. He distilled the salient arguments from these reports into a general order on 7 October. Suchet was to stay where he was; d'Erlon would take over the Army of the Centre, which Soult was to reinforce with a cavalry brigade and an infantry division. The Armies of the Centre and South would then push north, link up with the Army of Portugal, and tackle Wellington. When Soult protested that this was impossible because of his original orders from the Emperor, Joseph gave him just one alternative: to do as he was told, or hand over the Army of the South to d'Erlon and go back to Paris for trial. For once, Soult accepted that he had gone too far and he backed down. It was Joseph's greatest success since he had first had the job of trying to get the Peninsular Marshals to pull together. On 15 October the advance to the north began.

This new concentration put Wellington, as he himself later admitted, in 'the worst scrape he had ever been in'. He had taken a gamble which could only have had a fighting chance if the French did nothing – and in his time he had had ample opportunity of seeing how fast the French could move when they were up against it. What he had done was to push three divisions down to the Tagus to shield Madrid from the south and head north with the other half of his army to take Burgos, the lynch-pin in the French communications in the north. This would shut the Armies of the North and of Portugal out of central Spain, enabling Wellington to hasten south again and block Soult and Joseph with the aid of Hill's force from Estremadura. He hoped that the Spanish Army of Murcia and the British expedition from Sicily would keep Suchet's hands full while all this was going on.

This sort of strategy, based on dividing a smaller army and keeping a stronger enemy on the *qui vive* by hitting him from different directions with the fragments, was what Robert E. Lee used with dazzling success in the American Civil War, at Chancellorsville in 1863; and given a lot of luck, enemy inaction, and fast work by trusty subordinates it could achieve wonders. But Lee at Chancellorsville had all these advantages plus a battlefield measuring only 25 to 30 miles by 10 deep. Wellington in 1812 had to cover hundreds of miles of northern, central, and eastern Spain in his planning, with untrustworthy allies and subordinates who always needed his personal supervision to prevent them from making dangerous mistakes. At best, his plan for the autumn campaign of 1812 was based on an extremely dubious combination of long shots.

One setback sufficed to turn it into a house of cards and put Wellington in much the same position as Sir John Moore had been in at the end of 1808, before the retreat to Corunna. Wellington's troops reached Burgos without trouble on 16 September and occupied the city, but the French garrison in the castle refused to give in. Wellington was forced to sit down for a full-dress siege, but the luck which had carried him through at Rodrigo and Badajoz failed him this time. He tried five times to take the place, but each attack was beaten off and the casualty list rose to an alarming height of 2,000 — and casualties were the one thing Wellington dared not risk. And meanwhile his ring of covering forces around Burgos was sensing increasing pressure from the Army of Portugal, now under the command of General Souham and back in the game with a vengeance. It had been recruited back to a strength of 41,500 as a result of hefty drafts from the reserve force across the Pyrenees at Bayonne. Close at hand were the 11,000 men of the Army of the North, and coming up from the south were the 61,000 of the combined forces of Soult and d'Erlon. A terrifying trap was closing in on Wellington: 112,000 French troops, commanded by men who were out for revenge for the loss of Madrid.

If Wellington had had plenty of frightening lessons about the speed at which the French could move when pushed, the French had had equal opportunities to learn how Wellington could move like lightning when put in an apparently hopeless position. Raising the siege of Burgos castle on 21 October, Wellington raced his army back to the Douro in five days. His idea was to salvage as many as possible of the sensational gains of the summer, holding the Douro himself while Hill stood on the Tagus. But he failed on both counts. The French forded both rivers and forced both halves of Wellington's army to march for their lives. Hill abandoned Madrid on 31

October and made for the Guadarramas. The next halt line for the Allied Army was the line of the Tormes, shielding Salamanca – the position Wellington had taken when confronting Marmont in July. And it was there, after an extremely punishing series of long, hard marches, that Wellington and Hill joined forces on 9 November.

The initiative, however, remained with the French by virtue of the speed with which they had followed up and their superior numbers. Soult now lived up to character by starting an extremely promising manoeuvre which he was too cautious to convert into a decisive victory – *the* decisive victory, in fact, on which all immediate hopes in the Peninsula depended. On 14 November he pushed across the Tormes and turned Wellington's right flank, but he did it so obviously and with such hesitation that Wellington had all the time he needed to pull back again, this time to Ciudad Rodrigo, abandoning Salamanca in the process.

Once again it was stalemate. Both armies were in pretty bad shape after the autumn marching, and there could be no question of any dramatic moves during the winter.

The military stalemate granted a month of deluded security to Joseph's heavily-compressed kingdom. The campaign of 1812 had wrested sizeable portions from the Kingdom of Spain, but had strengthened the French hold over what was left. Andalusia, Estremadura, Galicia, and Asturias had gone; and the north-east swarmed with *guerrilleros* who made the problem of getting news from France worse than ever. But Joseph could once again play the monarch in his own capital: he returned to Madrid on 2 December, and this time there were 95,000 French troops shielding the city. Most accounts record that Madrid society under Joseph's regime was never gayer than during the winter of 1812-13.

When the next news did get through from Paris it was appalling. On 6 January, 1813, a copy of the grim 29th Bulletin, in which Napoleon admitted the disaster in Russia, finally arrived in Madrid (it is worth pointing out, as yet another comment on the difficulties the French had in their communications with Madrid, that a copy had got to London as early as 21 December). From this forbidding document it was obvious that Spain would be getting no more reinforcements for a long time, and this was confirmed by orders which finally arrived from Paris on 14 February. They radically shifted the balance of the French forces in the Peninsula, and amounted to a formal admission that the Imperial plan for Spain had failed.

As far as the Peninsular Marshals were concerned the most important step was the recall of Soult. Joseph had moved heaven and earth to get rid of Soult – but Joseph was not the cause of Soult's departure, nor was Soult sent home in disgrace. (Napoleon needed him badly for the decisive campaign of 1813 in central Europe.) Soult finally set off for France on 2 March – it took some time to assemble sufficient baggage-waggons to carry his impressive collection of Murillos and other art treasures which he had built up during his years in the Peninsula. Also recalled was General Cafarelli, who had put up a most indifferent performance as commander of the Army of the North. In a swift reshuffle Clausel took over the Army of the North and General Gazan, Soult's former chief-of-staff, was promoted to the command of the Army of the South. Far more serious, however, was the withdrawal of some 20,000 combat troops for service in Germany.

Also of vital importance was the totally new, defensive disposition which Napoleon laid down for Joseph's armies. Madrid was now to be no more than the extreme left of the French line, which was to be drawn back into the north-eastern provinces. Joseph was to shift his capital and headquarters from Madrid to Valladolid, and make his first objective for 1813 the stamping out of all *guerrillero* resistance in the northern provinces. There must be no future interference with the lines of communication with France.

And so it was that Joseph left his capital for the last time, not in a panic-stricken scamper caused by the approach of the Allied armies, but on the orders of Napoleon. He rode out on 17 March, followed by a vast train of courtiers, officials, and renegade Spaniards whose only safety was behind the shelter of French bayonets, and arrived at Valladolid on the 23rd.

With the French Empire menaced throughout its entire, top-heavy structure by a formidable new coalition of enemy powers after the disasters of 1812, every French soldier was literally worth his weight in gold to the French war effort. The net effect of these new measures for Spain should have been to cut the losses of the whole Peninsular venture, maintain effective hold of as large a bridge-head as possible on the far side of the Pyrenees, and release the maximum number of French troops to act as the backbone of the new *Grande Armée* which Napoleon was working overtime to create. But the Emperor, incapable as ever of grasping the military realities of the Spanish theatre, made this impossible for Joseph and Jourdan in 1813. His explicit order to smash the *guerrilleros* of Navarre was the big mistake, for it distracted from the main objective: containing at all costs, and if possible defeating, the army of Wellington. Every doctrine of concentration, of sticking to your objective, of bringing the maximum number of troops into action against the enemy where he least expects them, was flouted by Napoleon when he sent out his orders for the Spanish campaign of 1813 to Joseph and Jourdan.

What he did, in short, was to demand too much of two extremely mediocre commanders, and order them to make dispositions which could only mean that one big defeat would leave them with no alternative but retreat to the Pyrenees. And one big defeat was what they got. It was the result of another momentous gamble by Wellington which, if it had failed, would have been equally disastrous for his army.

As soon as he had got wind of the new French dispositions, Wellington knew for sure that the initiative would still be his in 1813. 'I propose to take the field as early as I can and place myself in fortune's way,' he wrote. But this did not mean that he was merely going to sally out and play his next campaign by ear. He laid an extremely daring long-term plan which had the Pyrenees as its final objective. One major gain of the 1812 campaign had been the capture of Santander on the Biscay coast, which had fallen during the heady months of June and July when Commodore Popham's naval squadron was rampaging up and down the coast of Navarre, raising havoc generally and keeping the Navarrese *guerrilleros* under Mina supplied with arms and ammunition. Santander was to play a key role in the leapfrog campaign which Wellington was planning in February-April 1813.

He would feint at Salamanca, but this time he would send the bulk of his army northward through the mountainous Tras Os Montes into Leon, around the French right flank. Next would come an eastward advance across the Esla and Carrion rivers towards the Ebro. This would put his troops in an ideal position for a radical shift of their main base — from Lisbon to Santander, using sea power. The transfer of base to Santander would vastly assist the supply of his army and prevent the French from doing what they had always been able to do before: force him to retreat by threatening his road back to Portugal. The French, he knew, could wreck this new plan in two ways. First, there was the danger that by intensifying their anti-*guerrillero* operations in Navarre they might get Santander back (although British sea power made this unlikely, it was a nasty possibility). Second, they might yet concentrate an army larger than Wellington's own, and concentrate it before he had the chance to defeat its basic components piecemeal. And if anything should go badly wrong during the march into Leon and he should suffer a major setback, Wellington knew that he would have no choice but to pull right back into Portugal and rebuild his army before having another try — which would give the French a vital respite in what promised to be the most crucial year of the whole war.

Once again, Wellington's best ally was Napoleon's interference and Joseph's dog-like attempts to carry out his brother's wishes. This time, however, Wellington would not be duelling with any of the stars of the Marshalate. All his old opponents — Junot, Ney, Massena, Bessières, Soult, Marmont, and Victor — had gone, and his opponents were Joseph himself and the lacklustre Jourdan.

Wellington held yet another trump card. Thanks to the Spaniards he could find out all he needed to know about what the French were up to, while the reverse applied to the French. Moreover, he was ideally placed to use what Montgomery has called 'wet-hen' tactics: keeping the enemy in the maximum uncertainty as to where the main blow would fall, and keeping this up for as long as possible. Hill was in Estremadura: did this mean that Wellington was planning a repeat performance of his 1809 Talavera campaign and a march on Madrid? Wellington himself, however, was at Frenada, near Ciudad Rodrigo: surely this meant that he would do what he had done when faced with Marmont the previous year, and advance direct via Salamanca? As the weeks went by and May drew on, wildly contradictory reports came in from the French Intelligence agents (unhappy men, these, trying to extract hard facts in the face of British secrecy combined with Spanish mendacity) which kept Joseph and Jourdan in a state of thorough confusion. Joseph finally decided to put the Armies of the South and Centre (units whose names had long since failed to bear any relevance to their actual geographical location in Spain) north of the Douro between Toro and Valladolid. He had 55,000 men there and he reckoned that they would be able to hold Wellington long enough for the Armies of the North and of Portugal to come up, 40,000 strong, and complete the ruin of the British and their allies.

The serenity with which Joseph contemplated the approaching campaign was, however, dangerously misplaced. He had made the unfortunate mistake of believing Napoleon's gross underestimation of Wellington's forces. Wellington was not down to his last 30,000 British troops: he had been heavily reinforced during the winter and spring and had some 52,000 British and 29,000 Portuguese, well equipped, fully recovered from the privations and exhaustion of the 1812 campaign, and eager for action.

When the axe fell, it came down hard and fast. In May Wellington set his columns in motion, preparing to march on Salamanca with Hill, who had come north over the Baños Pass. Meanwhile Graham set out on the long, painful 200-mile clamber through the Tras Os Montes with the larger half of the army. Wellington and Hill flung the single French division holding Salamanca — Villatte's — out of the town on 26 May. By 29-30 May Graham's divisions were out of the Tras Os Montes and had reached the Esla, which they crossed on the 31st. Zamora, on the Douro, fell on 1 June. Joseph's neatly-sited blocking army on the Douro had been taken in flank right at the outset of the campaign, and there was nothing for it but to retreat and try to hold the line of the Carrion river. Toro and Valladolid were evacuated on 2 June, and within 48 hours of the withdrawal of King Joseph from yet another of his capitals the two halves of Wellington's army had joined up, 81,000 strong, with the ball at their feet.

Giving the French army any time to pull itself together and make a stand was no part of Wellington's plan. The Allied Army set off in an exhilarating pursuit in which there always seemed to be one more river to cross — the Tormes, Esla, and Douro were followed in quick succession by the Carrion and Pisuerga. By 9 June Joseph was back in Burgos. He was prepared to stand and fight here, but Wellington was not going to oblige him. The Allies hooked round the northern flank of the French and forced them out again. This time Wellington's objective was the Ebro itself. He had already sent off orders to Corunna to send the first supplies into Santander and start stock-piling there.

In the French camp, a rift now began to open between Joseph and his chief-of-staff. Much has been said in disparagement of Jourdan — that he only hit peak form in the Revolutionary Wars (and then only once, at Fleurus, in 1794) and that by the time the Peninsular War began he was a hopeless old dug-out. It was true enough. But Jourdan had never forgotten the rudiments of the game, and in 1813 he had the exasperating job of trying to din them into Joseph. The latter, Jourdan found, was willing enough to talk about the necessity for an 'honourable' battle, but was perfectly incapable of understanding the logic of strategic withdrawal when necessary. Despite Jourdan's protests that Wellington was not going to be such a fool as to fight a battle at Burgos when he could manoeuvre them out of the town, Joseph dithered at Burgos for three days before making the inevitable decision to fall back on the Ebro.

Joseph evacuated Burgos on 12 June. The castle was blown up on the following day — a tremendous explosion which caused much interest in the Allied lines on account of its size. (One can only wonder why the French wasted so much powder. Their spread-out armies certainly needed it.) The new position taken up by the French was Miranda de Ebro, which Joseph reached on 16 June. He had already sent off appeals to Clausel for help and during the retreat to the Ebro three divisions of the Army of Portugal (Maucune's, Sarrut's, and Lamartine's) had joined the main army, strengthening it by some 15,000. Clausel was still tied down in his anti-*guerrillero* operations and it was not until 27 June that he had scraped together four divisions and was able to start off. Foy, on the Biscay coast, had two more divisions between Bilbao and San Sebastian, but it took him even longer to get ready to march to the King's aid.

Wellington, however, had crossed the Ebro the day Joseph reached it: 16 June. The crossing-point was some thirty-five miles away from the French HQ at Miranda de Ebro, and the Allied Army immediately set off for Vitoria.

When the news came in that Wellington was across the Ebro, Joseph and Jourdan — unfortunately for themselves — thought that he was setting his sights on Bilbao. Reille, commanding the Army of Portugal, was ordered to counter this phantom offensive. But Reille's line of march took him right across that of Wellington, and the result was an extremely punishing couple of miniature battles at Osma and San Millan which ruined Maucune's division and sent the Army of Portugal back the way it had come. The appalling speed of Wellington's advance was now beginning to dawn on the French commanders. Reille, thoroughly chastened by his defeats at Osma and San Millan, was in favour of shifting down the Ebro valley and joining up with Suchet. But once again Joseph clung to the letter of his orders from Napoleon. The whole campaign may have been one long disaster from the moment that Wellington's advance began, but he had a clear brief: keep the French lines of communication clear. With the British across the Ebro there could be no possible doubt as to where the next stand would be made. It had to be at Vitoria.

Jourdan tried desperately to make the King see reason. If he could gain a few more days Clausel and Foy would have time to weigh in with 30,000 men and prevent the main French army from having to fight a pitched battle on inferior terms. Joseph, however, was an amateur who had the last word. Being an amateur, he tended to plan his campaigns by the map — and the map showed him that Vitoria was not only an ideal focusing-point for the reinforcements of Clausel and Foy, but the last town of any importance west of the Pyrenees. But amateur strategy was not the only problem with which the French had to contend at Vitoria. There were in fact two armies involved in the campaign of 1813 — the combatant troops and the vast, disorderly shambles which in any other army would have been summed up as the 'baggage train'. In the case of Joseph's army it was some 20,000 strong, choking the road at the back of the army — hundreds and hundreds of waggons, carriages, pack horses and mules, flunkeys, cooks, fancy women and their escorts. It was a major source of demoralization for the fighting troops, who were starting to think that their main purpose was to defend these parasites. 'We were a travelling brothel,' complained a captured French officer.

By 20 June the French in Vitoria knew that they were

going to be attacked soon. Jourdan chose this moment to take to his bed with a high temperature and later claimed that if he had been well he would never have agreed to the dispositions of 21 June. Wellington's convergent attack on the 21st resulted in a complete victory which had been virtually won before a shot was fired. It was a *tour de force* by the British commander: an attack which simultaneously threatened the main French objective (Vitoria itself) and the vital line of retreat from that city. Joseph's dispositions had put his 57,000 men in an extraordinary position in which no rapid redeployment was remotely possible. And the aftermath of the battle dissolved in chaos on both sides, a chaos created by the French baggage train, which clogged the line of retreat of the French army and was luxuriously plundered by the victorious British.

In terms of casualties Vitoria was a small-scale battle, the Allies losing under 6,000 and the French not more than 8,500. Wellington was justly incensed that the plundering of the enemy baggage train robbed him of a battle of annihilation, but his troops were very tired after the scorching pursuit of the past weeks and could not resist the temptation to let off steam. Yet the results of the battle were momentous. Joseph had no alternative but to fall back to the Pyrenees (he can hardly have been consoled by Jourdan's comment — 'Well, gentlemen, you would have a battle; and it appears we have lost it'). By the end of June 1813 the French Army of Spain had concentrated on the line of the Bidassoa river and the western Pyrenees, 85,000 strong. On hearing of the disaster at Vitoria Foy had swept up the garrisons along the Biscay coast and force-marched his two divisions to rejoin Joseph's armies. Clausel's army beat a hasty retreat into France through the central Pyrenees, as did Suchet in the east.

Napoleon's reaction to the defeat was predictable — and for once correct. He deprived Joseph of his command, slapped him and Jourdan under house arrest, blamed them both in vicious terms for the defeat, and sent off Soult as 'my lieutenant-general and commander-in-chief of all my armies in Spain and in the Pyrenees'. In taking on this new command – for which he had angled for years – Soult, too, ran true to form. He issued a flamboyant general order telling the troops how they had been betrayed by their own commanders and how he would lead them to victory and the re-establishment of their honour, and planned an ambitious counter-offensive with the explicit aim of avenging Vitoria by recapturing the place.

Soult's immediate objective was to raise the sieges of Pamplona and San Sebastian, beat up the rear areas of the Allied Army, and capture as many of their supplies as possible before launching a limited offensive back into Spain. He took command on 12 July, and within ten days took the offensive. His attack collided head-on with Wellington's attempt to storm San Sebastian. The measure of how close Soult came to succeeding can be found in Wellington's curt comment 'it was a close-run thing' (Wellington's stock phrase, not unique to Waterloo, for saying that a battle had been really tense). On 27 July Wellington's desperately improvised defence at Sorauren village broke Soult's offensive; and from then on the French never regained the initiative.

For several weeks Soult's army was saved by political considerations. The 1813 campaign in central Germany had begun with Napoleon winning three impressive-looking victories at Lützen, Bautzen, and Dresden, and a truce had been agreed. News of this truce had been assiduously conveyed to Wellington, and it provided an effective brake on his plans to maintain the offensive. It was a deterrent, too, for there was no knowing whether or not Napoleon would be able to race reinforcements to Soult. Wellington therefore contented himself with a limited offensive during the later summer of 1813. San Sebastian was stormed on 31 August, forcing Soult to pull back across the Bidassoa. On 3 September Wellington heard that the truce in Germany was over and that Austria had combined with Prussia and Russia against Napoleon. He immediately prepared for the assault on the Bidassoa, which was carried on 7 October.

The storming of the Bidassoa, like Julius Caesar's crossing of the Rubicon, was a classic symbol. Effectively it marked the end of the Peninsular War. It took Wellington's army onto French soil. It set the stamp on the liberation of Spain. But it did not end the war. Soult, the selfish egotist who inadvertently had done so much to assist Wellington's patient erosion of the French supremacy in the Peninsula, fought on. He defended the river-lines of the Nivelle, the Nive, the tributaries of the Adour, and the Garonne. On 10 April, 1814, he fought a desperate battle at Toulouse before being forced to draw off from the city. Soult's adamant defence of southern France was instrumental in allowing Napoleon to fight his last-ditch defence of France in 1814.

The campaign in the south was Soult's, and Soult's alone. He got no help from Suchet, who surrendered before he did. Soult surrendered to Wellington on 13 April – a full week after Napoleon had abdicated as a result of pressure from Ney and the other Marshals in Paris. Of course it was a futile defence. So was Ney's epic performance during the retreat from Moscow in 1812. But the tenacity with which Soult strove to keep Wellington as far back as possible can never be forgotten. It was, after all, typical of the underlying professionalism with which the Peninsular Marshals – despite all their rivalries, despite all the meaningless interference from Napoleon – had managed to keep Wellington out of southern France for over four years.

CHAPTER TWELVE

BALANCE SHEET

It is only possible to try to sum up the performances of the Peninsular Marshals by first accepting that they fell into two categories. There were the short-term Marshals, the passers-through, the casuals; and the long-term Marshals, whose service in the Peninsula really counted for something. Matters become more complicated, however, when one realizes that both categories contained men of outstanding military talent as well as comparative incompetents — either honest plodders or commanders who were simply not up to their jobs. And this in turn is a comparatively sweeping condemnation, because warfare according to Peninsular standards was a game of which none of the Marshals ever really learned the rules in full. Still the fact remains that out of Napoleon's twenty-six Marshals over half served in the Peninsula at one time or another. How, then, did they measure up against the heart-breaking standards of the Peninsular War? And what happened to them?

Augereau must be ranked among the transients. His service in Catalonia was longer than most of the Peninsular Marshals (1 June, 1809 to 24 April, 1810) but it was devoted to a purely secondary theatre and was by no means distinguished at that. Augereau's star had already begun to wane before he went to the Peninsula: the destruction of his VII Corps at Eylau in 1807 was one of the first shadows to fall across the Napoleonic Empire. Augereau was put in command of XI

Corps in Germany in July 1812; and he served as Governor/ Commander of Berlin and Frankfurt during the opening half of 1813, when it seemed that Napoleon was going to succeed in the apparently hopeless task of keeping his grip on Germany. During the fateful Leipzig campaign of autumn 1813 Augereau commanded the XVI Corps of the *Grande Armée*, and in the last-ditch defence of France in 1814 he commanded the skeletal 'Army of the East', based at Lyons. A realist to the last, he threw over Napoleon in April 1814 and embraced the cause of the Bourbons — for which his name was struck from the list of Marshals on Napoleon's return during the 'Hundred Days', which culminated at Waterloo. Augereau got little thanks from Louis XVIII after Waterloo, however, and was deprived of all his privileges of rank in December 1815. On 12 June, 1816, he died on his estate at Haussaye.

Bessières had served two campaigns in Spain — in 1808-9 and again in 1811 — but his contribution to the Peninsular War was also slight. What Massena needed in 1811 was a back-up colleague who could help him pull the chestnuts out of the fire after the retreat from Torres Vedras. What he got was Bessières, and Bessières was simply not the right man for the job. He let Massena down badly at Fuentes de Oñoro, and even Napoleon sensed this. Bessières, when all is said and done, did best in his favourite position as the figurehead of the Imperial Guard, safely under Napoleon's eye. In this role he soldiered through the Russian campaign of 1812, only to be killed by a shell at Rippach in Saxony on 1 May, 1813 — the consequence, it has been argued, of his own folly in riding within range of a laid enemy gun. The one impressive glimmer he had shown in the Peninsula was as King Joseph's strong-arm man in the summer of 1808, when he beat Cuesta at Medina del Rio Seco.

In many ways, Lannes was the most tragic of the Peninsular Marshals. Certainly he was among the most successful. His victory at Tudela in December 1808 was instrumental in clearing the Emperor's path to Madrid, and

Lannes was also the man whose dogged determination broke the fanatical resistance of the defenders of Saragossa in the following February. Lannes was a tough and ruthless fighting man — it is hard to imagine him winning over the population of any Spanish province he might have been set to govern. But one can only conclude that Wellington was very lucky in that he never had to cross swords with Lannes. The latter's untimely death after being mortally wounded at Essling (he died on 31 May, 1809) removed one of the most formidable of all the Marshals from the scene.

Lefebvre, too, was a rarity among the Peninsular Marshals, though at opposite poles to Lannes when it came to efficiency. Lefebvre's blundering manoeuvres in northern and central Spain caused Napoleon to recall him in a fit of thoroughly-justified irritation. In the Austrian campaign of 1809 Lefebvre commanded the Bavarian corps of the *Grande Armée* during the lunge on Vienna, after which he was granted two and a half years of thoroughly well-earned rest. The Russian campaign of 1812 saw Lefebvre commanding the infantry of the Old Guard; he survived the rigours of the retreat, but was again unemployed in the campaigns of 1813. In 1814 Lefebvre was back in harness, again with the Old Guard, but like most of the other Marshals he faced up to reality and voted for Napoleon's abdication in April. Yet he survived Napoleon's comeback during the Hundred Days; Napoleon confirmed the title of Peer of France which Louis XVIII had given him; and it was still as a Peer of France that the tough old Marshal-Duke of Danzig died in Paris on 14 September, 1820. For Lefebvre it can be said that virtue was its own reward. No one could or did ever make him out to be a military genius. But no one could deny his sincerity and devotion to duty — not even Napoleon. There can be few higher compliments than that.

Macdonald had taken over from Augereau as commander in Catalonia, and his service in Spain extended from 24 April, 1810 to 20 September, 1811. Like Augereau, however, Macdonald contributed little to the French war effort in the

Peninsula. He certainly failed completely to pacify Catalonia, where the tradition of resistance to the invader was stronger than most. For the invasion of Russia in 1812 Napoleon gave him the extreme left-wing corps of the *Grande Armée* with St Petersburg as his objective. But Macdonald got stuck at Riga, where he had to mount a relentless but fruitless siege (he is foiled by the energy and resource of the redoubtable Hornblower in C.S. Forester's *The Commodore*) and retreat in December. In the campaigns in Germany of 1813 Macdonald was in the thick of the fighting as commander of XI Corps of the reconstituted *Grande Armée*, and he soldiered through the 1814 campaign in France before Napoleon gave him, Caulaincourt and Ney the task of negotiating with the Allied sovereigns on 4 April. He readily accepted service under Louis XVIII, becoming a member of the Council of War and a Peer of France. During the panic-stricken scramble to get out of Paris when Napoleon returned to France in 1815 Macdonald accompanied Louis XVIII to the French frontier, only to return to Paris and serve as a lowly grenadier in the National Guard. After Waterloo he returned to service under Louis XVIII, becoming a Minister of State and a Privy Councillor. Chief of all the offices which Louis XVIII lavished on Macdonald, however, was that of Grand Chancellor of the *Légion d'honneur*. (He later got the Grand Cross of the Order of St Louis and became a Knight Commander of the Order of the Holy Spirit, but the significance of his presidency of the *Légion d'honneur* set him apart.) As commander-in-chief of the French Army, Macdonald was responsible for its demobilization in 1815 — a task which he fulfilled as painlessly as anyone could have expected. Macdonald lived to a particularly ripe old age, not resigning his office as Grand Chancellor until 23 August, 1831. He finally died at his country estate at Courcelles-le-Roi on 25 September, 1840.

Moncey had been another of the Peninsular Marshals of 1808, in attendance on Joseph. His ineffectual venture against Valencia had been followed by service under Lannes at Tudela in December, and a notably incompetent attempt to take Saragossa before Lannes stepped in to clear up the mess. The Peninsula, in fact, was the last theatre in which Moncey saw active service in an independent role under Napoleon. In 1812-14 he had the duty of inspecting the National Guard, and as commander of the Paris National Guard during the siege of 1814 he led it in person, defending the *barrière de Clichy*. Louis XVIII confirmed him in the post of Inspector-General of Gendarmerie and named him a Peer of France, as did Napoleon on his return. After Waterloo Moncey lost his new-found title and added a further black mark to his name by refusing to preside over the trial of Ney, writing an exceedingly dignified letter to Louis XVIII in which he expressed his contempt for the entire proceeding. For this he was stripped of his titles and imprisoned for three months in the fortress at Ham. But Louis XVIII, that placid monarch, was not a man who bore grudges. In July 1816 he not only restored Moncey to his privileges as a Marshal but back-dated them to 1 December, 1815 – the time of the Ney trial. The final stage in Moncey's official resurrection came in March 1819 when he was once more named a Peer of France; and in April 1820 he was appointed Governor of the 9th Military District.

In 1823, however, one of the more ironic gifts of fate was dumped in Moncey's lap. It fell to him to command the French Army of the Pyrenees, invade Spain, and wage a brisk and efficient campaign which was one hundred per cent more successful than anything achieved during the Peninsular War of 1807-13. This time the French were not trying to oust the Spanish Bourbons but were intervening in a full-blooded civil war to restore them. The confusion of civil war obviously helped, but it was nevertheless astonishing that in under ten years Spanish memories of hatred against French intervention should have waned so much. Moncey had no trouble at all in overrunning Catalonia, beating Mina (the formidable ex-*guerrillero* leader who had been a constant plague to the French in the first Peninsular War), and taking

Barcelona and Tarragona. He returned to France in November 1823, his mission accomplished, scoring both the French Grand Cross of the Order of St Louis and the Spanish Order of Charles III for his success. Moncey's last position, like that of Macdonald, was an honorific one: Governor of the Invalides, which he became in December 1833. Like Macdonald, too, Moncey was granted a generous old age. He died in Paris in April 1842 at the age of eighty-eight.

Last of the short-term Peninsular Marshals was Murat, the peacock, conceited cavalry genius who had supervised the crushing of the *Dos de Mayo* back in 1808 and who had then quitted Spain before having time to see what he had started. He replaced Joseph Bonaparte as King of Naples on 15 July of that year, being proclaimed on 1 August. As the figurehead ruler of the southernmost extremity of Napoleon's Empire Murat was left pretty much to his own devices. Doubtless he frequently derived much gratification in comparing his own lot to that of the wretched Joseph in Spain. Murat made a great show of concentrating Neapolitan troops down on the Strait of Messina to invade Sicily and chase out the *émigré* court of the Bourbons of Naples, but without an invasion fleet all his sabre-rattling was null and void. He did, however, make one extension to his kingdom, capturing the island of Capri from a composite Allied force under – of all people – Sir Hudson Lowe, who later earned notoriety as the gaoler of Napoleon on St Helena.

In 1812, however, Murat was pitchforked back into the thick of the action for the Russian campaign, and showed that he had lost none of his fieriness on the battlefield – particularly distinguishing himself in the blood-bath of Borodino. After Napoleon left the rapidly-dissolving chaos of the *Grande Armée* to speed back to Paris, Murat, as senior Marshal, was named as replacement commander-in-chief, but he proved himself to be completely unable to cope with the horrors of the retreat. On 18 January, 1813, he handed over his command to Prince Eugène and went back to Naples. In many ways a weak and stupid man, Murat saw very clearly what was coming in 1815, and he opened secret negotiations with Austria and Britain which, he hoped, would save him his kingdom. But he served, again with brilliance, with the *Grande Armée* in the German campaigns of 1813, as much because he believed in hedging his bets as because a premature declaration for the Allies could have been fatal. Murat finally signed treaties with Austria and Britain in January 1814 and turned on Prince Eugène's forces in northern Italy, driving them back behind the Adige.

But after the return of the Bourbons Murat put himself in a fatal position, making himself an object of hatred both to the Bourbons who wanted Naples back and to Napoleon. Murat issued a manifesto to the Italian people, calling upon them to rise and fight for their independence. This got him nowhere. When Napoleon landed in southern France and returned to Paris, Murat went to offer his services to the Emperor on the eve of Waterloo. He was forbidden to enter Paris. After Waterloo he found himself at Toulon with a price on his head and took to sea in a coasting ship, reaching Corsica. A desperate bid to raise the subjects of his former kingdom by landing at Pizzo failed ignominiously and he was arrested. Within half an hour after receiving the death sentence from a special military tribunal, Murat found himself before a firing squad. Yet even after all the ignominy and moral squalor of his recent double-dealing, he still managed to conjure up a flicker of his old magnificence at the last. 'Spare my face,' he is said to have told the firing-squad: 'aim for my heart.' Such, on 13 October, 1815, was the end of Murat, the man who had set Madrid ablaze with patriotic fury back in 1808.

Alphabetical order is a good enough sequence in which to take the short-term Peninsular Marshals. For the other category, the Marshals who did most to make their mark on the course of the Peninsular War, another approach is advisable: a league table of merit, starting at the bottom and working up to the top. On this basis the first candidate for examination has to be Jourdan.

One of the worst sins of omission Napoleon ever made in his slap-dash approach to the Peninsular War was to sanction the employment of Jourdan in that theatre. The original reason was clear enough: Jourdan had been Joseph's chief-of-staff in Naples, and it seemed logical to send Jourdan to Spain when Joseph was translated to that kingdom in 1808. But this was rather like giving a novice horseman riding lessons on an animal that has never been ridden, so that they can both start together. As chief-of-staff in 1808 Jourdan proved completely unable to stop the first collapse in Spain which saw King Joseph and his court bolting in panic from Madrid. In the summer of the following year Jourdan refused to stop Victor fighting at Talavera, and the resultant defeat spoke for itself. Napoleon weeded Jourdan out of Spain in October 1809. But two years later he was back as Governor of Madrid, and from there to being Joseph's chief-of-staff again was but a step. By the time of the Vitoria campaign of 1813 Jourdan had not only proved himself to be the complete antithesis of what a good chief-of-staff should be: he was all aches and pains and negligent inertia.

Napoleon put Jourdan on the retired list in August 1813. It was high time, but Jourdan never accepted this. He turned his coat with alacrity when Napoleon fell in 1814, and again when Napoleon came back in the Hundred Days, and again after Waterloo. He was not unique: other Marshals and generals found it expedient to move with the times. But it was Jourdan who agreed to preside over the court which tried and condemned Ney in 1815 – a piece of soul-selling which leaves a nasty taste in the mouth. He got his reward: Bourbon ribbons and stars, the command of military districts for form's sake, and elevation to the rank of Peer of France. He became Governor of the Invalides in 1830, a post which passed to Moncey when Jourdan died in Paris on 23 November, 1833.

Victor runs Jourdan pretty close as prime candidate for the worst of the 'full-time' Peninsular Marshals. Victor is an interesting case. He was so mediocre. Yet there he was: a Marshal of the Empire, who led crack French troops into some bad defeats, but not a few victories as well. He was one of those tubby little red-faced characters who crop up now and again in history and who always seem to rake up trouble all round when they get sufficient power to do so. A driving need to prove to the world that they are far more important than appearances might suggest is probably the root cause.

Certainly this was true with Victor. He won some perfectly creditable victories of his own over the Spaniards at Espinosa, Ucles, Medellin, and Alcabon, although he made a mess of things under Napoleon's eye during the storming of the Somosierra Pass. But the Talavera fiasco was directly attributable to Victor and was the result of inflated military conceit getting its just deserts. Victor enjoyed another ripple of prominence during the occupation of Andalusia and then failed to take Cadiz. During the siege of Cadiz he was given a thorough hammering at Barossa, although he managed to maintain the siege. Had the Allies been able to open up Cadiz as a sally-port into southern Spain, the great French concentration which in 1812 put Wellington in 'the worst scrape he had ever been in' would have been impossible. The Allies failed to do so until the French raised the siege, however, and their containment in Cadiz was largely Victor's doing, even though this was perhaps because he was too short-sighted to know when he was taking on a task beyond his capabilities.

After his return to France in February 1812 Victor commanded the back-up corps of the *Grande Armée* — IX Corps — in Germany, but he was soon dragged into the Russian campaign in which, like Murat, he was utterly out of his depth. Victor was with the new *Grande Armée* during the German campaigns of 1813 and the defence of France in 1814, but Napoleon deprived him of his command when he failed to arrive on time for the battle of Montereau in February. When the bubble burst in April 1814 he went over to the Bourbons, but it should be pointed out that he was slightly less unpleasant about his coat-turning than Jourdan and others. Victor stayed with Louis XVIII during the Hundred Days and the Waterloo campaign, and was rewarded accordingly. After Waterloo, however, Victor showed himself in a less straightforward light as far as his old comrades were concerned. He was one of those who voted for the death sentence during the Ney trial, and was made president of the commission set up to examine the records of officers who had made the mistake of backing the wrong horse during the Hundred Days. In 1823, while Moncey was leading the Army of the Pyrenees to victory in Spain, Victor was War Minister in Paris. By 1830 he had earned himself a reputation at court as an expert on military affairs, a reputation which none of his professional colleagues could ever endorse. Victor finally died in Paris on 1 March, 1841.

Mortier, the big, hearty, simple Marshal, and certainly the most likeable of them all, comes next. His role in the Peninsular War can best be described as that of the ideal subordinate. This by no means implies that he was lazy. His corps marched through most corners of the Peninsula in its time, but its role was usually secondary: covering the siege of Saragossa, or Badajoz, or acting under Soult's orders in Estremadura or Andalusia. In the Peninsula he earned the reputation of a reliable corps commander who did what he was told. Massena could certainly have done with a team of Mortiers in Portugal in 1810-11. His promotion to the command of the Young Guard in Russia, Germany, and France in 1812, 1813, and 1814 was thoroughly deserved, and he fought on in 1814 until there was clearly no point in prolonging the agony. Louis XVIII gave him the 16th Military Division, the order of Knight of St Louis, and made him a Peer of France; but Mortier could not resist rejoining the Eagles during the Hundred Days. Napoleon appointed him to command the Imperial Guards cavalry, but illness saved Mortier from fighting in the Waterloo campaign.

When the Bourbon regime returned after Waterloo Mortier lost his peerage, but was a member of the court during the

Ney trial. It is pleasant to record that he abstained when the vote for the death penalty was cast. In 1816 he went into politics, being elected a deputy for the Nord Department in October with a handsome majority. Like the other surviving Marshals, Mortier received his title and decorations back after 1819, and he became a member of the Supreme War Council. In 1831 he was Ambassador to Russia, became Grand Chancellor of the *Légion d'honneur*, and was Ambassador to Russia again in 1832. For four months he was War Minister and President of the Council, but he resigned in March 1835 and resumed his functions as Grand Chancellor. His death came suddenly and tragically. He was in attendance on King Louis-Philippe when the anarchist Fieschi made his bomb attack on the King on 28 July, 1835. The blast spared the King — but not Mortier.

Next comes Ney, the most dramatic of the Marshals. He was the 'Bravest of the Brave' in the Napoleonic legend and 'old Red-Head' to the troops who worshipped him: the hero of Elchingen, Jena, Friedland, Borodino, and — virtually single-handed — of the retreat from Moscow. He was in the thick of the fighting in 1813 and 1814, and Ney, not Napoleon, was the key French commander at Waterloo. But he should never have been sent to the Peninsula. He would serve under a colleague, but he always needed Napoleon within reach to keep him in check. Ney was too fiery, too impatient, to adapt to the failures (or, in the Peninsula, the deliberate back-stabbing) of others. Ney would have backed Massena to the hilt if the Prince of Essling had thrown himself into the fray during the Torres Vedras campaign, but he could not stomach the lazy old cynic living on his reputation and flaunting his girl-friend on campaign as well. Quarrel after quarrel with Massena resulted until the latter was goaded beyond measure and sacked Ney.

Whole volumes could be written about Ney's superb performance in the Russian campaign. At Borodino he earned the title 'Prince of the Moskowa'. He *was* the retreat from Moscow, during which there were more blazing rows with his brother Marshals because of their callousness and incompetence. His indomitable fight with the rearguard of the *Grande Armée* is summed up by the story of how he staggered into Königsberg in January 1813, emaciated, red-eyed, and begrimed. 'Don't you recognize me?' he asked an astonished French officer. 'I am the rearguard of the *Grande Armée* – Marshal Ney!'

After Russia came Germany and the campaign in France – but by the spring of 1814 things had gone too far for Ney. He was the man who tackled Napoleon, forcing him to abdicate with the cutting ultimatum 'The Army will follow its leaders.' And with the return of the Bourbons the last eighteen months of Ney's life began. They make sad reading: his growing bewilderment at the cold-shoulder treatment by the popinjays at the Bourbon Court; his embarrassing boast to Louis XVIII that he would bring Napoleon back to Paris in an iron cage; the disciplinary contempt with which Napoleon greeted him before giving him the key command in the army of 1815. The Waterloo campaign, like the retreat from Moscow was all Ney, but something had been broken in him and only his battlefield hysteria remained. Napoleon had only himself to blame for letting Ney run wild at Waterloo.

Yet all was redeemed by the dignity and courage with which Ney faced his accusers after Waterloo. He knew that he would never be forgiven for his boast of the iron cage. But even Ney could not have guessed how many of his former colleagues among the Peers who tried him would vote him before the firing squad. Defiant to the last (it is superfluous to comment that he refused a blindfold), the 'Bravest of the Brave' faced his last volley in Paris on 7 December, 1815.

Suchet has often been hailed as the greatest of all the Peninsular Marshals, but his champions often fail to stress the fact that he could be as factious and bloody-minded – with headquarters or his fellow army commanders – as any of them. Nor was he uniformly successful in the field – even Victor had a better record against the Spaniards than Suchet, who also had the luck of never having to fight Wellington.

One thing certainly cannot be denied: Suchet was the only Peninsular Marshal who made a good job of pacifying and administering naturally rebellious Spanish territory. But this cannot be defended as an all-excusing virtue. Despite the myriad problems of the other fronts in Spain, Suchet tended to hang on to as many troops as he could and to warn off his colleagues from 'his' territory like a goldfish patrolling its tank.

Suchet's last two commands were in the south of France in 1814 and 1815. He went back to Napoleon during the Hundred Days and was given the command of the Alpine front. While the Waterloo campaign was rolling to disaster in Belgium, Suchet launched a diversionary invasion of Savoy, cut short by the news of Waterloo. Struck from the list of the Peers of France in 1815, Suchet was restored in 1819, but never returned to the active scene. Polished, polite and urbane, he lived out the last five years of his life without fuss, dying in his chateau near Marseilles on 3 January, 1826.

By any criterion, Marmont's performance in the Peninsula, although foreshortened by his wound at Salamanca, was an impressive one. He had the energy. He had the strategic sense. He knew how to mark down his main objective and concentrate on it. He co-operated gladly with his colleagues and received little thanks for doing so. One mistake – just one – landed him in bad trouble at Salamanca, but one can readily imagine Marmont picking up the pieces and carrying on if he had not been wounded. In addition, his earlier record in Dalmatia had proved that he was as able an administrator as Suchet. There can be no doubt that Marmont was a decided paragon among the Peninsular Marshals. He was only beaten once, while Soult was defeated at Corunna, Oporto, Albuera, the Pyrenees, Orthez, and Toulouse – but that defeat has always prevented him from getting his full due for his service in the Peninsula.

Yet there is a far more important reason. Marmont was the man who in 1814 entered into negotiations with the Allies for the surrender of his corps – an act which encouraged the Allied sovereigns to insist on the withdrawal of the Bonaparte dynasty from its claim to being the ruling house of France. For this the Duke of Ragusa was never forgiven – never. '*Raguser*' – to welsh – became a dirty word in the French language after 1815. Marmont also added to his unpopularity by voting for the death sentence in the Ney trial. He did his lackey service with the Bourbons like the other Marshals, but he always had the mark of Cain on him after the betrayal of 1814. After the Revolution of 1830 Marmont, who had narrowly escaped from being lynched by a Parisian mob, went into self-imposed exile and never returned to France. After wandering around Europe he eventually settled in Venice and died there, outcast and alone, on 3 March, 1852.

Massena and Soult remain. For Massena, one can only remember that he was the man who pushed Wellington as he had never been pushed before, that Wellington never dared take the slightest risk when Massena was in the field before him, and that Wellington never forgot the lessons he learned at Massena's hands. Massena was far and away the best field commander on the whole of the French side in the Peninsular War. And this although he was long past his physical peak, tired, cynical, and hampered by the most troublesome pack of self-opinionated subordinates who have ever plagued a commanding general. Massena's come-back after the retreat from Torres Vedras was a master-stroke which caught Wellington badly at Fuentes de Oñoro, but his underlings refused to obey orders and the chance was lost. It was Massena's last battle. Napoleon never forgave him. 'Well, Prince of Essling! So you are no longer Massena?' he barked when Massena reported to him after his recall. It was grossly unjust. Massena passed the rest of the war well out of the limelight, dying in Paris on 4 April, 1817.

Soult, therefore, is left as the principal claimant and the grounds are not so much efficiency as longevity. He was another man whom Wellington dared not ignore because he was always *there*. Although Wellington knew Soult's faults as a tactician, he also knew that Soult could react like lightning when necessary. Soult's faults in the Peninsular War are almost too numerous to list: selfishness, jealousy, *folie de grandeur,* mendacity, avarice, and a strong measure of idleness on occasion. But if Napoleon once called Soult the best strategic brain in the Peninsula, he was not far wrong. The ridiculous quibbles which Soult used to challenge Joseph's orders were not meant to be taken seriously. They were meant to sting, to infuriate. Soult's extraordinary patchwork mentality of cold professionalism breaking through spoiled and sulky petulance was largely the result of frustration with the command set-up. It was fitting that Soult and Wellington were the men who squared up for the last fight on the line of the Bidassoa in 1813. For Soult, however, the tragedy was that the moment when he had the authority he needed to co-ordinate the French war effort in Spain had come too late.

In the first chapter of this book, Ney, the front-line fighting general, was contrasted with Soult, the staff man. This contrast was seen for the last time in 1815, when Soult was Napoleon's chief-of-staff at Waterloo. After the second abdication Soult's career went much the same way as those of the other Marshals: in service with the Bourbons. Soult, however, turned out very differently. He lived on to become the Grand Old Man of France, taking charge of the chaos in Paris when the Bourbons were expelled, becoming War Minister, and serving as Ambassador Extraordinary at the coronation of Queen Victoria in 1838 (when Wellington accosted him with the arch greeting, 'Ah – got you after all these years'). But a greater honour yet awaited Soult. In 1847 he was named Marshal-General of France, a supreme rank which only three men had held before him: Turenne, Villars, and Saxe. Respected by all, the last Marshal of the original creation, Soult died at his ornate chateau, 'Soult-berg', on 26 November, 1851.

FURTHER READING

Individual biographies on the Marshals are surprisingly thin on the ground. Foremost among them, however, are *Marshal Massena* by James Marshall-Cornwall (O.U.P.) and *Marshal Ney* by Piers Compton (Methuen). On the Marshalate in general there are few more entertaining accounts than *Napoleon and His Marshals* by A.G. Macdonell (Macmillan). This is crammed with anecdotes and incidents ranging from the hilarious to the horrifying, and remains a classic introduction to the subject.

Napoleon's Marshals by Brigadier Peter Young (Osprey) takes a different approach; it consists of a collection of individual biographies. But for those with a zest for the 'Who's Who' presentation and a working knowledge of French there is no substitute for Georges Six's *Dictionnaire Biographique des Généreaux & Amiraux française de La Révolution Et De L'Empire*. This noble and invaluable work is published in two volumes, under the imprint of the *Librairie Historique et Nobiliaire Georges Saffroy*, of Paris, and its detail is fascinating. Early service, promotions, decorations, monetary awards and pensions, not to mention 'hairbreadth 'scapes i' the imminent deadly breach' galore, are faithfully recorded. A charming touch is being told where to look for the different names on the Arc de Triomphe.

Books on Napoleon and the rise and fall of the Empire are legion, but one of the best is Felix Markham's *Napoleon* (Weidenfeld & Nicolson). Two other titles serve as basic reference works for the wars of the Revolution and later of the Directorate which brought Napoleon to power as First Consul. These are *The French Revolution from Its Origins to 1793* by Georges Lefebvre (Routledge Kegan Paul), and *The War of the Second Coalition* by A.B. Rodger (O.U.P.).

Bertie Greatheed's diary, referred to in Chapter 3 on the subject of Junot, is superb first-person source material for Paris during the Consulate. It is a mixture of photographic memory and near-professional journalism (the description of the public guillotining is particularly sobering), plus the classic 'Englishman abroad' testiness over the shortcomings of Parisian society. Greatheed's diary was published in 1953 by Geoffrey Bles under the title *An Englishman in Paris: 1803.*

Michael Glover's *Legacy of Glory: The Bonaparte Kingdom of Spain* (Leo Cooper) is a must. It shows the appalling time which poor 'Brother Joseph' had while desperately trying to rule his kingdom, thwarted by the Peninsular Marshals on the one hand, Napoleon on the other, and impossible geographical distances in between. Details of the protocol of life at Joseph's court in Madrid are particularly interesting.

Although *Napoleon's Peninsular Marshals* is a deliberate attempt to look at the French side of the war, there is bound to be much indignation at my not quoting the inexhaustible list of excellent publications on Wellington. But there is one collection of letters from a British cavalry officer in Wellington's army which contains a fascinating survey of service life in the Peninsula. This is *Peninsular Portrait, 1811-1814 – The Letters of Captain William Bragge*, edited by S.A.C. Cassels (O.U.P.). These letters, showing how bad things frequently were for the British in Spain, certainly make one wonder what they could have been like for the French!

Nobody asked to think of further reading on this subject could fail to consider C.S. Forester's splendid novels on the Peninsular War. In *A Ship of The Line* Hornblower himself gets embroiled in a brisk little campaign on Spanish soil; but

Forester's masterpieces on the Peninsula are *The Gun* and *Death to the French*. *The Gun* covers the period between Napoleon's Spanish campaign of 1808-9 and the year 1811; *Death to the French* concentrates on Massena's invasion of Portugal in 1810. All three of these titles are available as Penguins.

INDEX

Note: Names of the Peninsular Marshals appear in capitals